# BAUHAUS

## 1919-1933 Weimar-Dessau-Berlin

Michael Siebenbrodt
& Lutz Schöbe

Authors: Michael Siebenbrodt and Lutz Schöbe

Layout:
Baseline Co Ltd,
33 Ter-33 Bis Mac Dinh Chi St.
Star Building, 6th Floor
District 1, Ho Chi Minh City
Vietnam

Photographical credits:
Abbreviations:
BHA Bauhaus-Archiv, Museum für Gestaltung, Berlin
SBHD Stiftung Bauhaus Dessau
SWKK Stiftung Weimarer Klassik und Kunstsammlungen

p. 11: Photograph Louis Held
p. 19: Photograph Hugo Erfurt
p. 20: Unknown photographer
p. 23 (top): Unknown photographer
p. 23 (bottom): Photograph Lucia Moholy
p. 26: Unknown photographer
p. 30: Unknown photographer
p. 32: Unknown photographer
p. 35: Photograph Emil Theiß, Stadtarchiv Dessau
p. 36: Photograph Howard Dearstyne
p. 37: Unknown photographer, BHA
p. 45: Photograph Umbo (Otto Umbehr)
p. 48: BHA
p. 65: Unknown photographer, BHA
p. 77: Photograph Louis Held Workshop
p. 88: Unknown photographer, BHA
p. 119: Unknown photographer, BHA
p. 121: Photograph Wolfgang Kleber,
    HOCHTIEF Essen / Anhaltische
    Gemäldegalerie Dessau / Stiftung
    Bauhaus Dessau
p. 123: Photograph Gunter Lepkrowski, BHA
p. 127: Unknown photographer
p. 130: © Bühnen-Archiv Oskar Schlemmer,
    Sekretariat, I- 28824 Oggebbio
p. 131: Unknown photographer, BHA
p. 132 (top): Unknown photographer, BHA
p. 132 (bottom): Unknown photographer, BHA
p. 133 (top): Photograph Edmund Collein or Heinz Loew, BHA
p. 133 (bottom): Unknown photographer, SBHD
p. 134: Photograph Gunter Lepkrowski, BHA
p. 135: Photograph Heinz Loew or Joost Schmidt
p. 138 (top): Unknown photographer, BHA
p. 138 (bottom): Photograph Erich Consemüller
p. 146: Unknown photographer, SBHD

p. 147: Photograph Walter Peterhans
p. 151: Unknown photographer
p. 152: Unknown photographer, BHA
p. 153: Unknown photographer, SWKK
p. 154: Reno/Foto-Atelier Louis Held, Bauhaus-Museum,
    Kunstsammlungen zu Weimar (KW)
p. 156: Unknown photographer, BHA
p. 158: Photograph Marburg
p. 159 (top): Unknown photographer, BHA
p. 161: Photograph Gunter Lepkowski, BHA
p. 162: Unknown photographer, BHA
p. 163: Unknown photographer, BHA
p. 166: Unknown photographer, BHA
p. 167 (top): Kicken, Berlin/Phyllis Umbehr, BHA
p. 167 (bottom): Unknown photographer, SWKK
p. 168: Unknown photographer, BHA
p. 169 (top): Unknown photographer, SWKK
p. 169 (bottom): Unknown photographer, SWKK
p. 170: Unknown photographer, BHA
p. 171: Unknown photographer, SWKK
p. 172: Photograph Erich Consemüller
p. 173 (bottom): Unknown photographer, BHA
p. 173 (top): Unknown photographer, BHA
p. 174: Photograph Jost Schilgen, BHA
p. 175: Photograph Marianne Brandt
p. 178: Universität zu Köln/Theaterwissenschaftliche
    Sammlung
p. 179: Staatliche Kunstsammlungen Dresden,
    Puppentheatersammlung, 1957
p. 180: Unknown photographer, SWKK
p. 181: Unknown photographer, BHA
p. 182 (left): Universität zu Köln/Theaterwissenschaftliche
    Sammlung
p. 182 (top): Harvard Art Museum
p. 182 (bottom): Germanisches Nationalmuseum
p. 183: Universität zu Köln/Theaterwissenschaftliche
    Sammlung
p. 184: © Bühnen-Archiv Oskar Schlemmer,
    Sekretariat, I- 28824 Oggebbio
p. 185: Photograph Erich Consemüller,
    © Bühnen-Archiv Oskar Schlemmer,
    Sekretariat, I- 28824 Oggebbio
p. 186 (top): Photograph Lux Feininger
    © Bühnen-Archiv Oskar Schlemmer,
    Sekretariat, I- 28824 Oggebbio
p. 186 (left bottom): Photograph Lux Feininger,
    © Bühnen-Archiv Oskar Schlemmer,
    Sekretariat, I- 28824 Oggebbio
p. 186 (right bottom): Photograph Erich Consemüller,
    © Bühnen-Archiv Oskar Schlemmer, Sekretariat,
    I- 28824 Oggebbio
p. 187: Photograph Marianne Brandt, BHA
p. 190: Unknown photographer, BHA
p. 191 (top and bottom): All rights reserved, SWKK
p. 194: All rights reserved, SBHD
p. 195 (top): All rights reserved, SBHD
p. 195 (bottom): All rights reserved, Stiftung
    Meisterhäuser Dessau
p. 196 (bottom): All rights reserved, SBHD
p. 196 (bottom): All rights reserved, SBHD
p. 197 (top): All rights reserved, BHA
p. 198: All rights reserved, SBHD
p. 199: gta archives / ETH Zurich: bequest of Hannes Meyer
p. 200: Junkers-Luftbild, BHA
p. 201: All rights reserved, SBHD
p. 202: All rights reserved
p. 203: All rights reserved/BHA
p. 214: BHA
p. 228: SWKK
p. 232: Photograph Paula Stockmar, BHA
p. 234: Unknown photographer: SWKK
p. 234: Photograph Lucia Moholy, BHA
p. 235 (bottom): Photograph Hajo Rose, BHA
p. 235 (bottom): Photograph Edmund Collein, SBHD
p. 236 (top left): Photograph Irene Bayer, SBHD
p. 236 (top right): Photograph Erich Consemüller, BHA
p. 236: Photograph Erich Consemüller, private collection

ISBN: 978-1-85995-626-7

Printed in Singapore

# BAUHAUS

## 1919-1933 Weimar-Dessau-Berlin

Michael Siebenbrodt
& Lutz Schöbe

PARKSTONE
INTERNATIONAL

# Contents

# Preface

The Bauhaus was one of the most important and momentous cultural manifestations of the twentieth century. There is no doubt about it. It is more than ever a phenomenon of global dimensions. Today, the Bauhaus is embedded in the public consciousness; it is held in high esteem and, depending on one's interests, occasionally glorified or denounced. But recognition and positive esteem are prevalent. The work of the Bauhaus artists enjoys universal admiration and interest in the great museums of the world. Their creative theories, if often taken out of their complex context, received and continue to receive attention in many renowned architectural and art education institutes, as well as in basic art lessons in education facilities. Bauhaus products – such as Marcel Breuer's famous tubular steel furniture – proceeded to become highly-traded design classics. Bauhaus buildings, such as the sites in Weimar and Dessau, are considered pieces of architectural history, and today they are part of Germany's cultural heritage. The Bauhaus went down in art history as the original modernist art school.

Now, almost a century after its foundation, it is still current. This is evident not only in the increased institutional interest in the school's work, an exhibition boom that hasn't worn off, and a multitude of new publications and unending media interest, but also in the area of theoretical architectural research, in which investigations into functionalism, a design concept closely connected to the Bauhaus, are on the increase. The creation of a new man for a new, more humane society was the Bauhaus's true goal. It remains historically unfulfilled. Are we to understand the intervention by philosopher and sociologist Jürgen Habermas regarding "modernism as an unfinished project" in this way, too?

This book limits itself to portraying the history of the Bauhaus in a more or less rough overview. The authors can thus make reference to a multitude of existing publications as well as to their own published writings on the subject. The claim is not to subject the Bauhaus to criticism on principle from a twenty-first century perspective but rather the intention simply to portray what *was*, in an objective argument of the most important points and with no claim to exhaustiveness, for this book is intended for the interested reader and not the knowledgeable expert. If this leads to the break up of unilateral ways of viewing the Bauhaus, that harmonious, consistent, conflict-free, "progressive" and non-traditional organisaton, the authors will consider themselves lucky.

The portrayal begins with references to the forerunners of the Bauhaus, places it in the context of the events of its time and describes the circumstances leading up to its foundation. In a brief overview, the authors present the internal structure of the school and its individual sites in Weimar, Dessau and Berlin, as well as the conceptions of its three directors, Walter Gropius, Hannes Meyer and Ludwig Mies van der Rohe. The following chapters inform the reader about the teaching and training structure of the Bauhaus and present the teaching concepts of its most important teachers. Attention is given to the Bauhaus workshops, their respective structures, the spectrum of achievements and the modifications by the different directors. These are followed by short chapters on general matters such as architecture, photography and visual arts in the Bauhaus, as well as on life and work at the school. A short overview of the effects and reception of the Bauhaus from its beginnings to the present forms the conclusion.

Special emphasis is placed on promoting the comprehension of connections, consequences, mutual influences and developments in a sequence of selected and matched images. In this way, the reader may have visual access to the Bauhaus through the language of its time.

The appendix, with its compressed chronology summarising the history of the Bauhaus and evoking parallel events in culture, politics, technology and science, allows for individual conclusions and the identification of links and references not included in the text.

A bibliography, with information about the most important literature on the Bauhaus in general, as well as on select topics, offers opportunities for further in-depth study of the subject.

# History of the Bauhaus

## Forerunners, Roots and History

The artistic and pedagogical achievements of the Bauhaus were revolutionary in Germany as well as in Europe as a whole. Its intention to renovate art and architecture was in line with other similar efforts, from which it drew numerous ideas for its own work.

Still, the school's historical significance cannot be overestimated. The Bauhaus did not develop in empty space. On the one hand, one of stereotypes of Bauhaus history is that the school broke with all traditions and started from scratch. On the other hand, there is a general trend to omit hardly any art movements or important artists of the late nineteenth and early twentieth centuries when discussing the sources of the Bauhaus.

The conditions leading to the development of the Bauhaus are, indeed, complex and widely ramified. Its sources in humanistic and social history reach back into the nineteenth century. Furthermore, the issue addressed by the Bauhaus has its roots in the Industrial Revolution, that lasting cataclysm beginning in England in the middle of the eighteenth century and resulting in industrial manufacturing and industrial society. This modernisation process had led to tensions in almost all areas of life: a radical change occurred when mechanical tools replaced age-old tools of the trade. For lack of new concepts, art and architecture reverted to a historical vocabulary of shapes, which increasingly led to contradictions. The changed conditions for the production of articles for daily use required a new design, now aligned with machine production. It took until the middle of the nineteenth century for the attempts at solving this problem to take concrete shape. The Bauhaus was part of a traditional line of initiatives and efforts called "modernism," which issued from here and strove to re-establish unity between the areas of artistic and technical production, which had been separated by emerging industrial production. The resulting social separation of the artist, his isolation and the fragmentation as well as the segregation of different types of art, was to be reversed. This led to the idea of the *Gesamtkunstwerk* (synthesis of the arts, unified work of art), a thought which, with different accentuation in earlier centuries, strove to synthesise in reality all the arts involved in construction and manual trades. In the nineteenth and early twentieth centuries, the idea of the *Gesamtkunstwerk* was allied with the utopian claim that it could further the solution of society's social and cultural problems on the basis of a unified aspiration.

## Art School Reform

The Art School Reform, which was concerned with the transformation of art academies into unified art schools, based artistic training on the manual trades and a general artistic elementary education. Gropius himself eventually saw the Bauhaus as a part of "reform ideas typical of the time", and as a new kind of school, whose fundamental pedagogical concept was based on reform ideas.

There were other attempts, before the Bauhaus and parallel to it, to implement in practise the goals of Art School Reform. Among these, the Art School in Frankfurt am Main must be mentioned, as well as the Obrist-Debschitz School in Munich, the Breslau Academy for Arts and Crafts, the Düsseldorf Arts and Crafts School, the Arts and Crafts School Burg Giebichenstein in Halle, the Reimann School and the Itten School in Berlin, the Folkwang School in Essen, the Arts and Crafts School in Bratislava, and finally the Higher Artistic-Technical Workshops (Vkhutemas) in Moscow.

Like the school in Moscow, the Bauhaus was an institution implementing the ideas of the Art School Reform in a unique way, consistently, imaginatively, completely, rigorously and in a sustained manner. According to Gropius, the Bauhaus was a matter of life for the people. In this comprehensive claim, which went far beyond architecture and design, lies *inter alia* its historical importance.

## Ruskin, Olbrich and Others

In his 1923 essay "Idea and Construction of the Staatliches Bauhaus (State Bauhaus)", Bauhaus founder Walter Gropius himself points to the sources which directly influenced him and the foundation of the Bauhaus. Gropius lists "Ruskin, Olbrich, Behrens, (Darmstadt Artists' Colony) and others in Germany, then finally the Deutsche Werkbund (German Association of Craftsmen)". In his own writings, John Ruskin (1819-1900), the English painter, art historian and social reformer, opposed the cluttered adornments of the past but also industrial production; he juxtaposed the alienating work on the machine with the ideal of the creative artisan of the Middle Ages. In his restoration efforts, which were extremely influential in England, especially in the second half of the nineteenth century, he postulated the production of things that did justice to the material, that were largely unadorned but still expressive, following the model of the Gothic style. Products made by machines, however, were "surrogates" according to him, soulless, "dead things". It was left to the writer, designer and founder of the Socialist movement in Great Britain, William Morris (1834-1896), and the Arts and Crafts movement associated with him, to put Ruskin's critical thoughts into practise and give further momentum to the arts and crafts reform. Morris designed novelties and interior furnishings, avoiding the misled ornamentation of the past. He and the Arts and Crafts movement saw the return to the qualities of manual trades as a way to react against the product design challenges of the Industrial Revolution. The products thus made in specially-founded arts and crafts companies were marked by simplicity, robustness, rusticity and great esteem for the material. Morris, himself a dedicated socialist, connected his design work and the associated reactivation of craftsmanship with a forced, yet illusory social assertion, which consisted of counteracting the decay of society by encouraging communal life, through joyful, manual and largely self-controlled work and the resulting good form. As a result of this, a conflict-free, blissful society should emerge, free from the rule of the machine.

Ruskin, Morris and the English Arts and Crafts movement are closely connected to the beginnings of modernist design in Europe, due to their criticism of the aesthetic appearance of machine-made products and their art reform based on the quality of the products of the manual trades. Allied with this movement were the efforts of the Scottish artist and architect Charles Rennie Mackintosh (1868-1928) and the Secession Movement in Austria with artists like Otto Wagner (1841-1918), Josef Hoffmann (1870-1956), Koloman Moser (1868-1918) and the architect mentioned by Gropius, Josef Maria Olbrich (1867-1908). Olbrich, architect of Vienna's Secession Building, rejected the traditional, conservative concept of art, which was founded on historicism, and tested, among other things, the idea of the unified work of art by designing new, futuristic buildings and living spaces.

Shortly thereafter, Olbrich also pursued this claim with the members of the Darmstadt Artists Colony, founded in Germany in 1899, of which German architect and designer Peter Behrens (1868-1940) was also a member. Behrens was one of the most influential founders of modern industrial design and modern functional industry culture. Walter Gropius, Ludwig Mies van der Rohe and Swiss architect Le Corbusier were among his collaborators. Peter Behrens is regarded as one of the most important forerunners of functionalism, which developed into one of the most important design principles of the Bauhaus.

In Germany, Richard Riemerschmid (1868-1957) and Bruno Paul (1874-1968) were also part of the group of artists becoming industrial designers by means of their *Typenmöbel* (batch production furniture) designs for the *Dresdner Werkstätten für Handwerkskunst* (Dresden Craftsmanship Workshops). The artist Henry van de Velde (1863-1957) followed suit in Belgium and later in Germany. He tried to renew art through manual trades without rejecting technology, then turned to arts and crafts, designing functional objects for industrial production and building houses as an expression of highly-cultivated artistic individuality. Free from the ballast of historic forms, using a system of lines sensitively calculated and derived from nature in order to demonstrate in a subtle manner the structure of an object or house and its functions, the objects designed by van de Velde still did not live up to the design requirements of batch or mass production. Van de Velde, whose Grand-Ducal Saxon School of Arts and Crafts, founded in Weimar, was one of the immediate forerunners of the *Staatliches Bauhaus*, was regarded, like the artists previously mentioned, as one of the most important representatives of Art Deco, a movement of artists who were aware of their responsibility towards society and wanted to avoid the advancing separation of artistic and consumer culture by melding them together into a new unity. The result was an original, yet exclusive concept, which eventually could not live up to the needs of a highly-developed industrial society.

## *Deutscher Werkbund* (German Association of Craftsmen)

Walter Gropius repeatedly emphasised that the Bauhaus emerged from the spirit of the *Deutscher Werkbund*. Founded by Hermann Muthesius (1861-1927) in Munich in 1907 as an association of artists, architects, businessmen and experts, and carried by designers like Peter Behrens and Walter Gropius, the *Deutscher Werkbund* tried to create a practical, effective connection between commerce, craftsmanship and industry, and the designing artist. On the basis of a positive assessment of social and technical industry potential and new products such as aircraft, fast trains, washing machines and automobiles, aesthetics were developed which emphasised usefulness and functionality as well as material appropriateness in architecture and consumer devices, in the spirit of an industrial culture for all. Emphasis was also placed on sustainable marketing of the Werkbund products in the media. Despite fundamental agreements among the members of the Werkbund, accord was never reached on specific questions, which ultimately can be traced to the processes of exploitation, alienation and objectification in a modern industrial society, closely connected to the production of goods.

## *De Stijl, Blauer Reiter* (Blue Rider) and *Der Sturm*

The Dutch artists' group *De Stijl*, founded in 1917 with constructivist design principles that were propagated in Weimar by painter Theo van Doesburg (1881-1931), immediately influenced the artistic development of the Bauhaus. The

Bauhaus's study of technology and industry was accelerated by *De Stijl*, and Gropius's and other Bauhaus artists' use of forms was in part aligned with the group for a sustained period of time. In the area of visual arts, the most important artists for the Bauhaus were those whose work was grouped around the *Blauer Reiter* and the magazine and gallery *Der Sturm*, founded by musician and art critic Herwarth Walden (1878-1941). These included the painters Paul Klee (1879-1940) and Wassily Kandinsky (1866-1944), who were later appointed Masters at the Bauhaus. These painters' specialities lay in the great sensitivity and vividness with which they reacted to the changing society and profound transformation of the scientific view of the world. Design methods considered appropriate responses to the contradictions of the time usually involved the rejection of the outdated concept of faultless rendering as well as a focus on abstraction and expression, cubism and futurism. An in-depth analysis of the artistic means of design as well as an exploration of their innate laws assisted in the search for a new intellectuality by means of cognitive progress on the basis of an enlightened rationality.

Politically, the Bauhaus developed after and in reaction to the 1917 October Revolution in Russia, the 1918 November Revolution in Germany and the end of World War I. The situation after the war and the radical political changes were general premises for the intended renewal of art and architecture. It is evident from Gropius's programmatic texts that the Bauhaus founder was clearly aware of this connection and that he himself, as many of his contemporaries and later comrades-in-arms, wanted to make a contribution to the creation of a new, democratic society. For Gropius, World War I was more than just a lost war. For him, his world had ended and in 1918, he was looking for radical solutions to the problems of his time. In the end, he was credited with making an attempt in his thinking to unify some of the most important cultural influences, impulses and trends of the past and present and to develop an image of the new world in synthesis. The Bauhaus was solidly anchored to this concept.

## The Staatliches Bauhaus in Weimar (1919 to 1925)

Probably no other school in Germany was so closely connected to the cultural, political and socio-economic developments of the Weimer Republic as the Bauhaus. The Bauhaus foundation date of 1st April 1919 coincided with the negotiations of the constitutional assembly in the Weimar *Hoftheater*, which adopted the so-called Weimar Constitution on July 31st. Only a few weeks after Hitler's seizure of power, on 30th January 1933, police searched the Bauhaus for Communist materials and closed it down, before the Academy was dissolved on 19th July 1933 in a final act of freedom of decision.

In between lay two site changes, in 1925 to Dessau and in 1932 to Berlin, as well as two changes of directorship, in 1928 to Hannes Meyer and in 1930 to Ludwig Mies van der Rohe, which were all politically motivated. Local parliaments always played a part in the development of the Bauhaus, the Thuringian Landtag in Weimar until 1925 and the Dessau City Council until 1932, and even longer with political activities and legal proceedings.

As early as March 1920, extremist right-wing military personnel and politicians led by Wolfgang Kapp (1858-1922) and Walther Freiherr von Lüttwitz (1859-1942) tried to destroy the young republic with a military coup (Kapp *Putsch*). This *coup d'état* was put down by a general strike during which numerous demonstrators were shot by the rebels. For those killed in Weimar, Gropius created the Memorial for the March Victims in the Main Weimar Cemetery in 1922, and in that same year he also designed a memorial plaque on the German National Theatre for the Weimar Constitution. The memorial for the murdered Karl Liebknecht (1871-1919) and Rosa Luxemburg (1871-1919), created by Ludwig Mies van der Rohe and commissioned by the KPD (Communist Party of Germany), was inaugurated in Berlin's Friedrichsfelde Cemetery in 1926. The poverty of the post-war years, which was dramatically increased by the reparations ordered by the Treaty of Versailles, led to the economic collapse of 1923. While the exchange rate for the Dollar to the Mark was still at 1:8 in January 1919, the figure fell to 1:50 at the beginning of 1920, to 1:200 in 1922, to 1:7,000 at the beginning of 1923, and until the currency stabilisation at the end of 1923, it was 1:4.2 billion! The period of economic upswing and relative stability–"the Golden 20s"–in Germany lasted from 1924 to 1929, when "Black Friday" at the New York Stock Exchange started a worldwide economic crisis on 25th October 1929.

The Bauhaus became the focal point of the *avant-garde* in education, design and architecture: in 1923 with the large Weimar *Bauhaus Exhibition and Attached Exposition of International Architecture*, in 1926 with the Bauhaus buildings in Dessau, in 1929/1930 with the *Travelling Bauhaus Exhibition*, and in 1930 with the German section at the *Exposition de la Société des Artistes Décorateurs*, led by Walter Gropius in Paris.

Discussions and conflicts within the Bauhaus in Weimar and the programmatic and structural changes often dramatically mirrored these connections: the Groß Case in 1919, the secession of former Art Academy professors and the refoundation of the Weimar Academy of Fine Arts in 1920/1921, Theo van Duisburg's *De Stijl* course and the Constructivist Congress in Weimar, the Gropius-Itten conflict and the foundation of a Bauhaus development co-operative in 1922, a Bauhaus limited company and the Society of Friends of the Bauhaus in 1924 up to the politically forced change of site to Dessau on 1st April 1925.

Building of the former Grand-Ducal Saxon Academy of Fine Art in
Weimar, architect: Henry van de Velde, 1904/11 (UNESCO World
Heritage Site)

Building of the former Grand-Ducal Saxon School of Arts and Crafts in Weimar, architect: Henry van de Velde, 1905/06 (UNESCO World Heritage Site)

## Between Vision and Reality: The 1919 to 1920 Construction Phase

After Belgian artist Henry van de Velde had submitted his petition for release from his post as Director of the *Großherzogliche Kunstgewerbeschule* (Grand-Ducal School of Arts and Crafts) to the Weimar Grand Duke on 25th July 1914, just a few days after the outbreak of World War I, his contract finished on 1st October 1915, the date that the school closed. As his successors, Van de Velde recommended to the Grand-Ducal Saxon State Ministry the German architect August Endell (1871-1925) and Walter Gropius, as well as the Swiss sculptor Hermann Obrist (1863-1927). Since October 1915, a lively correspondence had developed between Fritz Mackensen (1866-1953), the painter and director of the *Großherzoglich Sächsische Hochschule*

(Grand-Ducal Saxon Academy of Fine Arts) in Weimar, and Walter Gropius regarding the attachment of an architecture and visual arts department, of which Gropius was to be the head. He was staying in Weimar in December and was granted an audience with the Grand Duke to discuss the appointment. On 25th January 1916, Gropius, at the request of the Weimar State Ministry, submitted his *Suggestions for the Founding of an Educational Establishment as an Artistic Advice Centre for Industry, Trade and Crafts*[1]. One year later, the professorial staff of the Academy of Fine Arts submitted a list of reform suggestions to the State Ministry, particularly asking that the educational programme be extended to include architecture, arts and crafts and theatre arts.

On the 3rd November 1918, revolution began in Germany and reached Weimar five days later. On the 9th, the social Democrat Philipp Scheidemann (1865-1939) proclaimed the "German Republic" in the Reichstag, and two hours later Karl Liebknecht proclaimed his "Free Socialist Republic" at Berlin Castle. The Kaiser and all the German princes abdicated without any far-reaching radical social changes.

On 3rd December 1918, the first meeting of the November Group took place in Berlin. It was an association of artists and architects such as Lyonel Feininger (1871-1956), Wassily Kandinsky, Walter Gropius and Ludwig Mies van der Rohe, and also included Max Pechstein (1881-1955), Otto Dix (1891-1969), George Grosz (1893-1959) and Hans Poelzig (1869-1936), who wanted to make their contribution to the building of the young republic. Parallel to this gathering, the Working Council of the Arts was formed, including a group intent on reforming the education system led by architect Otto Bartning (1883-1959), with whom Gropius also collaborated. A central question was the creation of equal opportunities for all students by means of a unified school, in connection with the idea of a working school. Special emphasis was placed on the reform of fine arts academies. The results of these discussions were also expressed in an only slightly modified form in Walter Gropius's *Bauhaus Programme and Manifesto*, which appeared in April 1919 with Lyonel Feininger's woodcut on the cover. The reunification of all artistic principles in building, in combination with manual trades and workshop as educational fundamentals were the focal point of its aims and objectives. The Masters, Journeymen and Apprentices of the Bauhaus were to be closely in touch with industry and public life and strive for friendly relationships amongst themselves outside of classes as well as in them, with theatre, lectures, music and "ceremonious merriment at these gatherings."[2]

The first Bauhaus signet, the "matchstick star man", which led student Karl Peter Röhl (1890-1975) to win the student competition, was a special symbol of this departure from convention. It its centre is an abstract line drawing of a man with his arms raised, consciously following Leonardo da Vinci's (1452-1519) Vitruvian Man in a circle and square, but reminiscent at the same time of the Old Germanic double-rune "man-woman" with a circular head, which with its black and white halves represents the highest degree of abstraction of the Chinese *yin* and *yang*. This Bauhaus man carries a pyramid as the antique symbol of the unity of society, art and religion. He is orbited by the sun as a swastika, the Buddhist symbol of love, and the moon and stars—world cultures and world religions form the humanistic backdrop for the Bauhaus's visions of the future.

The foundation of the Bauhaus coincided with the first elections in the newly founded Free State of Saxony-Weimar-Eisenach on 9th

March 1919, and the formation of a new provisional republican government by the Social Democrats (SPD) and the German Democrats (DDP). In February and March, Gropius travelled to Weimar on several occasions for negotiations and gained support for his appointment as Director and the new name *Staatliches Bauhaus in Weimar* (State Bauhaus in Weimar) from the Fine Arts Academy staff. On 1st April 1919, the Weimar Lord Chamberlain's office signed the contract with Gropius and also agreed to the institution's renaming on 12th April.

In the merger of the former Academy of Fine Arts and the Academy of Arts and Crafts, Gropius had to take on the remaining professors of the Academy of Fine Arts, Richard Engelmann (1868-1957), Otto Fröhlich, Walther Klemm (1883-1957) and Max Thedy (1858-1924). The appointment of the new international faculty of avant-garde artists took all of four years. In 1919, Lyonel Feininger, Gerhard Marcks (1889-1981) and Johannes Itten (1888-1967) joined, then one year later Georg Muche (1895-1987). In 1921 came Paul Klee (1879-1940), Oskar Schlemmer (1888-1943) and Lothar Schreyer (1886-1966), then Wassily Kandinsky in 1922 and László Moholy-Nagy replacing Itten as late as 1923.

As early as the autumn of 1919, Bauhaus opponents in Weimar—conservative craftsmen, academic artists, members of the right-wing conservative educated class and politicians—formed the Free Association for City Interests and publicly attacked the "… Spartacist and Bolshevist influences" in the Bauhaus. At one such meeting the Bauhaus master student Hans Groß lamented the lack of a nationalist, "German-minded" leadership personality at the Bauhaus. The "Groß Case" led not only to the withdrawal of more than a dozen students and a complaint to the state government against the Bauhaus by forty-nine right-wing conservative Weimar citizens and artists, but also to the first mobilisation of Bauhaus supporters in the *Deutsche Werkbund* and the Berlin Working Council for the Arts. Walter Gropius countered the pamphlet against the Bauhaus by Emil Erfurth, chairman of the nationalist *Bürgerausschuss* (Citizens' Committee), with his own leaflet in the spring of 1920, supported by the Ministry of Education and the Arts.

On 30th April 1920 eight previously independent Thuringian free states joined together to form the district of Thuringia with Weimar as the capital. On 20th June the first state elections took place, which resulted in a coalition between SPD, USPD (Independent Social Democratic Party), and DDP led by August Fröhlich. The Bauhaus was put under the control of the Ministry of Public Education, Art and Justice. On 9th July Gropius gave a speech in front of the Thuringian parliament and participated as an expert in budget discussions. He took advantage of the

Lyonel Feininger, Cathedral of the Future, title page for the manifesto and programme for the Staatliches Bauhaus in Weimar, 1919

# PROGRAMM

### DES

## STAATLICHEN BAUHAUSES
## IN WEIMAR

**D**as Endziel aller bildnerischen Tätigkeit ist der Bau! Ihn zu schmücken war einst die vornehmste Aufgabe der bildenden Künste, sie waren unablösliche Bestandteile der großen Baukunst. Heute stehen sie in selbstgenügsamer Eigenheit, aus der sie erst wieder erlöst werden können durch bewußtes Mit- und Ineinanderwirken aller Werkleute untereinander. Architekten, Maler und Bildhauer müssen die vielgliedrige Gestalt des Baues in seiner Gesamtheit und in seinen Teilen wieder kennen und begreifen lernen, dann werden sich von selbst ihre Werke wieder mit architektonischem Geiste füllen, den sie in der Salonkunst verloren.

Die alten Kunstschulen vermochten diese Einheit nicht zu erzeugen, wie sollten sie auch, da Kunst nicht lehrbar ist. Sie müssen wieder in der Werkstatt aufgehen. Diese nur zeichnende und malende Welt der Musterzeichner und Kunstgewerbler muß endlich wieder eine bauende werden. Wenn der junge Mensch, der Liebe zur bildnerischen Tätigkeit in sich verspürt, wieder wie einst seine Bahn damit beginnt, ein Handwerk zu erlernen, so bleibt der unproduktive „Künstler" künftig nicht mehr zu unvollkommener Kunstübung verdammt, denn seine Fertigkeit bleibt nun dem Handwerk erhalten, wo er Vortreffliches zu leisten vermag.

Architekten, Bildhauer, Maler, wir alle müssen zum Handwerk zurück! Denn es gibt keine „Kunst von Beruf". Es gibt keinen Wesensunterschied zwischen dem Künstler und dem Handwerker. Der Künstler ist eine Steigerung des Handwerkers. Gnade des Himmels läßt in seltenen Lichtmomenten, die jenseits seines Wollens stehen, unbewußt Kunst aus dem Werk seiner Hand erblühen, die Grundlage des Werkmäßigen aber ist unerläßlich für jeden Künstler. Dort ist der Urquell des schöpferischen Gestaltens.

Bilden wir also eine neue Zunft der Handwerker ohne die klassentrennende Anmaßung, die eine hochmütige Mauer zwischen Handwerkern und Künstlern errichten wollte! Wollen, erdenken, erschaffen wir gemeinsam den neuen Bau der Zukunft, der alles in einer Gestalt sein wird: Architektur und Plastik und Malerei, der aus Millionen Händen der Handwerker einst gen Himmel steigen wird als kristallenes Sinnbild eines neuen kommenden Glaubens.

WALTER GROPIUS.

**D**as Staatliche Bauhaus in Weimar ist durch Vereinigung der ehemaligen Großherzoglich Sächsischen Hochschule für bildende Kunst mit der ehemaligen Großherzoglich Sächsischen Kunstgewerbeschule unter Neuangliederung einer Abteilung für Baukunst entstanden.

### Ziele des Bauhauses.

Das Bauhaus erstrebt die Sammlung alles künstlerischen Schaffens zur Einheit, die Wiedervereinigung aller werkkünstlerischen Disziplinen — Bildhauerei, Malerei, Kunstgewerbe und Handwerk — zu einer neuen Baukunst als deren unablösliche Bestandteile. Das letzte, wenn auch ferne Ziel des Bauhauses ist das Einheitskunstwerk — der große Bau —, in dem es keine Grenze gibt zwischen monumentaler und dekorativer Kunst.

Das Bauhaus will Architekten, Maler und Bildhauer aller Grade je nach ihren Fähigkeiten zu tüchtigen Handwerkern oder selbständig schaffenden Künstlern erziehen und eine Arbeitsgemeinschaft führender und werdender Werkkünstler gründen, die Bauwerke in ihrer Gesamtheit — Rohbau, Ausbau, Ausschmückung und Einrichtung — aus gleich geartetem Geist heraus einheitlich zu gestalten weiß.

### Grundsätze des Bauhauses.

Kunst entsteht oberhalb aller Methoden, sie ist an sich nicht lehrbar, wohl aber das Handwerk. Architekten, Maler, Bildhauer sind Handwerker im Ursinn des Wortes, deshalb wird als unerläßliche Grundlage für alles bildnerische Schaffen die gründliche handwerkliche Ausbildung aller Studierenden in Werkstätten und auf Probier- und Werkplätzen gefordert. Die eigenen Werkstätten sollen allmählich ausgebaut, mit fremden Werkstätten Lehrverträge abgeschlossen werden.

Die Schule ist die Dienerin der Werkstatt, sie wird eines Tages in ihr aufgehen. Deshalb nicht Lehrer und Schüler im Bauhaus, sondern Meister, Gesellen und Lehrlinge.

Die Art der Lehre entspringt dem Wesen der Werkstatt:

Organisches Gestalten aus handwerklichem Können entwickelt.

Vermeidung alles Starren: Bevorzugung des Schöpferischen; Freiheit der Individualität, aber strenges Studium.

Zunftgemäße Meister- und Gesellenproben vor dem Meisterrat des Bauhauses oder vor fremden Meistern.

Mitarbeit der Studierenden an den Arbeiten der Meister.

Auftragsvermittlung auch an Studierende.

Gemeinsame Planung umfangreicher utopischer Bauentwürfe — Volks- und Kultbauten — mit weitgestecktem Ziel. Mitarbeit aller Meister und Studierenden — Architekten, Maler, Bildhauer — an diesen Entwürfen mit dem Ziel allmählichen Einklangs aller zum Bau gehörigen Glieder und Teile.

Ständige Fühlung mit Führern der Handwerke und Industrien im Lande.

Fühlung mit dem öffentlichen Leben, mit dem Volke durch Ausstellungen und andere Veranstaltungen.

Neue Versuche im Ausstellungswesen zur Lösung des Problems, Bild und Plastik im architektonischen Rahmen zu zeigen.

Pflege freundschaftlichen Verkehrs zwischen Meistern und Studierenden außerhalb der Arbeit; dabei Theater, Vorträge, Dichtkunst, Musik, Kostümfeste. Aufbau eines heiteren Zeremoniells bei diesen Zusammenkünften.

DK 1/87

Walter Gropius, Manifesto and programme for the Staatliches Bauhaus in Weimar, 1919

opportunity to present the development of the Arts Academies into the Bauhaus, to reject political attacks and to lobby for the expansion of the completely insufficient Bauhaus budget.

Former Weimar Academy of Fine Arts professors Thedy and Fröhlich had been pushing for the secession of the painting classes from the Bauhaus since early 1920, and were joined by Engelmann and Klemm in October. They achieved the re-foundation of the academically oriented *Staatliche Hochschule für bildende Kunst* (State Academy of Fine Arts) in Weimar on 4th April 1921, which was established adjacent to the Bauhaus in the rooms of the former Fine Arts Academy.

This secession enabled long-overdue new appointments at the Bauhaus in 1921, and at the same time helped the Bauhaus make its mark. The printing, bookbinding, sculpting and weaving workshops had become operational in 1919; the furniture, pottery, metal and stained glass painting workshops followed in 1920. In January 1921 the first *Constitution of the Staatliche Bauhaus in Weimar* was published, which remained in effect (after a revision) until 1925.

In February, Johannes Itten had designed a habit-like Bauhaus uniform, which was not officially introduced. In the summer he visited the Zoroastrian Mazdaznan Congress in Leipzig and introduced its teachings at the Bauhaus together with Georg Muche, among other things including vegetarian food in the Bauhaus cafeteria. Alongside this American sect, which referred to the ancient Persian teachings of Zoroaster (Zarathustra), various life reformation movements, the *Wandervogel* youth movement, Socialist ideas and itinerant Christian preachers all played a role and tried to fill the void left by war and revolution.

This spiritual and practical reconstruction and formation phase is often called the expressionist phase of the Bauhaus. The five Bauhaus print portfolios, probably the most important graphics production of the Bauhaus, seem to fit into this "expressionist" picture. *New European Graphic Arts* showed fifty-six works by forty-nine participating artists from six countries as well as all the Bauhaus Masters. In reality, it reflects the pluralistic image of the European avant-garde from German expressionism to Italian futurism and Russian constructivism, as well as the Dutch *De Stijl*.

### On the Way to [Becoming] the Modern Academy of Design: The 1921-1922 Formation Phase

In 1922, Walter Gropius reorganised the Bauhaus Masters' duties. In particular, Johannes Itten's many duties and power were reduced; following Klee and Schlemmer, Moholy-Nagy took over the metal workshop in 1923, Klee took over the stained glass painting workshop, Kandinsky, after an interlude by Schlemmer, took over the

mural-painting workshop, Muche the weaving and Gropius himself the furniture workshop. At the same time, the Masters' Council, the Bauhaus's highest leadership body, discussed intensely the idea and structure of the Bauhaus. Klee provided a sketch showing the Bauhaus as a globe with a sun motif in the centre. The earth's axis bore two triangular pennants reading "propaganda" and "publisher" and referred to the Bauhaus Masters' media strategies, which decisively influenced the corporate identity and international aura of the Bauhaus with their Bauhaus print portfolios, Bauhaus books, the Bauhaus magazine, and with exhibitions and lectures.

The globe's outer ring listed the preliminary lessons, the preparatory course, as an important pedagogical invention for the preparation for regular studies in the Bauhaus workshops, which were described with material terms such as wood, stone, metal, etc. in the sun's rays. The workshop work was linked in this sketch to the artistic and natural science technical courses, such as nature studies, colour and composition theory, construction theory, material studies or material and tool theory. The representation of the sun was in the centre with the terms "construction and theatre," and referred to the unity of the arts and at the same time the promotion of all creative talents in the students. The official diagram of the course of studies dispensed with the symbols of sun and earth and with the central positioning of theatre, but on the other hand emphasised in its strict circular shape the seriousness of the three-level education, the one-semester preparatory course, the three-year manual trades training with the Journeyman exam and the practical training in construction in postgraduate studies.

Gropius was only able to implement regular architectural education with the appointment of Swiss national Hannes

Karl Peter Röhl, The first Bauhaus seal, "Matchstick Star Man", 1919

Meyer (1889-1954) to the Dessau Bauhaus in 1927. This change in the perception of the Bauhaus was also to be reflected in a new signet, which was designed by means of a competition between the Bauhaus Masters. Oskar Schlemmer's head in profile emerged as the winner. Again, man was in the centre, now reduced to the head as the centre of feeling and intellect in a geometrically abstract use of form typical of the industrial age. The Bauhaus's reorientation was substantially stimulated by the work of Theo van Doesburg (1883-1931) in Weimar. In 1917 Doesburg had founded the Dutch artists' association *De Stijl* with Piet Mondrian (1872-1944), which with its holistic approach deduced a canon of artistic means with right angles and primary colours complemented by grey, black and white—a modern style. In December van Doesburg had visited the Bauhaus, and he had moved to Weimar in 1921. From March to July 1922, he held his legendary *De Stijl* class in Karl Peter Röhl's studio in Weimar. More than twenty people participated, mainly Bauhaus students, from Walter Herzger (1903-1985) to Andor Weininger (1899-1986), but also some teaching staff: Josef Zachmann (born 1905), Erich Brendel and fellow artists from Jena like Max Burchartz (1887-1961) and Walter Dexel (1890-1973). On 25th September 1922, Theo van Doesburg also called the Congress of Constructivist International to Weimar, and was hoping to follow Itten into the Master's position he was going to vacate, but Gropius appointed Hungarian constructivist and concept artist László Moholy-Nagy (1895-1946) instead. Thus Gropius consciously avoided the dominance of any one style at the Bauhaus in favour of an open and pluralistic design concept, which was oriented not least on the new opportunities of print media and advertising, film, photo and electronic data transmission. The KURI group (Constructive-Utilitarian-Rational International) of Bauhaus students, led by Farkas Molnár (1895-1945), which had been formed at the end of 1922, also promoted the modernisation of the Bauhaus.

This period also includes the only larger municipal architectural project, the reconstruction of the Jena City Theatre in 1921/22, commissioned by Ernst Hardt, the Director of the German National Theatre in Weimar. In the course of this renovation, a fresco by Schlemmer was washed off the ceiling in the auditorium due to complaints by Dexel and van Doesburg, who replaced it with a painting in grey, peach and deep blue.

On 13th April 1922, the Bauhaus development co-operative was founded to overcome the lack of student and teacher studios and living spaces, but also to promote the construction of a new academy building with better workshop facilities. In June 1922 the Thuringian state government requested a comprehensive exhibition of the Bauhaus achievements and made the further allocation of funds dependent on it. Gropius scheduled this

Oskar Schlemmer, Seal of the Weimar Bauhaus, "Profile", 1922
© Oskar Schlemmer Archive and Theatre Estate

exhibition for the summer of 1923 and focused the forces of the entire school on this goal, which is why no new students were accepted at the Bauhaus at that time. The first Bauhaus art exhibition took place at the end of 1922 in Calcutta, India, initiated by the Indian poet and painter Rabindranath Tagore (1861-1941). More than 250 hand drawings and printed graphics by the Bauhaus Masters, among them theatre projects by Schreyer and numerous preparatory course works by Margit Téry, were presented.[3]

## "Art and Technology—A New Unity" and the 1923 Bauhaus Exhibition

The great Bauhaus exhibition took place in Weimar from 15th August to 30th September 1923, and included the publication of *Staatliches Bauhaus in Weimar 1919-1923*, an activity report which took stock of the formation work, the *Haus am Horn* as the only realised Bauhaus building in Weimar, the *1st International Modernist Architecture Exhibition* and a Bauhaus Week with concerts, lectures and stage productions in Weimar and Jena. Gropius gave the opening lecture, "Art and Technology—A New Unity", and thus focused the discussion on the Bauhaus's profile since 1921. At the same time he took up his own conceptions of the connection between art and technology of March 1910, which he had presented to the then-CEO of the AEG, Walther Rathenau, in the form of a programme for the Modern Builders' Association.[4]

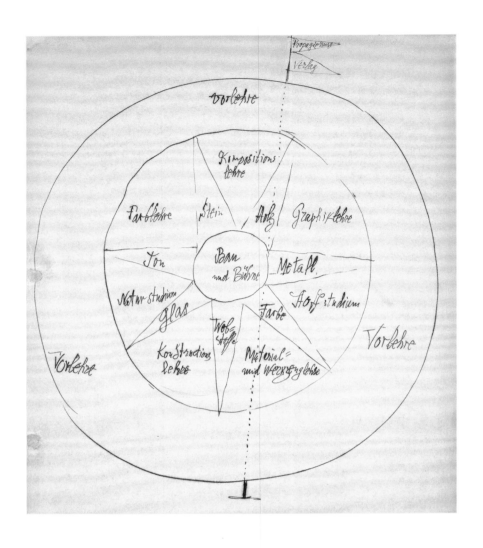

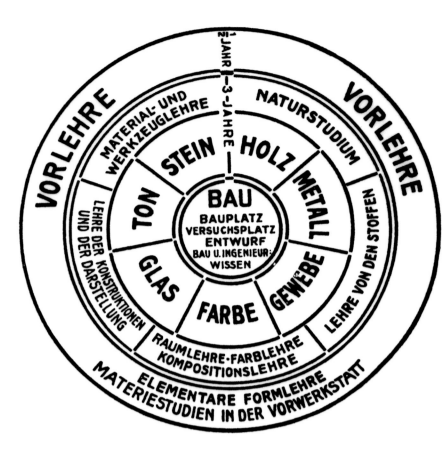

Paul Klee, Idea and structure of the Bauhaus, 1922

Walter Gropius, Model of studies at the Bauhaus, 1922

The German National Theatre in Weimar staged the *Triadisches Ballett* by Oscar Schlemmer, as well as concerts with works by Krenek, Busoni, Hindemith and Stravinsky. On 4th September the *Deutscher Werkbund* held a meeting in Weimar and was given repeat performances of Kurt Schmidt's *Mechanisches Ballett*, Oskar Schlemmer's *Figurales Kabinett* and Ludwig Hirschfeld-Mack's (1893-1965) *Reflektorische Lichtspiele*. The visual arts achievements of the students and teachers were presented in a comprehensive review at the Weimar State Museum.

Particularly in the workshops – the future "laboratories of industry" – many prototypes had been developed in the previous year, which made clear the transition from the manual trades to industrial technology. This included the "slat chair" by Marcel Breuer and a toy cabinet by Alma Buscher, the table lamp by Carl Jakob Jucker and Wilhelm Wagenfeld and a seven-branched candelabrum and seemingly minimalist floor lamp by Gyula Pap, the combination tea pot and mocha machine by Theodor Bogler and coffee pots by Otto Lindig in porcelain and ceramic, textile goods by Agnes Roghé, Hedwig Jungnik and Gunta Stölzl and individual wall hangings with form, material and bonding experiments.

The artistic interior design of the school buildings by Oskar Schlemmer, Joost Schmidt and Herbert Bayer as well as the director's office by Walter Gropius gave a multifaceted overview of the topics of colour and architecture.

The twenty Bauhaus postcards for the exhibition, based on designs of the Masters and students with 2,000 copies each, probably led to the first mail-art campaign in connection with the event programme. Train and railway station advertisements, posters and especially city maps made for an unusually professional advertising campaign.

This was all achieved while the German currency crashed completely in the summer of 1923, and 60% of the German population was unemployed. In October there were Communist uprisings in Hamburg, Saxony and Thuringia. Social Democrats and Communists also formed a "workers' government" in Thuringia, which was crushed when the *Reichswehr* (German army) marched into Weimar on 8th November. On the 23rd of that month the *Reichswehr* conducted a search of Gropius's house following anonymous political accusations. The political

Portrait of Walter Gropius, 1928, photograph by Hugo Erfurt

right in the Thuringian state government was questioning the organisation and operation of the Bauhaus as early as March 1924, while National Education Minister Max Greil defended the school.

In October, Gropius began negotiations with the president of the Thuringian National Bank regarding the foundation of a distribution company for Bauhaus products, the future Bauhaus Ltd. In connection with an intensification of production efforts in the Bauhaus workshops, Gropius wanted to try to free the Bauhaus from public financing and political influence and set up, if possible, a privately-owned company. On a smaller scale, this model had already been tested on students. Scholarships, grants and studios were awarded not only on the basis of social need, but also on the basis of achievement. Furthermore, the students received the sales proceeds of their products (less costs for material and machines) and were thus able to help finance their studies with qualified work, even before industry licensing fees had to be paid to employees and students of the Dessau Bauhaus.

This markedly practical approach in the production workshops meant yet another noticeable push for Bauhaus design work. High-quality furniture by Erich Dieckmann, tea and coffee sets by Marianne Brandt and Wilhelm Wagenfeld, and the Bauhaus chess set by Josef Hartwig were produced.

The third Thuringian state parliamentary elections on 10th February 1924 brought about a radical political change of course after the victory of the "Thuringian Order Union", an association of right-wing conservative parties (DNVP, DVP, and DDP). As early as 20th March the new Thuringian Public Education Minister, Leutheußer, informed Gropius that the contracts with the Bauhaus would not be extended. Attacks on the Bauhaus by the manual trade circle, the Weimar Artists' Council and the German nationalist bloc in the parliament increased, accompanied by the *Yellow Brochure*, an inflammatory pamphlet by former Bauhaus syndic Hans Beyer. On 9th April 1924 the Thuringian Finance Ministry determined the unprofitability of the Staatliches Bauhaus, which resulted in the government terminating its contracts with the Bauhaus from 31st March 1925 as a "precautionary measure." The final step in this cultural policy farce was the parliament's cutting of the budget from

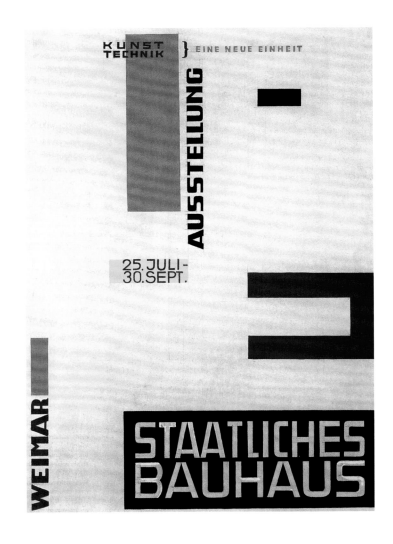

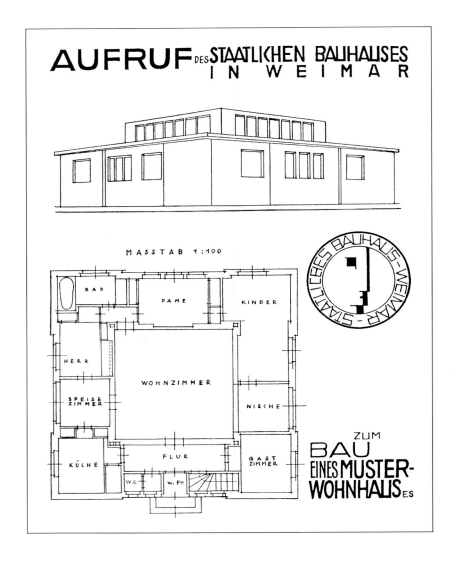

Georg Muche / Gropius Architecture Studio, *Haus am Horn*, north-west view, 1923

Call of the Bauhaus for the building of the *Haus am Horn*, 1922

Herbert Bayer, Project for the poster of the Bauhaus Exhibition, 1923

100,000 to 50,000 Reichsmark. A petition by more than six-hundred Weimar citizens in favour of the Bauhaus had just as little effect as the petitions by national and foreign artists, architects and organisations. Even the *Society of the Friends of the Bauhaus*, formed in the autumn of 1924, which included Nobel Prize winners such as Albert Einstein and Wilhelm Ostwald, could not persuade the state government otherwise. In an open letter dated December 26th, the Masters' Council declared the Bauhaus in Weimar dissolved from 1st April 1925 on the expiry of their contracts.

Walter Gropius, together with museum director Wilhelm Köhler, chose the best 165 workshop works from the 2,000 exhibits in the Bauhaus inventory for the National Art Collection in Weimar, works which today form the core inventory of the Bauhaus Museum—almost all of them twentieth-century design classics. The original photographic documentation from the Weimar Bauhaus is preserved at today's Bauhaus University in Weimar, as is the Bauhaus library with its approximately 500 volumes. The files of the Staatliches Bauhaus in Weimar are almost completely preserved in the State of Thuringia Main Archive in Weimar, and today form the basis of any serious Bauhaus research.

Herbert Bayer, Bills from the emergency currency of the Thuringia region, 1923

After making initial contact in February 1925, the Dessau City Council, headed by Fritz Hesse, decided to take on the Bauhaus in Dessau from 1st April of that year.

With the foundation of the State Academy of Crafts and Architecture in Weimar under the leadership of Otto Bartning on 1st April 1926, a second "Bauhaus chapter" began in Weimar, since 80% of the staff were Bauhaus graduates. It ended with a politically-motivated closure in the spring of 1930 by Nazi Minister Dr. Wilhelm Frick (1877-1946), who was executed in the autumn of 1946 and who is also responsible for the destruction of Bauhaus wall designs in the academy buildings as well as the shattering of the Bauhaus collection at the National Art Collection in Weimar.

## Bauhaus Dessau: Academy for Design (1925 to 1932)

Once it became known that the Staatliches Bauhaus in Weimar was to be closed, several German cities rallied to take it over. It had reached such a degree of fame that cities like Frankfurt-am-Main, Mannheim, Munich, Hagen, Hamburg, Krefeld, Darmstadt and also the City of Dessau wanted to house the school, should the need arise.

At the time Dessau was the capital of the State of Anhalt. Workers and employees of companies in the growing chemical and electronics industries lived there. These companies, while they may have been an incentive for the Bauhaus, were hardly apt for actual collaboration, as would soon be discovered. The Bauhaus community, and especially Walter Gropius, found the scenically delightful location of the city between two rivers appealing. Furthermore, they had a lot to catch up on culturally. Since there was a lack of apartments, the Bauhaus had good prospects of carrying out here its ideas of New Building, which had remained at the drawing-board stage in Weimar.

Dessau's mayor Fritz Hesse (DDP) had first heard of the Bauhaus in a newspaper article which he had received from Dessau's chief musical director Franz von Hoesslin in 1923. When the school had entered a state of crisis in Weimar in 1924, he sent the Anhalt state curator, Ludwig Grote, to Weimar; Grote returned with a favourable impression and encouraged Hesse to take over the Bauhaus. Following an initial on-site meeting with Wassily Kandinsky and Georg Muche on 20th February 1925, the Bauhaus made a commitment to move to Dessau. Dessau City and Anhalt government representatives for their part travelled to Weimar on 7th March 1925 to get an impression of the school. Henceforth the president of the *Landtag*, Heinrich Peus (SPD), and the city councillor and later parliamentary president Richard Paulick were so enthusiastic about the Bauhaus that a takeover

was considered in more concrete terms. Many Dessau politicians, such as the head of the city planning and building department Wilhelm Schmetzer and the head of the municipal planning and building department Theodor Overhoff, adopted a rather vacillating attitude towards the Bauhaus. Most of the politicians of the DNVP (German National People's Party) and the DVP (German People's Party), as well as wide sections of the middle classes, such as the Home Owners' Party and a citizens' association were opponents of the Bauhaus. Even during the initial takeover plans, the Bauhaus was attacked by these groups, but without success since a unique political situation had developed in Dessau. The SPD, classified as more right-wing within the political spectrum, had entered into a coalition with the liberal left-wing DDP (German Democratic Party) and on top of that had positive backing in the Anhalt free state. The KPD tried to exploit the Bauhaus as propaganda for their purposes from the start, and to influence it. The Dessau population, mostly industrial workers, adopted either a policy of wait-and-see or scepticism. Prominent representatives of the industries based in Dessau revealed themselves as supporters of the Bauhaus. Among those who turned toward new technological developments and were culturally open-minded was the scientist, businessman and aircraft engineer Hugo Junkers (1859-1935).

Quite differently from Weimar, narrower and more definite ideas were crystallising in this political and social sphere, which was favoured by a renewed upward economic trend; the city, as the new supporter of the school, expected from the Bauhaus an initiatory effect for its cultural and structural development.

After overcoming initial concerns on the part of some Bauhaus Masters, the city's intentions were largely in harmony with the wishes of Gropius and his comrades. The opportunities in Dessau were far beyond those of any other city. In March 1925, the Dessau city council decided to take over the school. That same month, the city's finance committee approved the construction of a Bauhaus building and the housing development for the Bauhaus Masters, and thus modified its earlier decision for the reconstruction of a local school for arts and crafts with which the Bauhaus was to merge.

The Bauhaus Masters had not anticipated this offer from Dessau. Lyonel Feininger, Wassily Kandinsky, Paul Klee, László Moholy-Nagy, Georg Muche and Oskar Schlemmer moved to Dessau, only Gerhard Marcks staying in Weimar. Not all the students followed. Former Weimar Bauhaus graduates who remained at the Bauhaus took over the workshops as Junior Masters, which actually would have allowed for the removal of the workshop leadership separation of Masters of Craft and Masters of Form. But since apprenticeships were to continue, the Master of Craft positions remained filled. Josef Albers ran part of the preparatory course as a Junior Master, Herbert Bayer was head of the typography workshop, Marcel Breuer ran the

Walter Gropius, Bauhaus buildings in Dessau, aerial view by Junkers, 1926    Walter Gropius, Masters' houses in Dessau, view from the north-west, 1925/26

Herbert Bayer, Bauhaus promotional brochure, 1927

furniture workshop, Hinnerk Scheper ran the mural painting workshop, Joost Schmidt was head of the sculpture workshop and Gunta Stölzl was in charge of the weaving workshop.

The Bauhaus spent seven years in Dessau. During this time buildings and products emerged which to this day continue to shape the image of the Bauhaus all over the world. The clarification process as to content, which had started with the Weimar exhibition in 1923, led to a consolidation in Dessau, on which even the forced change of site had a stabilising effect. The Bauhaus found unique support in Dessau. Here, it became an Academy for Design carried by the community; here, the workshops developed into "laboratories for industry." But in Dessau, too, there were conservative circles which did not like having the school in town. External and internal conflicts led to the fact that after Walter Gropius, there were successively two more directors. Political, social and economic developments in Germany eventually also had their effects on Dessau.

The new beginning came during a phase when the country was in an economic upswing; after 1929, the remaining years of the Bauhaus were characterised by rising unemployment and the battles of political forces which radicalised each other.

Since initially there was no building available which would have been large enough to hold the entire institution, provisional arrangements had to be made so that work could continue. This type of decentralised work corresponded to the situation in Weimar and did not seem to have hindered the new beginning in Dessau. With the express consent of the magistrate, Walter Gropius integrated his own architecture office and the Bauhaus administration into the old building of the Dessau School of Arts and Crafts (called the Technical Institute from 1926) with which a merger was planned in order to give the institution technical backing. Teaching began here on 14th October 1925, and on its upper floor, the plans and models for the construction of the Bauhaus building and Masters houses were created.

The workshops commenced their work on the upper floors of an annexe to a former Dessau mail-order firm which had been rented for this purpose. Individual studios were set up and art exhibitions organised. In the tower and other rooms of the former Leopold Dank Monastery (today's Museum for Natural and Pre-History), Wassily Kandinsky, Paul Klee and Oskar Schlemmer temporarily set up their studios, in which some of the classes also took place. Until their move into the Masters' houses, the Bauhaus Masters lived in the *Gründerzeit* (time of rapid industrial expansion) apartments which were situated in the northern part of the city, while the students mostly lived in the nearby district of Ziebigk. The relationship between the city and the Bauhaus was extremely ambivalent from the beginning. The ideas and new products of the Bauhaus obviously seemed to have asked too much of the majority of Dessau's population, who were reserved towards this innovative kind of institution and full of hesitant scepticism. The Bauhaus people, on the other hand, tried to reduce those feelings of resentment and misunderstanding by practicing openness and tolerance.

The Society of Friends of the Bauhaus also lent its support to this cause. Founded in 1924 by Walter Gropius to save the Bauhaus in Weimar, in Dessau it took over the important role of benefactor as well as mediator between the school and the city. As an association of intellectuals and industrialists close to the Bauhaus and a potential "association of sponsors", the Society of Friends of the Bauhaus also developed great influence and cultural charisma. It granted, for instance, an interest-free loan to make the Bauhaus's relocation from Weimar to Dessau more easily bearable. Furthermore the Society, whose membership grew to approximately five hundred in Dessau, financed the magazine *Bauhaus*, which was published beginning in December 1926, bought Bauhaus products, organised lectures as well as musical and theatre performances, initiated publications and arranged for annual gifts for the Bauhaus artists. The support also related to the provision of larger amounts or subsidies, for example for the free student meals.

## The Bauhaus Becomes an Academy

In the autumn of 1926 – the new school building had not yet been opened – the constitution was published. From that time, the Bauhaus was recognised by the Anhalt state government as the Academy of Design. Thus the Masters were henceforth called professors and the pupils, who now had the opportunity to gain the Bauhaus diploma, became students. The aims of the school were clearly defined in the constitution: first, "to shape the intellectual, crafts and technical abilities of creatively-talented human beings to equip them for design work, particularly construction", and second "to perform practical experiments, notably in housing construction and interiors, as well as to develop model types for industry and manual trades."

The holistic and comprehensive Bauhaus pedagogy was continued and reinforced. In Weimar the institution had been regarded as a pedagogical project for which the prestigious School for Arts and Crafts was a forerunner. The city of Dessau had remarkable school traditions to offer as well. A 1927 edition of the newspaper *Dessauer Zeitung* effusively reminded its readers of a "… Dessau Bauhaus 130 years ago" and referred to the General Preparatory Education Establishment for Mechanical Trades and Fine Arts for Dessau planned by the classicist architect Friedrich Wilhelm von Erdmannsdorff (1736-1800) in the eighteenth century. The Dessau *Philanthropin*, one of the most important schools founded in the eighteenth century, can in the broadest sense be seen as a regional forerunner of the Bauhaus on the basis of noticeable intellectual correlations. The Dessau education system, too, did not remain uninfluenced in the following period by these rich educational, political and reformist pedagogical traditions. In the second half of the 1920s there was, for instance, talk of a time of "pedagogical reforms and new reorganisation", while "student practical education, independence and self-administration, connection of individual subjects, physical education, [and] teacher co-operation" were seen as "new values".[5] The Bauhaus, that experimental school from Weimar which was very aware of this tradition, was able to continue this.

Apart from preparatory courses and workshop education there was also more complex instruction in natural science subjects as well as sports at the Dessau Bauhaus. In 1927, Walter Gropius was finally successful in appointing the Swiss architect Hannes Meyer, who would subsequently build and head the architecture department. Finally it was officially possible to educate architects in a two-level programme involving the completion of a builder's apprenticeship and work in the building studio. The lack of a building department or an architecture class as an appropriate conclusion of the Bauhaus curriculum had been recognised as a defect from the beginning. It was only later, with the establishment of an architecture department and the recognition of its academy status, that a renewed change of the teaching profile was brought about. Architecture was now above everything else. Almost all workshops were combined in the department of "Construction and Interior Furnishing." The advertising and, finally, the theatre departments remained separate areas. To this the "Seminar for Free Sculpting and Painting Design" was added, a course which was mainly run by Wassily Kandinsky and Paul Klee and later continued as a "Free Painting Class."[6]

## Laboratories for Industry – Workshop Work

Balanced economic and pedagogical considerations had preceded the structural changes as well as reorganisation of the curriculum in 1929. Among other things, this resulted in the fact that some of the Weimar workshops such as stained glass, painting, and bookbinding were not reinstated in Dessau. The stone sculpture and woodcarving department became a plastic workshop and the graphic printing department was replaced by the printing and advertising workshop. While it was possible in the new Dessau building to renovate the remaining workshops partially according to modern ideas, this was not true for the ceramics workshop, which was not continued in Dessau.

The interim solution in the city described earlier ended in October 1926 when the workshops moved into the Bauhaus building. After the opening of the new school building with its attendant publicity in December of the same year, all practical, manual trade subjects could be more strictly systematised and even more impulses from science could be picked up. With the orientation of workshop education towards industrial design, Gropius's principle of "nature research" was raised to a didactic model. According to it, a thing is defined "by its nature. In order to design it so that it functions – a container, a chair, a house – its nature must first be researched."[7] This approach was one of the things that created completely new jobs at the end of individual educational paths. The Bauhaus attempted to conceive serial production appropriate for industrial manufacture in the so-called "laboratory workshops", which were to be offered as high-quality and affordable mass products to a broad class of consumers. A precondition to the purchase of such furniture and objects for daily use, however, was the potential buyer's declared aesthetic belief in an industrially-based culture. Appropriate PR work was launched which included a stronger use of Bauhaus Ltd, which had been founded in 1925. It was mostly concerned with the marketing process for the products developed in the Bauhaus and with furthering collaboration with industry.

Industry and the beginning of urban construction were thus the focus of interest for the Bauhaus in Dessau. The central German industrial zone in which the Bauhaus had established itself offered more opportunities than ever before to push the combination of art and technology into a "new unity", and to connect the technical know-how of industrial production with the aesthetic modernism of the Bauhaus designs. But a broader collaboration between the Bauhaus as a "laboratory for industry" (as Gropius put it) and sectors of the industrial economy did not come about. Comprehensive collaboration with the gas device and aircraft manufacturer Junkers, for instance, would have been obvious in many areas, such as dwelling construction, aircraft interior furnishing, advertising and marketing or furniture construction. But the collaboration was reduced to individual projects and partial influencing. The reasons for this may have been less the lack of mutual support and respect than the differing economic interests of the company and the school, as well as the competitive situation which was eventually created by the avant-garde exploratory spirit of both parties.

## Planning and Building

The opportunity to build was one of the decisive reasons for Walter Gropius and the Bauhaus moving to Dessau. Here, many Bauhaus projects for which the city or co-operatives acted as clients could be carried out from the beginning. On the basis of this, municipal as well as residential buildings were created in rapid succession between 1925 and 1929, for which architect and Bauhaus director Walter Gropius coined the name "Bauhaus buildings." Designed in Gropius's private construction offices or together with teachers and students at the school and executed by regional contractors as well as in the Bauhaus workshops, a broad spectrum of modern architecture was created which to this day attracts interested visitors from all over the world. This includes the Bauhaus building itself, the Masters' houses, the former unemployment office and housing developments in Törten, a district in the south of the city. Yet Gropius's buildings, especially the housing developments in Törten, were extremely controversial at the time. Problems of structural physics and finance, as well as aesthetic aspects, were intensely discussed in daily newspapers and technical publications of the mid 1930s. In the articles, objectively existing defects reported by the inhabitants as well as aesthetically and politically-motivated negativity and concerns about a new type of design of space and object played a part. Furthermore, Gropius's buildings in Dessau had often been used as examples of the radicalism of modern architecture without concern for location or history. It was ignored that especially the housing developments in Törten and the Masters' houses bore an unapparent but subtle relation to the history of architecture and regional particularities, a reception of the English garden-

# semesterplan

| | 1. semester | 2. semester | 3. semester | 4. semester | 5. semester u. folg. |
|---|---|---|---|---|---|
| **1** architektur<br>a. bau<br>b. inneneinrichtung | *vermittlung der grundbegriffe der gestaltung*<br><br>allgemeine einführung:<br>a) abstrakte formelemente analytisches zeichnen — ca. 2 std.<br>b) werklehre, materialübungen — ca. 12 std.<br><br>allgemeine fächer:<br>a) darstellende geometrie — ca. 4 std.<br>b) schrift — ca. 2 std.<br>c) physik oder chemie — ca. 2 std.<br>d) gymnastik oder tanz (fakultativ) — ca. 2–4 std. | für fortgeschrittene:<br>baukonstruktion — ca. 4 std.<br>statik — ca. 2 std.<br>übungen — ca. 2 std.<br><br>*einführung in die specialausbildung*<br>praktische arbeit in einer bauhauswerkstatt — ca. 18 std.<br><br>vorträge und übungen:<br>a) primäre gestaltung der fläche — ca. 2 std.<br>b) volumen raumkonstruktion — ca. 2 std.<br><br>allgemeine fächer:<br>a) darstellende geometrie — ca. 2 std.<br>b) fachzeichnen — ca. 2 std.<br>c) schrift — ca. 2 std.<br>d) physik oder chemie — ca. 2 std. | spezialausbildung<br>prakt. arbeit in einer werkst. 18 std.<br>a. bau — baukonstr. 4 „<br>statik 4 „<br>a. entwurf 4 „<br>veranschlag. 2 „<br>baustofflehre 2 „<br><br>b. inneneinrichtg. — praktische arbeit in einer werkstatt, mit entwerfen, detaillieren, kalkulieren 36 std.<br>fachzeichnen 2 „<br><br>*spezialausbildung unter bevorzug. der theorie* | entwurfsatelier mit anschließender baupraxis<br>einzelvorträge über baukonstruktion eisenbetonbau statik wärmelehre installation veranschlagen ausschreibung normenlehre<br>sonderkurse über stadtbau verkehr wirtschaftliche betriebsführung<br><br>praktische arbeit wie im 3. semester 18 std.<br>gestaltungslehre fachzeichnen fachwissen<br><br>*reifere (siche abteilungsplan 1a vorbedingung 1–3) können bereits nach dem 1. semester auf antrag an den lehrgängen des 4. semesters teilnehmen.* | wie im 4. semester<br><br>wie 4. semester selbständige laboratoriumsarbeit in der werkstatt 36 std.<br><br>*erhöhte spezialausbildung mit wachsender selbständigkeit der aufgaben.* |
| **2** reklame | | | einführung in das werbewesen untersuchung der werbemittel praktische übungen | wie im 3. semester und einzelvorlesungen über fachgebiete | selbständige mitarbeit an praktischen werbeaufgaben |
| **3** bühne | | | werkstattarbeit gymnastisch-tänzerische, musikalische, sprachliche übungen | werkstattarbeit choreographie dramaturgie bühnenwissenschaft | werkstattarbeit, selbständige mitarbeit an bühnenaufgaben und aufführungen |
| **4** seminar für freie plastische und malerische gestaltung | | | korrektur eigener arbeiten nach vereinbarung selbstwahl der meister praktische arbeit in einer werkstatt 18 std. | wie im 3. semester ohne werkstatt | wie im 4. semester |

Masters of the Bauhaus on the roof of the Bauhaus building on the December 4th, 1926, photograph taken using automatic shutter release (l-r: Josef Albers, Hinnerk Scheper, Georg Muche, László Moholy-Nagy, Herbert Bayer, Joost Schmidt, Walter Gropius, Marcel Breuer, Wassily Kandinsky, Paul Klee, Lyonel Feininger, Gunta Stölzl, Oskar Schlemmer)

Bauhaus Dessau, Semester plan, 1927

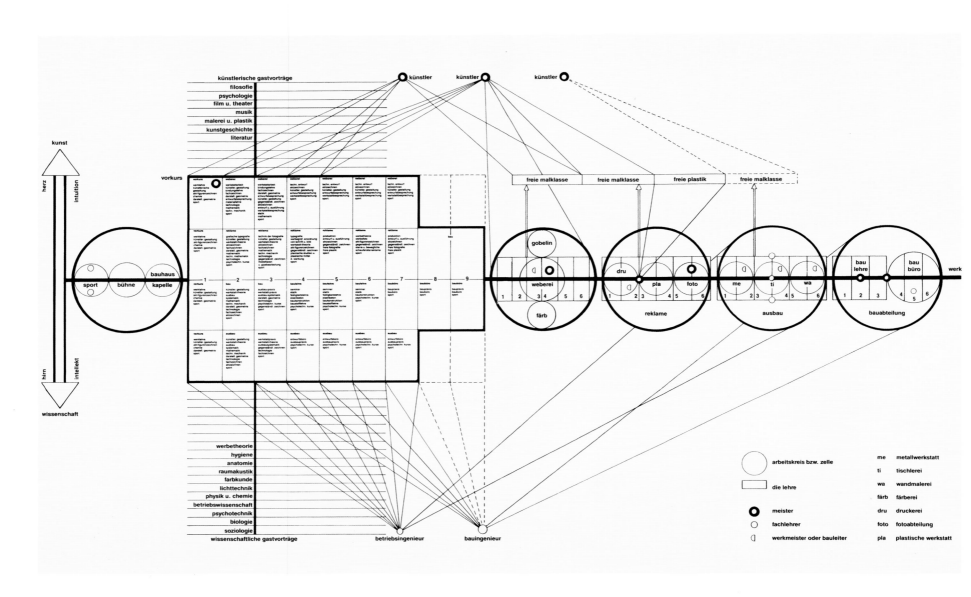

Hannes Meyer, Bauhaus Dessau, Model of the organisation, 1930

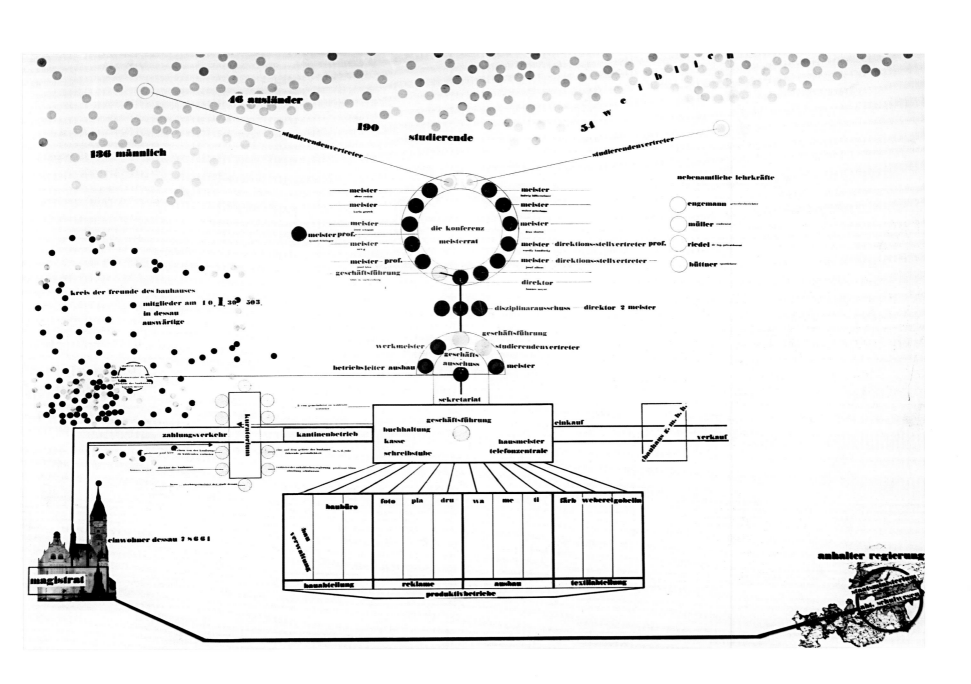

Hannes Meyer, Model of the Bauhaus organisation and its links with the outside world, 1930

city-movement and the late 18<sup>th</sup> century garden empire in Dessau-Wörlitz.

In the experimental climate of the Bauhaus in Dessau, a number of visionary plans were created which related to urban concepts and projections. One of the reasons for this was the general desire to develop the city of Dessau from the "royal city of yesterday" into a "city of industry and traffic" in order to overcome its "previously very conservative"[8] attitude toward cultural matters and to conserve its cultural identity as it confronted the modern industrial age. The Bauhaus was assigned an important role in this transformation process. Despite ample hostility and obstructions, the Bauhaus in Dessau had without a doubt become a place of experimental questioning and momentum for the development of the city of Dessau and beyond. Its international fame and general reputation grew particularly after the opening of the new school building and the construction of further Bauhaus buildings. Both then and now up to seven hundred visitors a day would travel to Dessau to visit the Bauhaus and its buildings.

## The Hannes Meyer Era

Swiss architect Hannes Meyer became the new director in 1928. This was preceded by a period of limited donations and a stagnation of good relations between the city of Dessau and its modern institute. The results were dismissals and further limitations imposed on the already very restricted workshops. The precarious situation worsened when the Bauhaus Ltd, despite intense efforts, could not find new customers for its newly-developed products; necessary income was missing. Criticism of the Bauhaus increased. It now came also from representatives of the SPD and there were even tensions with the mayor of Dessau, Hesse. This transferred to parts of the population, whose reservations against the Bauhaus increased as well. Dessau's lower middle class in particular considered what was carried on in the school as a danger to public order. The Bauhaus was denounced as a breeding ground for "cultural bolshevism" and avoided by many Dessau citizens.

Gropius was constantly busy with battles for the survival of the institution, and when internal problems also increased he gave up. He resigned from his position as director of the Bauhaus and suggested Hannes Meyer as his successor. Gropius stated that he wanted to build more, and considered again, this time somewhere else, the foundation of a "housing construction factory." The Bauhaus, so he thought, was firmly established and no longer required his leadership. It can be suspected that Gropius saw his goals fulfilled particularly in the pedagogical sector with the establishment of an architecture department and that he was now lacking

Hannes Meyer before the drawing table, c. 1926

motivation for further school experiments. Along with Gropius, László Moholy-Nagy, Herbert Bayer and Marcel Breuer also left the school.

Hannes Meyer took office as Bauhaus director on 1st April 1928. In the 1920s, he had been one of the most prominent representatives of a radical scientific functionalism with ideologically left-wing views. On the basis of his *Weltanschauung*, he reformed the education and workshop production of the Bauhaus and subjected the school to profound restructuring. Under his leadership, the metal, furniture and mural-painting workshops were combined into the "Interior Furnishing Workshop", while the "Advertising and Marketing Workshop" included the formerly independent workshops for printing, advertising, exhibitions, photography and sculpting. Workshop production was oriented in general toward "people's household goods", expanded into a production operation and pushed so that teaching, experimentation and production for a real market were fused. "Necessities, not luxuries", was Meyer's motto. The Bauhaus, whose products Meyer had earlier criticised as "sect-like and aesthetic"[9], should more than before be "a combination of workshop work, free art and science".[10]

When Hannes Meyer succeeded Walter Gropius, what was supposed to be avoided at the Bauhaus had already been extensively established: the "Bauhaus style." Even chequered underwear advertised the Bauhaus style. How had this happened? Gropius proclaimed his design principle of nature research on the basis of the unification of art and technology in 1925. This nature analysis was, however, not carried out according to empirically scientific criteria in the Bauhaus under Gropius, as was discovered by Gropius researcher Winfried Nerdinger. The nature of an object, according to Nerdinger, was sought for in its purpose. By equating purpose and nature, the purposeful form was aestheticised without further questioning, and that initially meant geometric forms.

Thus the products which were meant to serve the "new man" in a "new time" were subject to a vocabulary of geometric forms based on the design theories of art teachers, and Meyer initially sought to fight the "Bauhaus style" after taking office as director.[11] He put forward an analysis of social and economic questions which should eventually form the beginnings of the design process. Yet he did not succeed in fully communicating his approach, so it found its way into only a few elements of design practise. On the one hand, previously lacking engineering sciences were integrated into the curriculum, but on the other hand, the expansion of the art classes of the teachers of the Bauhaus and the "free painting classes" by Klee and Kandinsky eventually meant less of an integration and more of what seemed like the intentional exclusion of a specific field of learning. For Meyer, "art was strangling life" in the Bauhaus of his predecessor, which is why he wanted to limit the artists' influence. The path was to lead "from formal intuition to construction science education".[12] Meyer wanted education at the Bauhaus to be functional, constructive and collectivist, thus conditioning the school for the times ahead.

The nine-semester education system was structured as follows: Mondays were reserved for music education, while scientific subjects were scheduled for Fridays. In the time between, work was carried out all day in the workshops, reminiscent of a factory setting. Saturdays were reserved for sports. A specialisation then followed in the architecture department, which Meyer had subdivided into construction theory and building department. The two educational goals were now called "artist" or "production or construction engineer." Work and classes in the workshops as preparation for work in architecture thus corresponded completely to Walter Gropius's original approach. Under Meyer's leadership, the school's limits were stretched when the number of students increased to two hundred, whose acceptance into the school was facilitated by the exclusion of some of the most talented people. The reason for this was the intention, according to the pedagogics of the

Bauhaus to enable the "real" integration of a maximum number of people in society. In many points Meyer agreed in principle with the conceptual approach of his predecessor. Thus, for both men, building was a truly social development of "organisation of life processes" (as Gropius put it). But where Meyer's concept was different from Gropius's was in its affinity towards co-operative movements and the associated views going back to Swiss pedagogue Johann Heinrich Pestalozzi regarding the sense in building "small circles"–family, work associations of artists and designers. For Gropius, the principle of nature research applied, while for Meyer the systematic determination of the need was the basis of design. From the basis of this concept, Meyer did not only design his architecture but also organised the "vertical brigades" within which students of different levels of education worked on one project from the drawing board to the building site. In terms of enthusiasm for co-

Adolf Hofmeister, Cartoon of Hannes Meyer's dismissal, 1930

Portrait of Ludwig Mies van der Rohe, c. 1931

convey to the general public. In fact, the general public did not permit it. When an organised group of Communist students, which had been banned under Hannes Meyer's directorship following outside pressure, eventually called publicly for participation in the "world revolution" and 60% of the school's students participated in a KPD demonstration, the relationship between the Bauhaus and the Dessau city elders, who feared a loss of votes with such a "red Bauhaus", became intolerable. With the support of anti-communist Bauhaus teachers such as Josef Albers and Wassily Kandinsky, who saw their positions threatened by Meyer's restructuring, and also of Walter Gropius, who disliked Meyer's criticism of the Bauhaus, as well as the mayor Fritz Hesse and his state curator Ludwig Grote, Meyer was discharged from his post of director of the Bauhaus in August 1930. Initially, Meyer successfully fought the discharge but resigned from his post as a result of an arbitration settlement.

## The Ludwig Mies van der Rohe Era

Hannes Meyer, fallen into political and governmental disfavour, had after his discharge taken critical stock of his Bauhaus time in an open letter to the Mayor of Dessau entitled *My Discharge from the Bauhaus* and shortly thereafter had gone to Moscow with a "red Bauhaus brigade." In his post, he was succeeded by the German architect Ludwig Mies van der Rohe. Earlier, the attempt to reinstall Gropius as director had failed, as had the appointment of architect Otto Haesler (1880-1962), suggested by Gropius.

Ludwig Mies van der Rohe had drawn attention to himself one year earlier with the design of the German pavilion for the World Exposition in Barcelona. In 1926/1927, he directed the planning of the Weißenhof housing development in Stuttgart, a unique summary of achievements of the so-called *Neues Bauen* (New Building), with the participation of seventeen leading modern architects from all over Europe. With Mies van der Rohe, the Bauhaus was to focus on teaching at a time when economic and thus political problems intensified in Anhalt following a spreading world economic crisis and the increasing instability of the Weimar Republic. At the time of his installation, he announced: "I do not want marmalade, not workshop and school, but school." Politically, the Bauhaus was no longer to make itself visible. The school was temporarily officially closed and reopened for the autumn 1930 semester. What remained of the Bauhaus were the name and the building. Everything else was changed in agreement with the city: budget, programme, constitution, content and structure. The students had to reapply. Some were expelled, the politically radical sifted out. School fees were increased, living studios closed. "Five of the most deserving foreign Bauhaus students" were expelled by the

operatives as well as for building commissions, the city of Dessau provided a good opportunity with the commission of the *Laubenganghäuser* (Balcony Access Houses). Other buildings produced from 1928 to 1930, such as the complex for the Federal School of the ADGB (General German Federation of Labor Unions) in Bernau near Berlin and the Nolden House in the Eifel were also successful. The exhibition *Bauhaus Housing for the People*, which had been designed by the Bauhaus and was travelling the country in order to open up a market for Bauhaus products, gained much attention but not the hoped-for sales. Only the Bauhaus wallpaper created by Bauhaus students in Dessau in 1929 became a sales hit.

Hannes Meyer failed. This failure was mainly a result of the fact that he had permitted a left-wing political radicalisation to develop within the student body starting in 1928 and was not able to mediate the process enough to prevent damage to the institution's image. The school's practise of open discourse, its general love of experimentation, including discussion of political and social problems was, as it turned out, hard to

Iwao Yamawaki, *The Attack on the Bauhaus*, collage, 1932

Dessau magistrate without explanation.[13] In April 1931, Paul Klee (1879-1940), one of the most important teachers, left the Bauhaus in order to take up a teaching position at the Düsseldorf Fine Arts Academy. Shortly thereafter the only Junior Master, Gunta Stölzl (1897-1983), also left.

Mies van der Rohe did not strive for new experimental education methods at the Bauhaus. The social reference which may have applied to the designs of Gropius and Meyer did not play an important role for Mies van der Rohe. In spite of this, he continued many things begun by his predecessors. This included the adoption of the changes to the workshop structure initiated by Meyer. The experimental approach of Mies van der Rohe lay in the quality of new architectural designs themselves.

He deemed all other areas dependent on architecture and, based on this conclusion, he developed the specifics and a variety of educational propositions. His aim was not social efficiency, but the highest aesthetic and constructive quality. The art of building, a term that had been frowned upon earlier, became used again in everyday language and meant that not only the purpose but also the values and humanistic components were of importance. The architectural education now had an even more central role than under Hannes Meyer, with its studies reduced to six semesters, even though the previously characteristic combination of theory and practise had been lost.

Only Ludwig Hilberseimer (1885-1967), who had been appointed by Hannes Meyer, was able to include a practical approach in his classes. Even though technical education was not overly emphasised, the Bauhaus took on more similarities with a regular Technical Academy for Architecture with subdivisions of art and workshop, whose productions had been all but obliterated and reduced to the production of models for industry purposes. Mies van der Rohe himself taught, as Hannes Meyer did before him. His team was reinforced by the appointment of interior designer Lilly Reich (1885-1947) in the spring of 1932, who took over the department of interior furnishing. Starting from the fourth semester the students had the opportunity to attend instruction by the Bauhaus director, the so-called "Construction Seminar." The influence of Mies van der Rohe, for whom architecture was mainly the commanding control of space, material and proportion, had lasting effects on his students' understanding of architecture.

### The Closure of the Bauhaus in Dessau

Mies van der Rohe had tried to keep the Bauhaus politically neutral. Still, the school remained a thorn in the flesh of the National Socialist Party, which was gaining strength at that time. In the Bauhaus's end-phase in Dessau, relations with the city had reached their nadir. The NSDAP declared its fight against the Bauhaus, which was now denounced as a "Jewish dive" and for the party embodied an intellectual opposite to its own world view, one of its central topics. The budget was cut further so that the school became largely dependent on licence income and was hardly able to survive.

In May 1932 the parliamentary elections in Anhalt led to the fall of the state government, which had up until then been in favour of the Bauhaus, and the right-wing gained the majority. Anhalt thus became the first German state with a government led by National Socialists, who seized the opportunity to weaken the Dessau magistrate with a targeted personnel policy. On 8th July 1932, Paul Schultze-Naumburg, the National Socialist Prime Minister Alfred Freyberg, and other city and NSDAP representatives including Fritz Hesse, who was still mayor, visited the Bauhaus. Just a few days after this visit, the NSDAP, who in the Dessau city council elections of November 1931 had become the strongest party, proposed the closure of the institution. Hesse and four Communists agreed with the proposal, while the Social Democrats abstained. Thus the dissolution of the Bauhaus was sealed. Student protests with petitions in newspapers and to the *Reichspräsident* (national President) were as ineffective as a tour with more than nine hundred people from Chemnitz, who had specially travelled there by train.[14] On the last day of September 1932, the Bauhaus left Dessau.

## Bauhaus Berlin: Free Education and Research Institute (1932-1933)

On the basis of a settlement which Mies van der Rohe was able to reach with the Bauhaus Masters against the dissolution order, the city of Dessau was forced to continue to pay the teachers until 1935, let the Bauhaus keep furniture and equipment on loan and transfer the patents and utility models issued to the school as well as any rights form licensing agreements to van der Rohe as the last Bauhaus director. With that and the tuition income there was at least a material possibility that the school might continue its existence, for which the two Social Democrat cities of Leipzig and Magdeburg had lobbied. Mies van der Rohe, however, had already, prior to the closure of the Bauhaus in Dessau, had the intention of continuing the school as a private institute in Berlin, should the necessity arise. In the former telephone factory of J. Berliner at the corner of Siemensstrasse and Birkbuschstrasse in the Steglitz district of Berlin, he found the necessary rooms, which were provisionally outfitted and equipped mainly by the students. A small building with a glass roof housed the workshops, while theoretical instruction and classes in painting and photography were set up in a two-storey building.

In Berlin Mies van der Rohe provided the Bauhaus with the suffix "Free Education and Research Institute." The studies now lasted seven semesters. With the exception of Alfred Arndt and Joost Schmidt, who had not been taken on because of their political positions, the entire teaching staff and more than one hundred students moved to Berlin. As early as October 1932, thirty-five new applications were also registered, so that the school had again reached four-fifths of its Dessau enrolment. Since the institute's status was that of a private establishment, the authority now lay with the director, which was noted accordingly in a study guide. Mies van der Rohe wanted to continue in Berlin the content of the working programme which had been developed in Dessau. Wassily Kandinsky headed the free painting class and Josef Albers took over as a crafts teacher; Walter Peterhans was in charge of photography, Hinnerk Scheper directed the training in colouring, Lilly Reich ran the weaving and interior furnishing seminar, the engineer Alcar Rudelt headed the instruction in structural engineering and modern building construction, Friedrich Engemann ran the construction of buildings and interiors, and Ludwig Hilberseimer oversaw the subjects of building studies and urban development. Ludwig Mies van der Rohe himself ran a construction seminar.

"It is our goal," he explained, "to educate architects in such a manner that they command all the fields which touch onto architecture, from small residential apartment construction to urban development ... as well as all the furniture and down to textiles."[15]

The Bauhaus building in Dessau as NS-Gauführerschule (Nazi-regime School for the training of ministers of different regions), 1935

Thus Mies van der Rohe also strove – as did Walter Gropius in Weimar before him – for a type of synthesis of the arts in building. Under this premise oriented on "the needs of the masses" and striving for a "refinement of quality and taste",[16] he also sought collaboration with industry, for which the workshops were to develop models. Mies van der Rohe placed great importance on the courses taught by visual artists. In addition to the contributions of Kandinsky and Peterhans, he insisted that Albers also teach drawing from nature.

## The Closure of the Bauhaus in Berlin

When, at the beginning of 1933, Adolf Hitler was appointed *Reichskanzler* (German Chancellor), reality slowly set in at the Berlin Bauhaus and thoughts about the survival of the school started to be considered. In the same way that progressive museum and academy directors were subsequently attacked and works of modern art removed from museums, attacks against the Bauhaus also increased. On 11th April 1933, a police raid of the rooms of the Berlin Bauhaus took place upon the petition of the Dessau Attorney General, who was already investigating Hesse, the mayor. Supposedly "incriminating material" was seized, students temporarily arrested and the building sealed. Even though, thanks to the efforts of Ludwig Mies van der Rohe and several students, a reopening with concessions to the new state was eventually possible, the faculty of the Bauhaus declared the school dissolved on 20th July 1933. Economic and, primarily, political reasons made continuation impossible.

Bauhaus Berlin in a former telephone factory, 1932, photograph: Howard Dearstyne

The reasons for such a vehement rejection were primarily in the programme of the institution, which had always been considered "left-wing" and thus not compatible with the reactionary nationalist and racist cultural policy of the Nazi regime. The questioning of traditional academic forms of education, the turning towards industrial production and thus turning away from the manual trades (on which the lower middle classes were dependent) were from the beginning a thorn in the side of conservative forces. On top of this came the international composition of the faculty and the student body, and finally the social claims which were associated with the Bauhaus programme.

After the dissolution of the Bauhaus, Mies van der Rohe occasionally ran seminars on questions about the art of building with a small circle of former Bauhaus graduates in his private studio. Finally, in 1938, he became Director of the Architectural Department at the Amour Institute, which would

become the Illinois Institute of Technology in Chicago. Several Bauhaus graduates followed him there. Walter Gropius had left Germany earlier for England, together with Marcel Breuer. From there, he transferred to the Harvard Graduate School of Design in Cambridge, Massachusetts in 1937. Hannes Meyer, who had gone to the USSR after his discharge as Bauhaus director, later worked in Switzerland for some time, as well as in Mexico. Wassily Kandinsky emigrated to Paris as early as 1933. Paul Klee returned to his hometown of Berne the same year. Also in 1933, Josef Albers went to the USA and became one of the first Bauhaus teachers to teach at Black Mountain College in North Carolina. László Moholy-Nagy became head of the "New Bauhaus" in Chicago in 1937, where several Bauhaus graduates worked in the years following. Lyonel Feininger, too, emigrated in 1937 to the USA with Herbert Bayer, while Johannes Itten was drawn to Zurich in 1939.

Bauhaus teachers Oskar Schlemmer, Georg Muche and Gerhard Marcks, whose works had been categorised as "degenerate", however, stayed in Germany. A large proportion of Bauhaus graduates and former students got by in the Third Reich in some form or other, often moving between conformity and resistance. Some of them were unable to find work in any architectural office or advertising company, while some made careers for themselves. Politically active opponents of the National Socialist system and Jewish students were forced into exile or subject to prosecution. Some lost their lives in prison or concentration camps, such as Susanne Banki, Friedl Dicker-Brandeis, Lotte Menzel and Hedwig Slutzki in Auschwitz, Willi Jungmittag in Brandenburg and Josef Knau on the concentration ship *Thielbeck*.

Moving into the Bauhaus Berlin, 1932

Article from a Berlin local newspaper on April 12, 1933 about the police search of the Bauhaus

# II
# Preparatory Course and Basic Design Education

# The Preparatory Course

The preparatory course, also called the preliminary course or basic course, was among the most important pedagogic achievements of the Bauhaus, developed by Johannes Itten and continued by László Moholy-Nagy and Josef Albers. As an idea, the preparatory course was not a Bauhaus invention. The tradition of preparatory course teaching in artistic education goes back to the nineteenth century and is closely connected with the process of art school reform at the beginning of the twentieth century. As a trial or introductory semester, the preparatory course at the Bauhaus formed the basis for the introduction of young people of varied educational backgrounds to academic studies in the principles of design, and thus to break with all old educational privileges. The successful completion of the preparatory course was necessary for acceptance into one of the Bauhaus workshops. Those interested in the Bauhaus had the opportunity to test themselves in the preparatory course to see whether they had any aptitude as a designer. At the same time they had the opportunity—without the constraints of a regular course—to explore their leaning toward a certain field of studies or material in the different workshops. During this "self-finding course", imagination and creativity were "tested" as well as sensitivity, diligence, stamina and team work.

The students had the opportunity to learn together the new jargon for designers and to further develop it. The numerous foreign students—up to 33%—were able to perfect colloquial language and technical terminology before starting regular specialist courses. Not least, the informal work of the preparatory course and the resulting close acquaintances between the students formed the basis of future interdisciplinary project work and teamwork at the Bauhaus. The preparatory course mainly consisted of form, colour and materials instruction, which was given by the art teachers at the Bauhaus. Almost throughout, the painters Wassily Kandinsky and Paul Klee taught basic and elementary aspects of form and colour studies. Classes such as "Figure Study" and "Calligraphy" were part of the preparatory course; later, students also received instruction in the basics of natural science or descriptive geometry.

Johannes Itten set himself three goals for his preparatory course teaching:

1. To free the creative forces and thus the artistic talent of the students. Individual experience and insights were to lead to real work. The students were to free themselves step by step from all dead conventions and pluck up the courage to do their own work.

2. To make the students' choice of profession easier. Materials and texture practise were a valuable aid in this. Every student found out after a short period of time which material attracted him, whether glass, wood, stone, clay, metal or spinning products, stimulating him to creative activity.

3. Students were to be taught the basic laws of artistic design for their later artistic professions. The laws of form and colour opened the world of the objective to the students. In the course of their work, objective and subjective form and colour problems could intermingle in various ways.

… It was important to me when teaching artistic means of expression that the different temperaments and talents felt individually addressed. Only in that way could a creative atmosphere beneficial to original work emerge. The work was to be "real"…[17]

Itten had tested his pedagogical and artistic experiences, which he had gained in his teacher training in Berne, from art studies in Geneva and at the Stuttgart Academy with Adolf Hölzel, and in a private school in Vienna since 1916. It was there that he had met Walter Gropius in the artists' circle around Alma Mahler. Johannes Itten's preparatory course was, literally, mental training. Body and soul were to be adjusted to design work with breathing and concentration exercises. Out of resting concentration Itten developed exercises for moving concentration. Thus, he had students draw charcoal circles on pieces of packing paper with both hands, in the same and in opposite directions, circling to the left or to the right. The same exercise was repeated with parallel lines. To increase the level of difficulty, one hand was to produce uniform lines, the other rhythmic ones. These exercises seem to be comparable to those of a percussionist with his instrument in order to achieve the perfect rhythm, but also in order to be able to portray his own sensitivities and emotions. Not without reason was Gertrud Grunow appointed to the Bauhaus from 1919 to 1923 to teach "harmonisation studies", to introduce the basic relationships of tone, form and colour.

Itten tied in sensitivity training with this mental training. He had touch-boards assembled from various materials for students to feel and be able to recognise materials with their eyes closed.

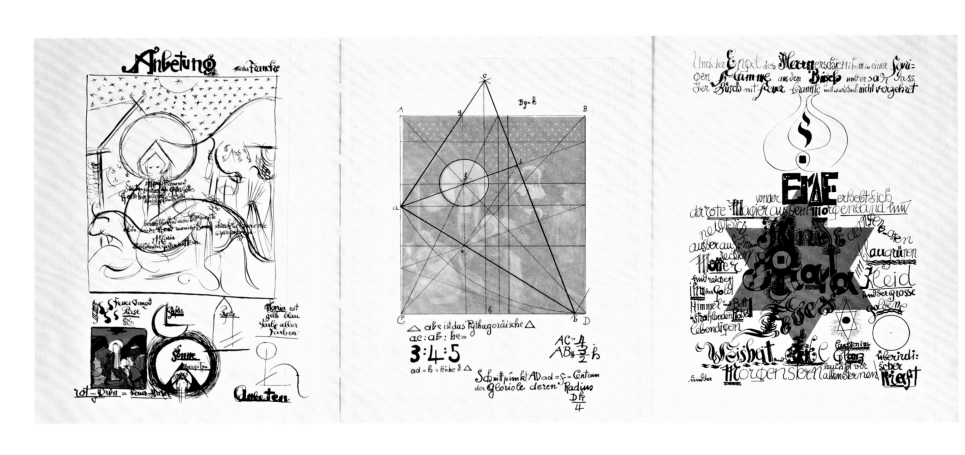

Johannes Itten, Veneration of Master Franke, print from *Analyses of the Old Masters*, in *Utopia. Dokumente der Wirklichkeit (Documents of Reality)* I/II, edited by Bruno Adler, Weimar 1921

The schooling of the sense of touch, the examination of the characteristics of materials and surfaces became the basic experience of design work. The training of hand and eye was in the focus of the obligatory exercises with grey-scales, where as many different shades between black and white as possible were to be produced with charcoal or chalk.

The systematic training of all the senses in order to know and understand one's environment better was one of Itten's pedagogically practical concepts, as was the "nature research" demanded by Gropius in order to advance to new problem-solving approaches. This also included the analysis method as presented by Itten in his 1921 publication *Analysis of Old Masters*. He used mathematical processes when analysing historic works of art in order to record measurements and proportions in a scientifically exact manner. At the same time, he used abstraction drawing–often with a large number of variations–to make clear the different aspects of the composition. Finally, he also included language as an individual medium of analysis with its range of possibilities from objective description to subjective reflection.

Yet nature studies were not neglected in the preparatory course either, but rather formed the basis for any design. Exact observation of nature, as well as exact graphic reproduction of the material, was taught. As early as his portfolio *10 Original Lithographs*, which

had been published in Vienna in 1919, Itten referred to the connection between the model in nature and abstraction. Plant motifs, mountainous landscapes, futuristically enlivened human figures as well as non-objective compositions showed different levels of abstraction and at the same time a pluralistic approach to art. Demanding exercises dealt with the human figure in motion. The model repeatedly carried out a movement or characteristic posture which was portrayed as a "movement rhythm", sometimes combined to form a contrast pair such as Rudolf Lutz's *The Young Woman* and *The Old Man*, created around 1919.

The aim of materials studies was the graphic depiction of the characteristics of various materials from memory in almost-photorealistic perfection. Materials studies led to an increased examination of different materials–often free materials from nature or household and workshop garbage and remnants–into the three-dimensional field of plastics and construction. This is demonstrated by *Würfelplastik/Lichtplastik (Cubic plastic/Light plastic)* by Theobald Emil Müller-Hummel of 1920 or Nikolai Wassiljew's *Spiral-Turm (Spiral Tower)* of approximately 1920, constructions made of tin cans, metal strips and wires on a pedestal. Of the material collages, reliefs and preparatory course "plastics", hardly any originals are preserved, and only a few were photographically documented, fourteen of which are in the original photo documentation archive of the Weimar Bauhaus. A particularly characteristic example is Erich

Dieckmann's material study of 1922, a material collage in a box of approximately 60 x 50 x 5 centimetres with briquette, pieces of bark, board elements trimmed in colour, peat, hay behind wire mesh, bundled grass blades, woven plant fibre and plant parts in a glass tube. Some of the works were reconstructed, such as the *Material Study–Composition of Different Materials for the Observation of the Complementary Effects of Different Materials* by Margarete Willers (?) around 1921 and the material study by Moses Mirkin from 1922 of wood, a glass cylinder and a saw blade. This playful and unprejudiced dealing with materials, colours, forms and design options can also be called "creativity training."

Itten's contrast theory, which he also transferred to colour and form theory, also proved to be a knowledge-theoretic model. Thus, he worked through a multitude of contrasts in his preparatory course: wide/narrow, thick/thin, large/small, black/white, a lot/a little, straight/curved, sharp/dull, vertical/horizontal, diagonal/circular, high/low, plane/line, plane/solid, line/solid, smooth/rough, hard/soft, still/in motion, light/heavy, transparent/opaque, continuous/interrupted, etc. He also included the seven colour contrasts inspired by Hölzel: hue contrast, light/dark contrast, cool/warm contrast, complementary contrast, simultaneous contrast, saturation contrast and extension contrast.

On the basis of colour courses with Itten, Klee and particularly Kandinsky, the Bauhaus Journeyman Ludwig Hirschfeld-Mack (1893-1965) developed his colour seminar in the 1922/1923 winter semester, which was published in 1923 in the Bauhaus book as a Kandinsky course with colour charts by Hirschfeld-Mack. With this colour seminar, the basic artistic education reached its first peak in 1923 with the aim of developing a uniform and universally-applied design language.

Itten's pedagogical practise of an art education by means of subjective experience and objective recognition encountered resistance as early as 1922 in the Bauhaus, when discussions regarding the development and reorientation of the academy towards design and architecture, following Gropius's motto "art and technology–a new unity", began. In addition to individual artistic creativity, the ability to work in a team and various scientific-technical aspects were now part of the academy's list of requirements.

Beginning in 1921, Georg Muche taught the preparatory course in rotation with Itten, and from 1923 to 1928 it was run by László Moholy-Nagy, supported by Josef Albers, who ran the preparatory course workshop in the Weimar Reithaus. Both focused the preparatory course more on the requirements of the workshop, which were increasingly to develop prototypes as "laboratories for industry." This became particularly evident in construction studies, where Moholy-Nagy examined topics like structural engineering and dynamics, balance and transparence. Spatial experience and spatial structuring were the focus of Moholy-Nagy's instruction with eight lessons per week. Albers, in the workshop class with eighteen lessons per week, taught a basic understanding and feeling for the connection and the correlation between materials, construction, technology, function/purpose and form with simple materials and tools. A characteristic example of the Moholy-Nagy/Albers preparatory course was the *Floating Construction* hanging on a string like a mobile and made of varnished wood and glass by Irmgard Sörensen in 1924. The construction, with its slot-and-tab connections, allowed for the relative shifting of individual elements with ever-changing states of balance to reach a formal optimum. Glass was not only tested as a transparent design element but also as a construction element with load-bearing characteristics. Probably in Albers's workshop class in 1923/1924, a tricycle with a sail and a curved wooden mast to which the sail was attached by a string was developed. The lightest construction and adequate use of specific material characteristics marked this toy design.

In Dessau, Albers taught twelve lessons on four mornings during the first semester, and Moholy-Nagy taught four lessons per week in the second semester, before Albers took over all lessons in 1928. Albers adapted many elements of the Itten course which he himself had attended, but created a completely new system. From 1927, students were no longer allowed to work with materials they had chosen themselves, but now followed the order (set by Albers) of glass, metal and paper before combinations of materials were to be explored. Albers explained the exercises on metal and paper surfaces: "The materials must be worked in such manner that no waste occurs; economy is the highest principle. The final form results from the tensions of the cut and folded material."[18]

Hannes Beckmann, who took the prep course in 1929/1930, described his first lesson as follows:

> Josef Albers entered the room with a bundle of newspapers under his arm, which he had distributed to the students. Then he turned to us and said: "Ladies and gentlemen, we are poor, not rich. We cannot afford to waste time and materials. We must make the best out of the worst. Every piece of work has a certain source material, thus we must first examine what this material is like. For this purpose we will–without yet producing anything–experiment with it. For the moment, we will prefer skill to beauty. [...] Remember that you will often achieve more by doing less. Our studies are meant to stimulate your constructive thoughts. [...] I also want you to respect the material, to design it meaningfully and always consider its characteristics. If you can achieve this without aids such as knife, scissors and glue, even better. Have fun."

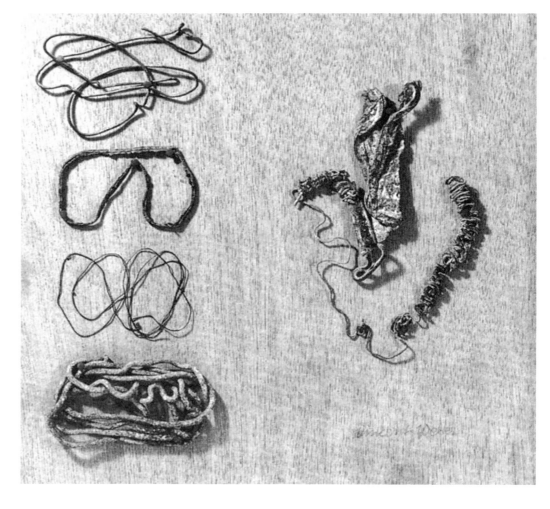

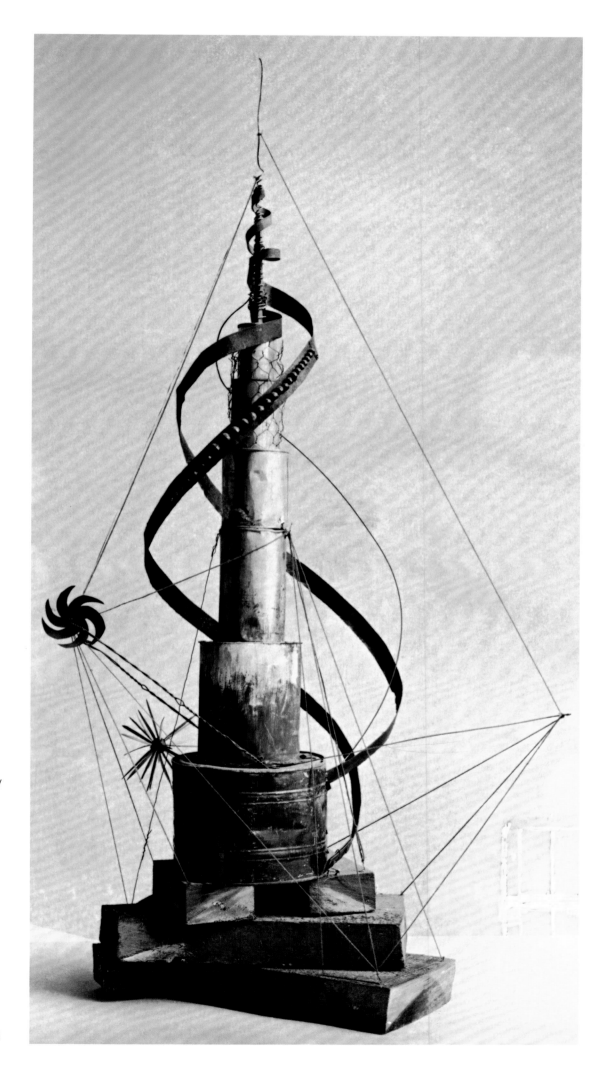

Anonymous, Texture study from the preliminary course with Johannes Itten, collage, 1919

Theobald Emil Müller-Hummel, *Cube sculpture/light sculpture* from the preliminary course with Johannes Itten, 1919/20

Rudolph Lutz, Study of composition and structure from the preliminary course with Johannes Itten, 1919

Vincent Weber, Study of matter (2), 1920/21

Nikolai Wassiljew, *Spiral tower* from the preliminary course with Johannes Itten, c. 1920

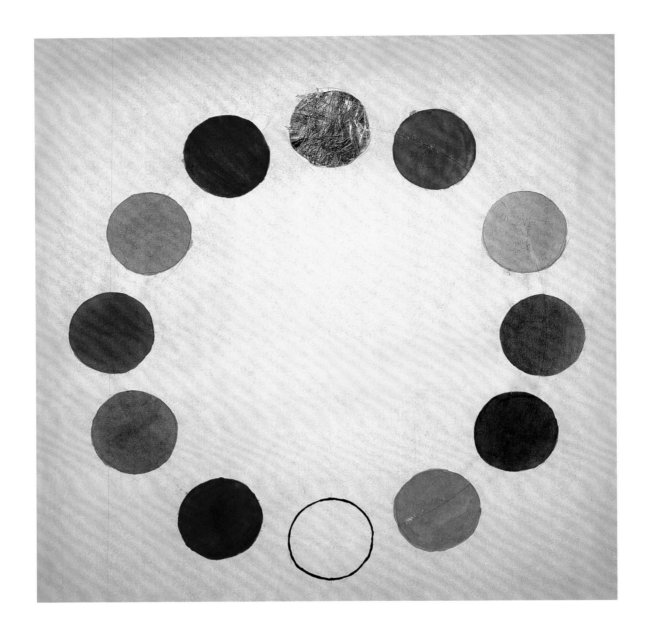

Hours later he would return and have us spread out the results of our efforts. Masks had appeared, boats, castles, aeroplanes, animals and various cleverly thought-out figures. He called it all kindergarten stuff [...]. Then he pointed to a creation that looked very simple; a young Hungarian architect had produced it. He had done nothing but fold the newspaper lengthwise so that it stood upright like a wing. Josef Albers now explained to us how well the material had been understood, how well it had been used and how natural the folding process was, particularly for paper, because it made such a pliable material stiff, so stiff that it was able to stand up on its smallest side—on the edge. [...] The preparatory course was like group therapy.

By means of the tangible comparison of all the solutions that the other students had found, we learned very quickly to find the most desirable solution of an exercise. And we learned to criticise ourselves; this was deemed more important than the criticism of others.[19]

In 1927, Bauhaus Journeyman Erich Consemüller was commissioned to make photographic documentation of the Dessau Bauhaus with approximately 300 images. The fifty-five published images of the preparatory course show more than 120 works which allow for a systematic overview: drawings, material collages, touch boards, cut and folding exercises in paper, tin metal and cellophane, construction and solidity studies as well as plastic material exercises with wires, straws and thin wooden sticks.

Construction paper, an inexpensive plane material, became the favourite experimentation device. Folding did not only develop plastic grid lines, but at the same time a three-dimensional distortion of the sheet. Veritable folding works were made from paper, such as were later executed in concrete in hall constructions or have been used in product design as lamp shades until this day. Folding and cutting produced three-dimensional plane creations which have played a role in—among others—Marcel Breuer's façade elements in architecture since the

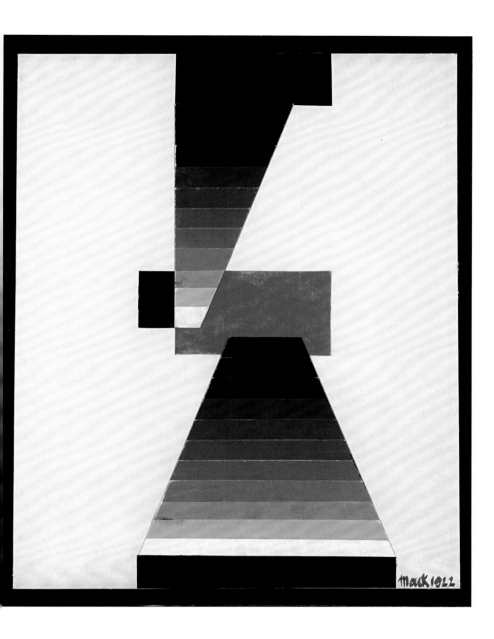

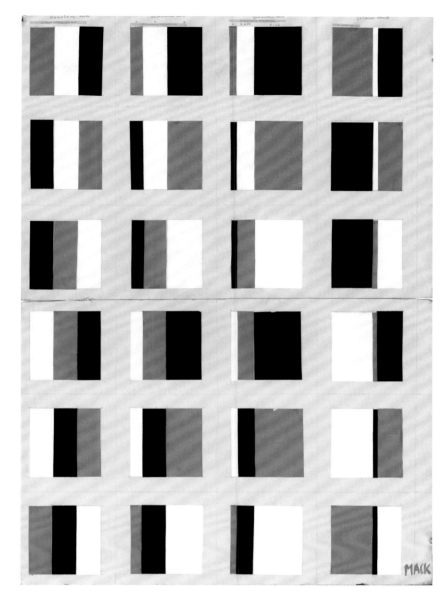

Alfred Arndt, *Chromatic circle* after Gertrud Grunow, date unknown

Ludwig Hirschfeld-Mack, *Definite Red*, 1922

Ludwig Hirschfeld-Mack, *Proportions in White, Black and Red –* Monotone Arithmetic and Geometric Series and the Golden Ratio, 1922/23

Teaching of the preliminary course with Josef Albers, 1928/29 photograph: Umbo (Otto Umbehr)

Karl Hermann Haupt, Collage from the preliminary course with László Moholy-Nagy, 1923

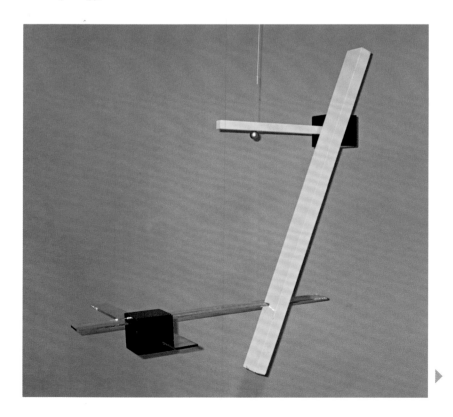

Franz Ehrlich, Material relief on the theme of structure, texture and touch from the preliminary course with László Moholy-Nagy, 1927 (?)

Irmgard Sörensen, *Floating construction* from the preliminary course with László Moholy-Nagy, 1924 (Reconstruction)

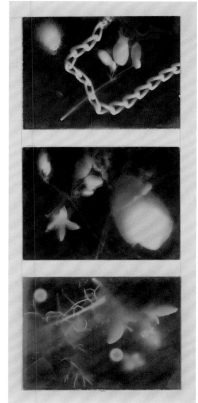

Margaretha Reichardt, Dolls from the preliminary course with Josef Albers, 1926

Konrad Püschel, Photographic compositions from the course with László Moholy-Nagy, photogram, 1926

Konrad Püschel, *Three balls of paper, folded and placed one inside the other*, material study from the preliminary course with Josef Albers, 1926

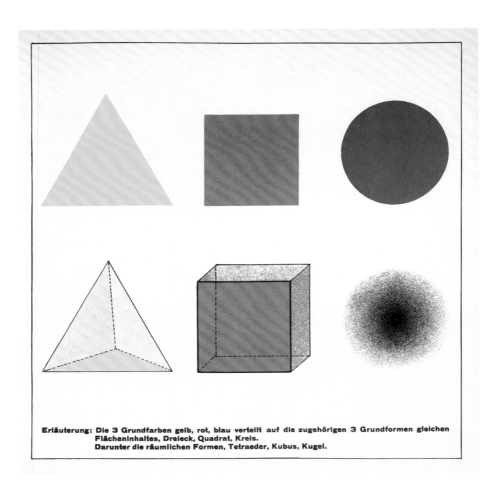

Erläuterung: Die 3 Grundfarben gelb, rot, blau verteilt auf die zugehörigen 3 Grundformen gleichen Flächeninhaltes, Dreieck, Quadrat, Kreis.
Darunter die räumlichen Formen, Tetraeder, Kubus, Kugel.

Wassily Kandinsky, *The Three Primary Colours Spread over Three Elementary Shapes*, 1923

1950s. Konrad Püschel developed three paper balls, folded and mounted inside each other. Tower constructions made of paper, and sometimes pulled-apart hanging structures were executed in numerous variations, while Paul Reindl and Werner Zimmermann experimented with corrugated cardboard.

One of the most impressive results of these examinations was Alfons Frieling's *Metal Plastic* made of aluminum, with the caption: "Emphasis on material economy (produced without waste from a rectangle, strongest solidity test, highest-possible height), work economy (one tool: metal scissors—apart from pedestal mounting—one work process: only scissor cut, without any bending)."[20]

Glass was tested in the preparatory course as an unusual construction material as well as for its optical characteristics of transparence and reflection. Sticking and clamping constructions made of thin wire or drawing pins became construction elements of glass towers. The stacking of thin glass planes, sometimes also with coloured glass, as "glass architecture" was probably inspired by Albers's glass works and Mies van der Rohe's glass high-rise buildings.

Despite occasional questioning, personnel and structural changes—or perhaps because of these—the preparatory course at the Bauhaus continued to give the most important encouragement of teamwork and creativity in a school of invention.

## Wassily Kandinsky's Course

After the Bauhaus Masters' Council decision on 15th March 1921 that every Master could give his own form lessons, Paul Klee and Wassily Kandinsky made particular use of this change in policy. Especially in the instruction given by Paul Klee (beginning in 1922) and Wassily Kandinsky (beginning in 1922/1923), both of whom independently and pronouncedly dedicated themselves to the subject of colour, the "basic language", a "grammar of artistic elements" or the "ABC of means of expression" for aesthetic inner-institutional communication as requested by Gropius was researched and developed. Their courses, which were obligatory for every student, had central importance, since these colour and form theories eventually extended into the workshops and the construction field.

Wassily Kandinsky dedicated a great deal of attention to colour theory in his complex, theoretical instruction programme, which was also delivered in a decidedly "teacher-centred" manner. He was able to draw upon the many insights that he had already published in his 1921 book *On the Spiritual in Art*.

As part of the elementary instruction, his colour seminar "Introduction to Abstract Form Elements" was one of the compulsory Bauhaus courses and stayed the same in its basic structure from 1925 onwards.

Itten had already taught colour. This preliminary instruction was supplemented in the 1922/1923 winter semester with the unofficial colour seminar of Bauhaus student Ludwig Hirschfeld-Mack. With this, he reacted to the great interest that Bauhaus students had in colour as a means of design and thought that colour was under-represented at the Bauhaus.[21] It was Hirschfeld-Mack's aim to stimulate research work in a casual manner through his colour seminar for Masters, Journeymen and students and to connect form studies and manual trades in order to work towards a collaborative working environment. The discussion and mutual exchange within the seminar was obviously focused on *Elementary Colour Systems and Their Immanent Principle of Order* and *Studies on Individual Phenomena of Colour with Regard to Virtual Movement Energies and Form Tendencies*.[22]

Stimulated by the contrast theory of German painter Adolf Hölzel, who had also taken his ideas from Itten's course, Hirschfeld-Mack invented the optical colour mixer in order to demonstrate the connection between quantity and intensity contrasts on the basis of the optical mixing by movement (rotation) of coloured areas. It was based on Itten and Kandinsky's suggestion that Hirschfeld-Mack's seminar should also discuss the binding assignment of the three primary colours red, yellow and blue to the basic shapes circle, triangle and square. The result of an experiment in perceptual psychological field research, carried out in the mural-painting workshop under the leadership of Wassily Kandinsky, showed that the majority of all those asked (both Bauhaus insiders and outsiders) associated the square with red, the triangle with yellow and the circle with blue. This not-undisputed colour/shape assignment would later, especially through Kandinsky's course, develop into dogma and have a style-forming effect, as it were, on the art and workshop production of the Bauhaus. The colour/shape analogy substantially contributed to the establishment of a Bauhaus myth geared towards it, which continues to this day.

Although fed by different sources (Goethe, perceptual psychology, esotericism), over the years Wassily Kandinsky arrived at his own expression of colour theory which corresponded to his personal views and his manifold interests in this medium. In contrast to Itten, Kandinsky had not determined a hierarchic system of colour relationships. Neither did he use colour models for demonstration, such as Itten's colour star or Klee's elementary star of the coloured plane. Rather, Kandinsky focused on the examination of colours and the systematic order of colour circles and colour series. Following an isolated analysis

Marianne Brandt, *Contrasts (Relativity of the Point)*, study from the course with Wassily Kandinsky, 1923

of colours, Kandinsky, led by an idea of aesthetic synthesis, went over to depicting the colour/shape relationship. "Colour and shape temperatures" became decisive categories for this, which at the same time opened up the opportunity for mutual assignment. From this grew the association of the three basic shapes circle, triangle and square with blue, yellow and red.

In his consideration of the harmony of colours, Kandinsky also referred in his lessons to Wilhelm Ostwald's measuring colour theory. Obviously, he agreed with Ostwald's understanding of harmony tied to a metric order system: "...harmonic or belonging can only be such colours whose characteristics have certain simple relationships".[23]

The rational exploration of artistic design basics was also the focus of the second, almost even more important part of Kandinsky's instruction, "analytical drawing." "Analytical drawing" is considered a paradigm of Kandinsky's art pedagogy. The sensitisation of perception was also investigated here, as well as the development of "constructive picture organisation" skills. The drawing of self-made still lifes made it possible for intrinsic forces and tensions to be discovered in any given object as well as its general structure. "... Education for clear observation and clear representation of correlations",

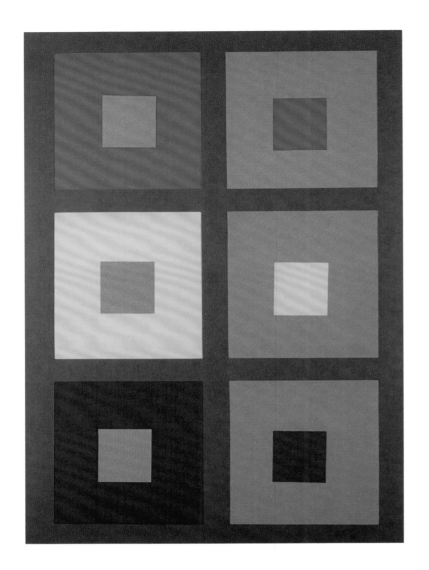

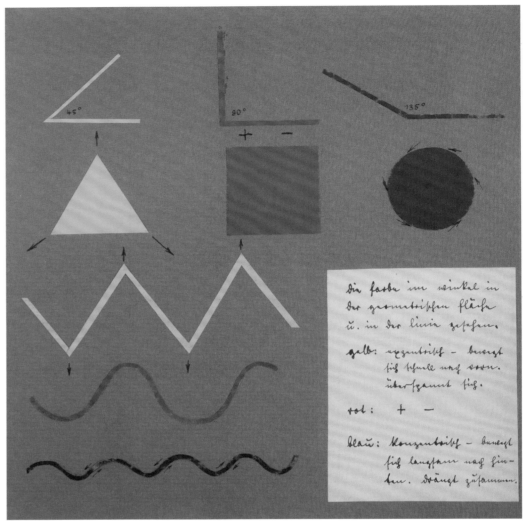

Reinhold Rossig, *Colour Contrasts (simultaneous contrast of the primary colours)*, study from the course with Wassily Kandinsky, 1929/30

Reinhold Rossig, *Colour viewed at an angle, on a geometric surface and in a line*, study from the course with Wassily Kandinsky, 1929

Kandinsky wrote in the Bauhaus magazine in 1928. Simple furniture and other objects for daily use, draped textiles etc., were arranged in "still lifes", graphically captured and abstracted in a step-by-step process according to formal tensions that could be felt and portrayed in a diagram. The objects could only be guessed at at the end, or were stuck in the memory. With form and colour, a new quality of overall composition was to emerge which came close to the nature of abstract painting, for which Kandinsky had fought in Russia many years earlier. The artist managed to summarise this and other insights he had gained from the "analysis of elements in painting" in a series of Bauhaus books beginning with the volume entitled *Point and Line to Plane* in 1926.

It is less known that a new theoretical course for the students of the fourth semester was set up at the beginning of Hannes Meyer's directorship under the leadership of Wassily Kandinsky, which would continue into the directorship of Ludwig Mies van der Rohe. The course is listed in the Bauhaus prospectus *Young People Come to the Bauhaus* of 1929. The course labelled "Artistic Design" dealt expressly with the examination and analysis of the relationship between art, architecture and technology. To this end, Bauhaus products were critically

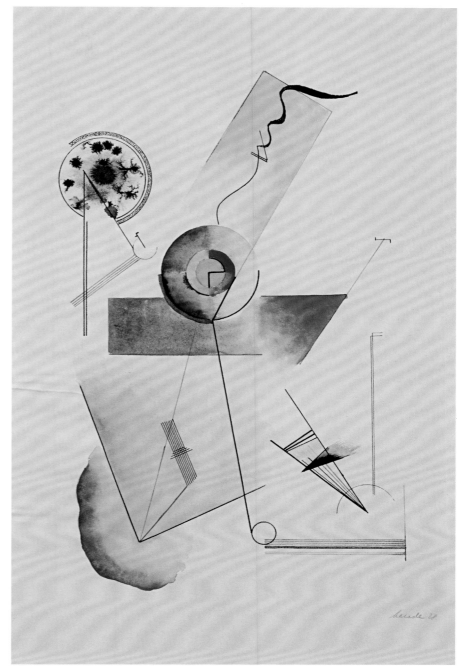

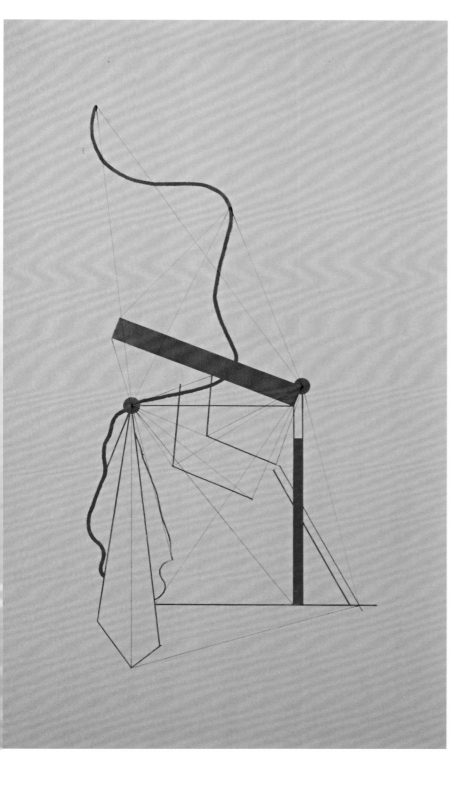

August Agatz, *Analytical drawing*, second stage, study from the course with Wassily Kandinsky, 1927

Erich Mende, *Still Life*, study from the course with Wassily Kandinsky, 1928

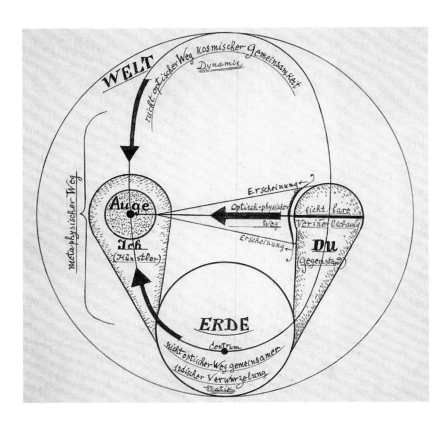

WELT
nicht optischer Weg kosmischer Gemeinsamkeit
Dynamik
metaphysischer Weg
Auge
Erscheinung
Optisch-physischer Weg
sicht bare
Verinnerlichung
Ich
(Künstler)
Erscheinung
Du
(Gegenstand)
ERDE
centrum
nicht optischer Weg gemeinsamer
irdischer Verwurzelung
Statik

Paul Klee, Diagram entitled *Me-You-Earth-World*, illustration for the essay *Wege des Naturstudiums (Ways of Studying Nature)*, 1923

discussed, but the specifics of old German paintings as well as those from other countries were also questioned and the relationship of abstract to objective art demonstrated. Kandinsky seized this opportunity to critically examine the design principle of functionalism which was widespread at the Bauhaus. Yet no significant effects of these discourses, held in Kandinsky's class, on the design of objects for daily use in the workshops at the Bauhaus can be determined. More than that, the course was probably more of an expression, a reaction to the growing interest in practical design work and the student criticism of the artistic classes associated with it.

Looking back, Kandinsky's instruction in design fundamentals necessary for a free and applied creativity, including colour theory, was considered of central importance in the Bauhaus teaching system. Its years of acceptance were credited to the fact that his "metaphysically transcendent" but yet "logically deductive" and "strictly rational" theory was unspecific in content, and practical applications were not included.[24] This kind of context-independent instruction of design principles considered "absolute" and thus prescribed was not free from the "danger of paralysis in schematic formalism". In this, as well as the conscious negation of scientific discoveries of his time, lay a conservative element, despite all the obvious progressivism.[25] Klee and Kandinsky's form and colour theory was primarily, as Oskar Schlemmer stated, a key to their own realm but also an aid for the students' design practise, "since beyond the framework of form and the colour scale begin the imponderables: the immeasurable, incalculable, mystical …"[26]

## Paul Klee's Course

Paul Klee, an important expressionist artist, joined the Bauhaus without much teaching experience, supposedly upon the recommendation of Johannes Itten. He demonstrated great interest in new forms of artist education and the development of an individual theory suitable for form instruction at the Bauhaus.

Paul Klee taught design theory from 1921 to 1932 as part of the preparatory course and parallel to it. If Kandinsky's instruction in the most elementary ideas of colour and form was considered a contribution of "rational irrationalism", this was also true of Klee's theory. For him, too, the theories of colour and form were the most important thematic emphases within his teaching spectrum. Analytical examination of the elements of form, from point to line to plane and eventually to space, was, in contrast to Kandinsky, oriented towards the process character of work. This also applied to the treatment of basic shapes. Mirroring, form twisting, proportioning etc. tested the students' abilities to organise planes. By adding colour the process gained complexity, and unlimited possibilities of design variation opened up. Furthermore, there were questions of balance and movement, of structure and rhythm, etc., which were discussed in his lessons in order to explore the laws of function in design elements in comparison with physical laws or the laws of music. Klee shared his own experience of painting and drawing with his students by presenting his works. Through them he explained composition criteria so as to render understandable the construction and effect of his art, the organic connection of the picture elements and the forces emanating from them. At first he painted actual sample pictures in order to demonstrate his theoretical instruction. These lessons, which also contained composition problems, were always tied to a particular type of examination of nature; Klee was never concerned with representation of external apprearances, the "ends of form", as he called them, but with artistic semblances of the "formative forces" of nature. At the same time, he was careful to connect his theoretical approach with holistic ideas which had a cosmic reference.

Colour theory was used to test and experience the laws of colour relationships and colour movements. After isolated initial difficulties, obligatory classes in the subject of colour began only in 1922, three years after the foundation of the Bauhaus, with Klee's "Artistic Form Theory." Between 1919 and 1922, colour was not systematically taught at the Bauhaus. The subject was rather among the "supplementary subjects" to "Form Theory", which at the time still seemed conservatively academic and was a part of the basic elements of Bauhaus pedagogy along with the training in manual trades. Johannes Itten, who called himself a "master of colour", was the only Bauhaus teacher concerned with an aesthetic colour theory as part of his preparatory course teaching prior to 1922.

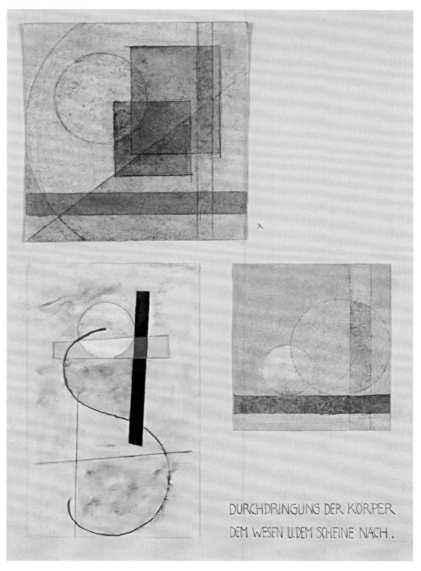

DURCHDRINGUNG DER KÖRPER
DEM WESEN U. DEM SCHEINE NACH.

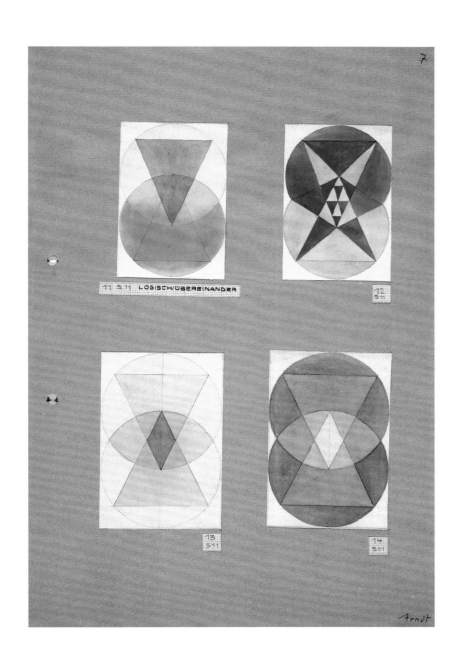

11 5.11 LOGISCH/ÜBEREINANDER

Arndt

Gertrud Arndt, *Logical layering*, study from the course with Paul Klee, 1923/24

Margaretha Reichardt, *Interpenetration of Bodies according to their Nature and Appearance*, study from the course with Paul Klee, 1928

Magda Langenstraß-Uhlig, *Chromatic Triangle*, study from the course with Paul Klee, 1925

Konrad Püschel, *Movement of the centre in the square (yellow), and on the outside (red)*, study from the course with Paul Klee, 1925/26

Reingardt Voigt, *Economy of Means, Complementary, Combined, Pushed, Rotated and Mirrored*, study from the course with Paul Klee, 1929/30

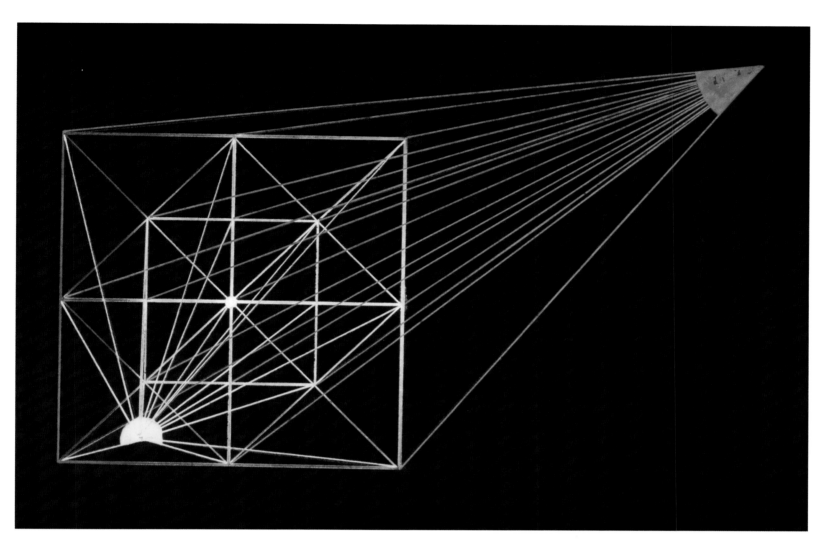

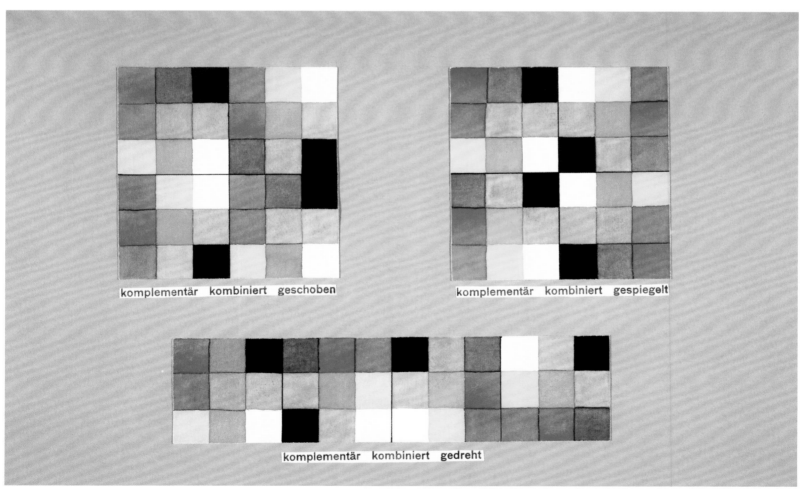

komplementär kombiniert geschoben

komplementär kombiniert gespiegelt

komplementär kombiniert gedreht

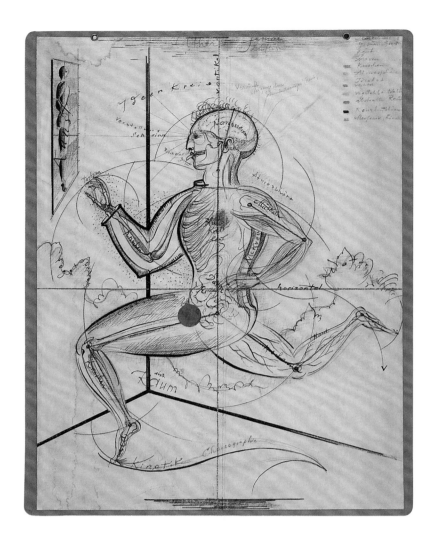

Oskar Schlemmer, *Man in the Circle of Ideas*, 1928/29
© Oskar Schlemmer Archive and Theatre Estate

For Paul Klee, colour theory was part of his "Artistic Form Theory", which he taught beginning in the 1921/1922 winter semester. All the Bauhaus classes, which had been subdivided into the dual system of form and manual trades theory, were differentiated, broadened, objectified and objectivised over the course of time in view of economic and socio-political realities. Klee, who gave crucial support to the Bauhaus through his contributions to basic artistic theory, developed his teaching programme "Artistic Form Theory" into "Design Theory" in 1924 to react to the increasing scientific-technical-economic orientation of the later Bauhaus in Dessau, calling it "Artistic Design Theory." In the methodical, sometimes academically-conservative set up of exercises and lectures, yet focusing on playful elements in his classes on colour during the 1922/23 winter semester, he integrated the ideas of Goethe, Runge, Delacroix and Kandinsky. The rainbow, as "an isolated incident of a scale of pure colours", according to Klee, served as his starting point; from there he reached the "circular symbol where pure colours truly reside".[27] In contrast to Kandinsky and Hirschfeld-Mack, Klee started from blue, yellow and red as the three basic colours and determined, by means of pendulum movements, their reach into the periphery of the colour circle in order to finally arrive at his "canon of colour totality" according to his process of analysis and synthesis. Klee's colour theory was based on movement theory principles, and this was his original contribution. His polar thinking was oriented towards balance and a harmonic, integral whole.[28]

In contrast to Kandinsky, whose teaching varied only slightly over the years, Klee continually developed the content of his teaching. In Dessau his teaching load increased when he took on a painting class in May 1926, and by the addition of the form instruction to the weaving workshop that he had to direct from 1927's winter semester. Klee, like Kandinsky, had been wishing for his own painting class for some time; the necessity to take on the form instruction in the weaving workshop arose from the departure of Georg Muche, who had fulfilled this duty until then. Klee impressed on the weavers further aspects of his colour theory and laws with regard to design on planes, then had them complete black-and-white scales, for instance, and varying light/dark relationships before the actual textile design began. Unity and balance in composition and colouration, the "creation of unity from the many", which to Klee represented perfect design practise, were the decisive criteria.

This corresponded completely with his understanding of art, which, bare of any dogma but against the contemporary reality marked by crisis and contradiction, was focused on totality and harmony, and found itself beyond the ordinary, so to speak, in a cosmic balance. Klee's colour theory, in which he tried to mediate between mathematic-scientific and intuitive-emotional views, influenced only in a minimally-researched manner the formal aesthetic as well as methodical (analysis-synthesis-process) workshop production of the Bauhaus–provided that the students working there were successful in following the complex thought patterns of their Master.

## Oskar Schlemmer's Course

Oskar Schlemmer, a painter, sculptor, theatre artist and theorist positioned between Expressionism, Dadaism, Constructivism, New Objectivity and Surrealism, was among those teachers in the early years of the Bauhaus who, due to their versatility, were busiest. Thus Schlemmer at times headed several workshops as Master of Form (mural painting, stone sculpting, metal workshop and woodcarving) until he was appointed head of the Bauhaus theatre in 1923. Here, he also taught the subject of "Theatre Theory" from 1926.

From 1921 Oskar Schlemmer, like Paul Klee and Georg Muche, occasionally also taught figure study. He presupposed drawing abilities, and on this basis he expected the objective representation not of the scientifically correct but of the essential and prominent on the basis of previous detailed study of muscle and bone structure as well as its function in the overall bodily system. Free from obvious control and correction, this rather unconventional class, in which the teacher himself also participated in drawing and the students themselves were models, was not concerned with the image of the static model but the representation of the moving figure, lines of light and shadow etc. In 1926/1927 "Figure Study" became the more complex "Figure Drawing." The schematic representation of the human body by means of line, plane and basic geometric shapes on the basis of measure, number and proportion focusing on skeleton and musculature was the most important criterion for this course, which in Dessau often took place on the Bauhaus stage with relaxing gramophone music. In 1928 this type of graphic nature study, which was far from a special form of nature imitation but rather, in the spirit of Goethe, contained the quest for a certain "style", became part of the class "Man." It was concerned with the development of an edifice of theories, with the development of a holistic image of man, within which formal and biophysical as well as philosophical aspects were discussed. The focus on this topic closely corresponded to Schlemmer's artistic calling. The reference to man as the starting and ending point of all pedagogic and practical design efforts, the formation of a new man for a new society, was one of the most essential aims of the Bauhaus. Schlemmer incomparably expressed this humanistic concern of the Bauhaus in his artistic practise and in his teaching. As an artist and teacher he succeeded in overcoming and balancing, with this complex reference to man as the primary orientation for action, the potential conflict imminent within the Bauhaus, which resulted from the constant striving to unify artistic individuality and objective design claims, metaphysical, esoterically orientated will for art and pragmatic orientation toward action.[29]

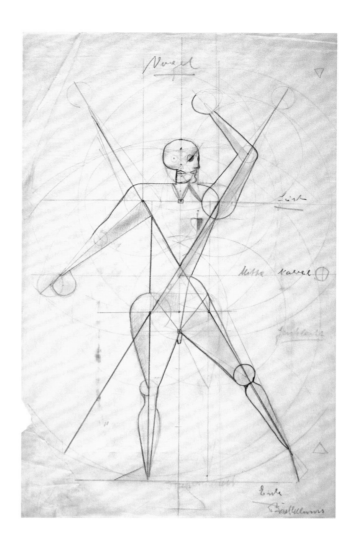

Klaus Barthelmess, Drawing of a Nude, study from the course with Oskar Schlemmer, c. 1922

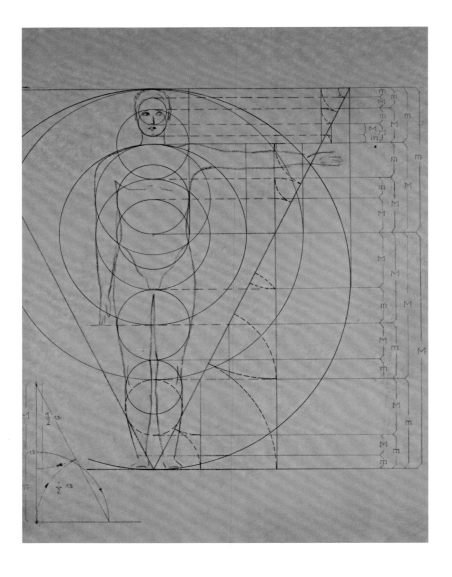

Friedrich Engemann, *Canon of Human Proportions* drawing after Albrecht Dürer's *Four Books on Measurement*, study from the course with Oskar Schlemmer, 1927

Walter Köppe, *Composition I*, study from the course with Oskar Schlemmer, 1928

In the formal, graphic part of the instruction on Man, which was directed towards those students who had already completed the two semesters of the preparatory course, Schlemmer

> … discussed the schemes and systems of the linear, plane and bodily-plastic: standard measurement, proportion theory, Dürer's measurements and the Golden Ratio. From this, the laws of movement developed, mechanics and kinetics of the body, within itself as well as in space, in natural space as well as in cultural space (building). The latter naturally carries particular weight: the relationship of man with dwelling, its furnishing and the objects.[30]

The focus on the unspoiled, the impersonal, the bringing out of the typical by reduction to geometric forms, including the human body, in order to demonstrate its tectonic structure, its bodily volume, are the hallmarks of this first part of more complex teaching. It ended with the analysis of figural depiction in old and new art. In Schlemmer's examination with man as an ideal, an abstract being reduced to a canon of forms, free from individual differentiation, there would lie the danger of negating man by ideal-typical reduction as a social being and in his historical determination, were it not concerned with the recognition of the type as precondition for the comprehension of the individual.

The formal teaching part was followed by a scientific (biological) part, which discussed issues such as the origin of life, the structure of cells, the mechanics of the human body, its organ functions etc., up to socio-hygienic issues. Birth, growth and death were introduced to the students as a type of *Theory of Life Activities*.

To Oskar Schlemmer, the philosophical part of his often parallel classes appeared of particular importance. Here, systems of thought from antiquity to the modern age were the topic of discourse. In this part of his class Schlemmer also presented his view of the world, which largely followed the philosophy of the Romanticist Ricarda Huch (1873-1913) and was characterised by a striving for an integral whole. Thus, he saw man as a creature of nature in the unity of body, soul and spirit embedded in a scientific, psychological and ideological system.

With his classes on *Man*, Schlemmer wanted to convey something like an "ideology" to the Bauhaus students, which should ideally enable them to react appropriately to contemporary trends and the demands of the day. This intention partly explains the universalistic approach and the claim to totality of Oskar Schlemmer's classes, which went beyond the boundaries of subjects. Rainer Wick critically points out that the extent and claim of the lessons overtaxed the teacher as well as his students, and that in the end such a claim to totality could not be realised by any one individual in the twentieth century.

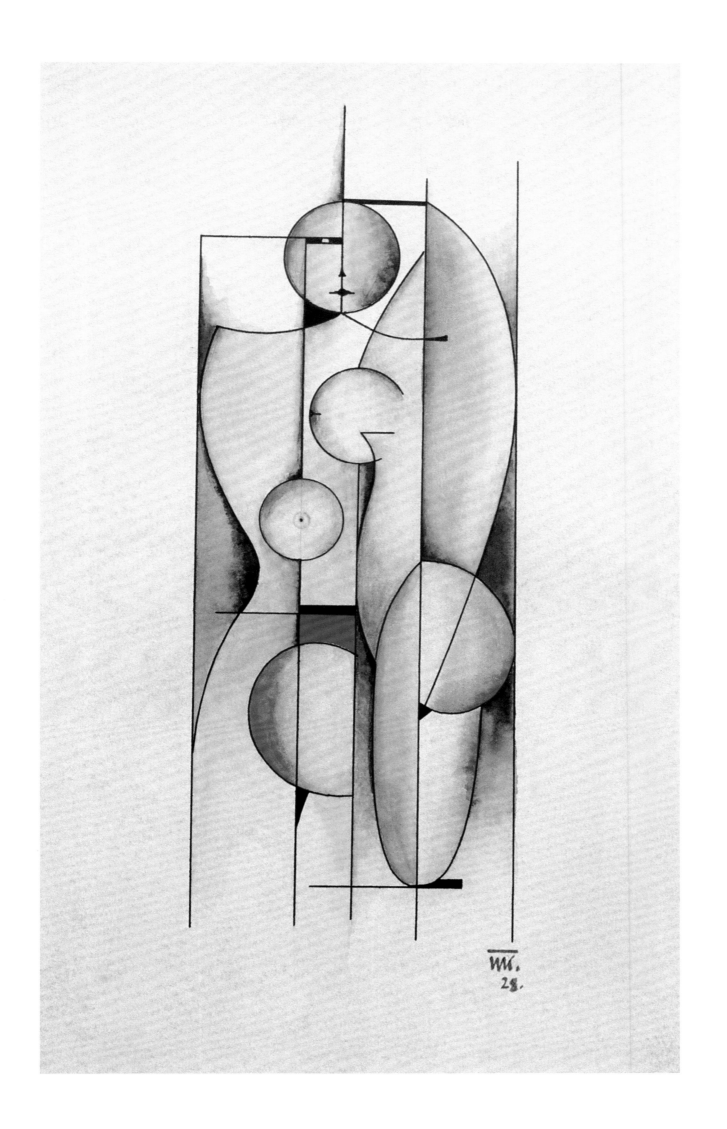

Reinhold Rossig, *Grotesque font*, study from the
preliminary course with Joost Schmidt, 1929

This touches on a seemingly controversial principle of the Bauhaus idea, according to which totality of life was to be reconstructed by and with the education of universally instructed generalists in a highly differentiated industrial society based on the division of labour.[31]

## Joost Schmidt's Course

The painter Joost Schmidt came to Weimar shortly after the foundation of the *Staatliches Bauhaus* to start a sculpting apprenticeship with Johannes Itten and Oskar Schlemmer. Soon he was excelling with remarkable achievements such as the woodcarvings on the residence designed by Walter Gropius and Adolf Meyer for the industrialist Sommerfeld in the Berlin suburb of Dahlem in 1920/1921. As an apprentice, he was put in charge of the vestibule design in the main building of the Weimar Bauhaus on the occasion of the Bauhaus exhibition in Weimar in 1923. Reliefs emerged which varied basic geometric shapes such as spheres, cylinders, cones and their relationship to one another by penetration and perforation. Furthermore, Schmidt stood out with some sensational achievements in applied graphics, such as the design of a poster for the Weimar Bauhaus exhibition. After occasional engagements on stage and with due regard to its technical equipment, the examination of the relationship between space and body and the analysis of writing, advertising and typography became the main focus of his subsequent teaching at the Bauhaus in Dessau.

Shortly after Joost Schmidt had passed his Journeyman examination as a sculptor while still at the Professional Trades Association in Weimar in 1925 – the Bauhaus had already moved to Dessau – he was appointed to the Bauhaus teaching staff as a "Junior Master" and entrusted with the leadership of the plastic workshop. He also had to teach in the printing workshop, which at that time was headed by Herbert Bayer, who had been appointed Junior Master like Schmidt. As part of the preparatory course obligatory for all new students, Joost Schmidt taught calligraphy from 1925. This special instruction covered two semesters and was expanded into a complex design theory over the course of time. In 1929, by which time Oskar Schlemmer had already left the Bauhaus, Schmidt also took on the vacated course in figure study and drawing in addition to his many other teaching commitments. With the forced closure of the Bauhaus in Dessau, Joost Schmidt's association with the school where he had spent ten years of his life also ended.

The appointment of Joost Schmidt and other Bauhaus graduates as Junior Masters placed significant emphases within the teaching and education structure of the Bauhaus. The teaching staff, which had been instructed in formal-artistic as well as technical crafts matters, developed their own teaching content and programmes, which were now and again dramatically different from those of their former teachers. In Joost Schmidt there was a Bauhaus graduate who, like Herbert Bayer and Josef Albers, had moulded his own form language based on abstraction on the basis of his own Bauhaus education and derived from various artistic fields.

Werner Kubsch, *Malays in the Royal Circus*, study from the preliminary course with Joost Schmidt, 1928

The calligraphy classes, which he started to build in the Dessau Bauhaus and which supplemented the courses by László Moholy-Nagy or Josef Albers, Wassily Kandinsky, Paul Klee and Oskar Schlemmer, initially contained a simple enabling of the writing and construction of lettering. For this purpose, the conditions and principles of lettering form and lettering image were examined in detail. The composition of lettering forms from circle, square and rectangle, their changeability, the variety of sizes and variability in bar weight, as well as the examination of concretely applied references were the main topics along with the treatment of colour and plane, in an isolated manner, in its reference to lettering and in general advertising work. Traditional lettering and those in general use were subjected to critical analysis. Later, aspects of language, expressive psychology, social, optical, technical and economic considerations were added. Matters of social relevance (lettering leads to collective form) did not remain excluded. Like his colleagues Albers and Bayer at the Bauhaus and several typographers outside the school (Kurt Schwitters, Herbert Post), Joost Schmidt also strove for an urgent reform of lettering. To this end,

he attempted to develop a simple typeface that would meet the demands of standardisation and international communication.

Joost Schmidt developed his obligatory calligraphy class, which had continued the earlier Weimar efforts of Dora Wibiral and Lothar Schreyer, into a teaching programme for the basic course in 1928; this seemed to have an integrating effect on the areas of theory and workshop that seemed to be drifting apart at the time. If for other artists there was a close interrelation between artistically aesthetic practise, its theoretical analysis and teaching, for Joost Schmidt the students were at the centre of his teaching concepts. On the basis of systematic mediation, he tried to free and develop the students' creative talents. Variety and complexity of human appearance and human action played important roles. The demonstration of connections, determinations and mutual dependences, from the elementary to the complex, refers to ideological aspects that were considered fundamental for design work in the dialectics of rationality and intuition, emotion and intellect. Possibly such general reflections preceded the actual design exercises. Exercises on plane segmentation as well as on the design of formal and thematic contrasts, which were intended to develop creative thinking and the skills of combination theory, were followed by an introduction to methods of perspective drawing, studies in the geometry of the human body as well as exercises on colour theory. It is remarkable that Schmidt, like his Junior Master colleague Hinnerk Scheper, who was head of the mural painting workshop in Dessau, largely oriented himself in his teachings on colour toward the colour rules of Chemistry Nobel Prize winner Wilhelm Ostwald, which were geared towards scientific exactitude. The knowledge he himself had gained in the field of artistic colour theory just a few years earlier in classes with Johannes Itten, Wassily Kandinsky and Paul Klee, however, was hardly reflected. This corresponded to a general desire for standardisation and scientific approach, which started in earnest at the Bauhaus in 1928.

Schmidt was different from his teacher colleagues at the Bauhaus in his tendency towards the authentic, the systematic, logical and factual as well as scientific laboratory work. Yet he always kept the "psychological whole" of man in his mind, man who he tried to localise in the range between "earthly" and "cosmic", and as part of the "all-space" with the help of adequate, sometimes esoteric, life philosophies.

Schmidt's teaching concept, which from the beginning had been based on an applied, contrasted theory of combination of elementary forms and bodies in a differentiated relationship with space, was subject to continuous expansion and renewal. Once again, artistic work and the claim to teaching within a programme based on an elementary way of thinking and a universalistic frame of reference blended into one. Thus, another complex design theory emerged at the Bauhaus, which aimed to prepare students exhaustively for their future professions.

# The Workshops
Pottery Workshop

The Bauhaus ceramics workshop, which was called the Pottery Shop, was established in 1920 under the leadership of sculptor and Master of Form Gerhard Marcks and Master of Craft Max Krehan in Saale, near Dornburg; by 1925, it had developed into one of the most creative and productive Bauhaus workshops.

At first Walter Gropius and Gerhard Marcks endeavoured to collaborate with the J. F. Schmidt stove factory in order to establish a ceramics workshop in Weimar, but this attempt failed in spring 1920. With the pottery shop of the Krehan Brothers, which was rich in history, a suitable partner was identified in Saale, twenty kilometers away, and Max Krehan was made the Master of Craft in the autumn of 1920. The state of Thuringia provided a studio for Marcks and living quarters for the students in Dornburg Castle's former stables.

While Krehan's workshop mostly focused on training on the potter's wheel and the production of traditional forms with so-called *industry fires (Wirtschaftsbrände)*, experimental container ceramics were created in the stable workshop. In May 1923 the Bauhaus took over Krehan's workshop as its production

workshop. Thus an early reaction to the changing structure of the Bauhaus into a modern academy of design was implemented in Dornburg in a timely fashion, and the thesis of "art and technology—a new unity" was put into educational practise. The most talented students, Journeymen Theodor Bogler and Otto Lindig, established ties to the Thuringian porcelain manufactory and championed a targeted effort towards the transition from manual trades at the potter's wheel to the ceramic casts of "industrial technology." Bogler developed the prototypes for kitchenware displayed in the *Haus am Horn* in Weimar on the occasion of the Bauhaus Exhibition in summer 1923 in the stoneware factory Velten-Vordamm. At the beginning of 1924, Lindig took over the technical side and Bogler assumed the business leadership of the pottery workshop.

In 1919, Marcks made use of ceramic materials for sculpting experiments with *Small Clay Samples*, in 1920 for manger figurines with coloured glaze, and in 1924 for the statuette of the *Small Thuringian Mother*. Around 1921 he created a portrait of Otto Lindig on an oven tile in the form of a reliefed caricature for the Pottery House in Dornburg. Among these early experiments was also Otto Lindig's sixty centimetre tall *Light Temple* of around 1920, a tower-like light sculpture, which is only preserved in a photograph, while Bogler's thrown manger figurines are fully preserved.

In addition, Marcks painted ceramics by Krehan and his students with objective motifs or colourations reduced to a few strict lines. The communal lifestyle of the Bauhaus community in Dornburg can be witnessed in Bogler's drinking cups, with the portraits of Bogler and Lindig painted by Marcks, as well as a *schnapps* bottle by Marguerite Friedlaender-Wildenhain, which Marcks decorated with a tomcat and the saying "Of the Tomcat at Night, Beware!!", "Tomcat" being German slang for "hangover"!

Gerhard Marcks prompted the students to experiment with form, but also to analyse the Thuringian pottery tradition with its typical forms and decoration, additionally confronting them with archaic vessel forms which had accompanied human development for thousands of years and could be studied at the Weimar Museum for Pre- and Early History. Influences from architectural history and building form theory like those conveyed by Gropius in his lectures found their formal expression in the strict double can by Bogler and Lindig of 1922, while a group of calabash-shaped jugs and cans by Lindig point to an exploration of African and Asian vessel forms. The ideas of building and mounting flow into these ceramics, on whose lid-shaped tops filling holes were placed as individually-thrown forms. Furthermore, disc-shaped elements gave structure to two high cans with lids by Lindig, which with their ambitious form language and complex production are more reminiscent of modern sculptures than simple objects for daily use.

Inspired by Japanese ceramic vessels, Theodor Bogler started to develop his design family of cans and storage containers with the basic mathematical shapes of cylinder and hemisphere in 1923. With these he also took the technological leap from the potter's wheel to cast ceramics. At the beginning stood his *Combination tea pot with eccentric fill opening* which was labelled "L1" as the first chosen prototype of the Bauhaus pottery workshop. Bogler combined the pot's functional elements—body, spout, fill opening and handle—into a great number of form and use variations. The spout, for example, was attached to the cylindrical body at different heights or the fill opening was placed in the middle or at the back edge—sometimes with an additional funnel. The handles show the largest number of variations, starting from the traditional arch-shaped ceramic handle through a trumpet-shaped tubular handle to a movable bow handle made of metal or wickerwork with ceramic loops. These industrially-produced pots were sometimes issued with glazes that were irregularly spread over the surface, which thus again turned a mass product into a unique piece. The peak of this developmental series was the six-part mocha machine,

which was made in 1923 at the Oldest Volkstedt Porcelain Factory and supplemented with a five-part, hand-thrown variation with black engobe decoration.

The students themselves tested their products for durability, simple functionality and how easy they were to clean. After an additional critical assessment of the form, the best products were chosen and suggested as prototypes for industrial production.

The sales figures of these ceramics with their strict, avant-garde, mathematical forms remained far below expectations. Since the students were able to have direct contact with the customers and receive feedback at the 1923 Bauhaus Exhibition, the Leipzig Grassi Fair and other events, they quickly recognised the public's lack of understanding and reservation regarding the new, technological form language. And they reacted immediately with ceramics which drew on the more organic forms of classical examples of around 1800. Lindig thus started to develop a group of pots and vases (L10 to L16) with elegant, bulbous forms on which synthetic grooves were intended to invoke associations of the manual production on a potter's wheel, even though all products were cast in stoneware or porcelain. Lindig did without this decoration on his coffee pot (L19) and thus created a timeless design, the cliché of the "Bauhaus style." In this way, he started a development in the design area which was continued at the Bauhaus Dessau under the leadership of Hannes Meyer.

Among the students of the Bauhaus pottery workshop were Werner Burri, Gertrud Coja, Johannes Driesch, Lydia Driesch-Foucar, Marguerite Friedlaender-Wildenhain, Thoma Gräfin Grote, Margarete Heymann-Marks, Herbert Hübner, Johannes Leßmann, Wilhelm Löber, Else Mögelin, Eva Oberdieck-Deutschbein and Renate Riedel.

Otto Lindig continued the traditional line of the Bauhaus pottery workshop as head of the ceramic teaching workshop in the State Building Academy of Weimar in Dornburg from 1926 to 1930, and Marguerite Friedlaender taught at the Arts and Crafts School Burg Giebichenstein in Halle from 1925 to 1933.

Despite the successful development of numerous products and prototypes, which were not without influence on the development of ceramics in the twentieth century, the ceramics workshop was not continued at the Bauhaus in Dessau. Obviously, the revolutionary potential of this workshop regarding modern casting technologies and for new metal and plastic materials was not recognised. Experience with solid objects of revolution flowed into the education at the newly created sculpture workshop, which was headed by the Bauhaus graduate and Junior Master Joost Schmidt from 1925 to 1930.

View inside Max Krehan's ceramics teaching workshop in the Bauhaus
Weimar in Dornburg, 1924

Gerhard Marcks, Glazed tile with a portrait of Otto Lindig for a kiln in the Pottery House in Dornburg, c. 1921

Max Krehan (Form), Gerhard Marcks (Decoration), Handled bottle with
a representation of an ox-drawn plough, 1920/21

Theodor Bogler/Gerhard Marcks, Double-spouted pot, 1922

Theodor Bogler (model), Aelteste Velten-Vordamm earthenware factory (production), Crockery for the *Haus am Horn* (trial house for the Bauhaus Weimar), 1923

Theodor Bogler, Two combination teapots (L 6), 1923

Theodor Bogler and Otto Lindig, Parts of a crockery set (L 4, L 42, L 12), 1923

Theodor Bogler (model), Volkstedt porcelain factory (execution), Mocha machine in six pieces, 1923

Otto Lindig, Covered pots and jugs (L 66, L 30, L 21, L 25), 1923

Otto Lindig, Two coffee pots in earthenware and porcelain (L 19), 1923

# Bookbinding

The bookbinding workshop of the Bauhaus constituted an exception among the Bauhaus workshops. As it had done with the weaving workshop, the Bauhaus made use of a workshop of a former arts and crafts school which had been operated by master bookbinder Otto Dorfner as a private business since 1915. Being an extremely well-versed master of his craft, Dorfner trained apprentices in his workshop as well as external technical students. From 1919 to 1922, at least twenty-three apprentices, visiting students, participants in trial semesters and technical students, sometimes more than ten per semester, trained with Dorfner. In 1920 alone, Fritz Baumann, Elisabeth Schweitzer, Karl Umlauf and Werner Voigt took their examination for the master craftsman diploma, followed by Paul Klein in 1922. They had all studied at least one semester at the Bauhaus.

Differences of opinion in pedagogic matters between Masters of Form Paul Klee in 1921 and Lothar Schreyer during the winter semester of 1921/1922 led to the discontinuation of Dorfner's contract with the Bauhaus at his request in March 1922. While Dorfner advocated well-founded education in the manual trades, the visual artists at the Bauhaus pleaded for greater creativity and room to experiment. The hierarchy between Masters of Form and Masters of Craft at the Bauhaus may also have contributed to this separation.

Otto Dorfner, however, continued to work for the Bauhaus and took over the manual execution of numerous print-graphic portfolios. The focal points were the five portfolios of *Bauhaus Prints* and *New European Graphics*, published from 1921 to 1924. The artistic design of the portfolios, with hand-made cover papers designed by Lyonel Feininger, Ludwig Hirschfeld-Mack and Josef Albers, was the work of Lyonel Feininger. The ten portfolios of the "preferred" edition were produced on full parchment, the two hundred portfolios of the "normal" edition on half-parchment. The 1923 master's portfolio of the Staatliche Bauhaus also contained half-parchment portfolios from Dorner's workshop according to Feininger's instructions, as well as the *Twelve Wood Cuts* by Lyonel Feininger in 1920. Kandinsky's famous collection of prints from 1922, *Small Worlds*, contained full-parchment portfolios from the Dorfner workshop with gold embossing, while Gerhard Marcks' parchment portfolios of

*Edda's Wieland song (Das Wielandslied der Edda)* of 1923 were completed with imprinted black writing. The same year Oskar Schlemmer's *Game with Heads (Spiel mit Köpfen)* was published in a Dorfner portfolio. Around 1923 also, the albums were made which were to hold the photo documentation of the Weimar Bauhaus, with its more than 450 photographs.

Otto Dorfner also evolved as an artist during these years. While expressionist trends with star motifs and acute-angled elements played a major role in 1919/1920, Dorfner increasingly designed his full-leather covers with fine rectangular gridlines and *sans serif* typefaces with asymmetrical compositions on the book cover. Only rarely did Dorfner approach the material experiments of his Bauhaus students; one such example is the 1928 cover of Johannes Schlaf's *Cosmos* with book covers made from wood grain. His book covers were always integral works of art which complemented the book's content with high artistic quality on the cover, endpaper, title and cut. Dorfner conveyed this rich experience from 1926 to 1930 as a teacher of lettering design and book covers at the State Academy for Crafts and Architecture, the successor school of the Bauhaus in Weimar, for whose publications he also oversaw the design.

After Dorfner left the Bauhaus, the student Anni Wottitz re-established a small bookbindery workshop and continued her bookbinding experiments, which she had practised in the Dorfner workshop for five semesters. Her book covers show influences from experience in Itten's preparatory course with materials studies and material collages as well as ethnographic ideas from the Bauhaus library or Theo van Doesburg's *De Stijl* class with its clear geometric compositions. She used, for instance, bark fibre, seed capsules and shells for her book cover of African fairy tales, in combination with African embroidery and a paper collage in red, black and violet as an endpaper to contrast with the sand-coloured bark fibre. Wottitz gave Knut Hamsun's *Pan* a dark-stained wood cover, which she tied with a light-coloured cord, combined with a contrasting endpaper made of gold paper. She bound Karl Widmaier's *The Dictator* with a cardboard cover, covered in wrapping paper with a self-constructed title type band. Her cover for the complete works of Hölderlin, Volume 3 also dates from 1923: a half-leather binding in red Morocco leather and wood marquetry in black, red-brown and golden wood veneer with a strictly square composition.

Friedl Dicker and Franz Singer followed similar design principles with their cover of *Chorus Mysticus*, made of wood veneer and parchment with a calligraphic design of the title in the centre. The writing is formed into a motif with an "O" as the crowning sun motif with a white circle of light and a red "M" with gold serifs in the centre. The photo documentation of the bookbindery workshop also shows covers with textile appliqués, material combinations or calligraphically-decorated papers.

The transformation of book designs into individual works of art for books which had special meaning to their owners had been practised at the Bauhaus by Johannes Itten since 1919/1920 with the support of Otto Dorfner, as seen in Martin Buber's *Ecstatic Confessions* with its parchment cover with red metal foil and calligraphy on the spine. The parchment cover of the *Hafis* songs, on the other hand, bears a free calligraphic design with curved letter forms on its front cover.

Resembling one of Johannes Itten's pieces of preparatory course work, the Bible cover by Johannes Driesch is decorated with images of Christ and St John on the cover, which was scratched, cut, coloured and gilded in black and brown leather on cardboard.

In the estates of the Weimar Bauhaus students, sometimes entire libraries with book covers made in the Dorfner workshop can be found, such as in Karl Peter Röhl's or Eberhard Schrammen's. With more than fifty handmade covers, Schrammen's library allows a glimpse into the spiritual world of the early Bauhaus as well as an overview of the different bookbinding techniques, mostly in half-leather and half-parchment binding with a multitude of coloured papers. Schrammen's friendly relations with Dorfner are also documented in his *Sketchbook for Otto Dorfner* of 1919/1920, with numerous drawings and caricatures that evoke life at the early Bauhaus.

Some of the most recent discoveries are experimental covers handmade by students in Dorfner's workshop, which remain preserved until this day as part of the former Bauhaus library in the library of the Bauhaus-University Weimar.

Otto Dorfner, Rainer Maria Rilke, *Das Marienleben*, book cover, 1920

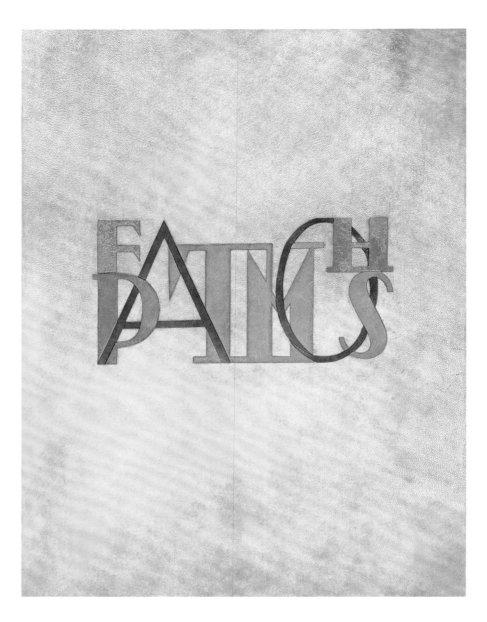

Friedl Dicker and Franz Singer, book cover in wood and parchment for *Chorus Mysticus*, 1923

Anni Wottiz, book cover for Friedrich Hölderlin: *Patmos*, Utopia Publisher and Printing, 1922

Otto Dorfner, Portfolio IV: Master of the Staatliches Bauhaus in Weimar, from the series: *New European Graphic*, 1923

**Stained Glass Painting Workshop**

The stained glass painting workshop at the Bauhaus in Weimar had special status because it had only one student and, from 1923, one Journeyman, Josef Albers. It was established in October 1920 by Johannes Itten with support from the Weimar stained glass painting company of Ernst Kraus, who earlier had already executed Itten's *Tower of Fire*, a cubic construction wrapped in stained glass elements and Asian temple bells—one of the very first colour, light and sound sculptures ever.

Beginning in 1922, Paul Klee ran the workshop as Master of Form, while Journeyman Josef Albers took on the duties of the Master of Craft. The glass assemblies *Figure*, *Rhine Legend* and *Window Image* by Josef Albers have been preserved since as early as 1921, free, non-subjective compositions made of waste glass following Itten's preparatory course.

During his attendance of Theo van Doesburg's *De Stijl* class in Weimar, Albers's compositions become more constructive, such as the *Grid Image* of 1922 over a consequent grid of squares. The stained glass windows to the entry room of the director's office in the Weimar Bauhaus building were also produced at that time. Comparable stained glass window designs by Peter Keler and Andor Weininger are preserved from 1922/1923.

Albers executed important stained glass windows in Gropius's buildings, such as the Sommerfeld House of 1921 and the Otte House in Berlin of 1921/1922. In 1923/1924 he carried out a large commission with six windows of coloured opaque glass in the stairway of the Leipzig Grassi Museum, and in 1924 he also designed the stained glass windows for Ullstein Publishing in Berlin, which were installed in 1926. Since all these stained glass windows were destroyed, only the preserved stained glass images of the years 1925/1926, made of sand-blasted opaque glasses with strict grid and colour structures, with transparence and overlapping, allow insight into Josef Albers's design intentions. With their transparence and geometric strictness, they demonstrate a kinship to paintings and prints by László Moholy-Nagy. There are also interesting similarities to textile work of the same time period at the Weimar Bauhaus by Margarete Köhler, Ida Kerkovius, or Gunta Stölzl and not least by his wife, Anni Albers.

Even though the stained glass painting workshop was not re-established at the Bauhaus in Dessau, Josef Albers continued his experiments with glass, and produced more works, including his combination type made of glass of 1928/1931.

Johannes Itten, *Tower of Fire*, 1920 (Reconstruction by Michael Siebenbrodt, 1996)

Josef Albers, *Rhine Legend*, image on glass, 1921

Josef Albers, *Grate*, 1922

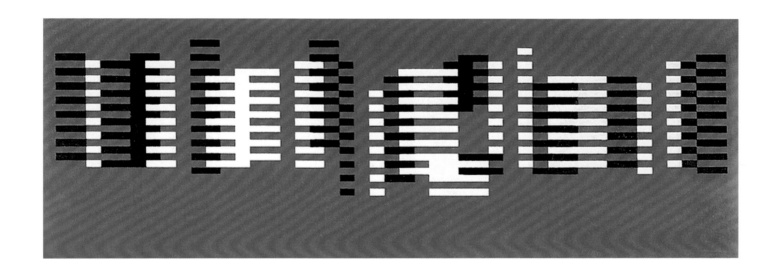

Josef Albers, *Fugue*, image on glass, c. 1925

# Graphic Print Shop

In 1919, very soon after the foundation of the Staatliche Bauhaus in Weimar, the Graphic Print Shop commenced its teaching and production operations on the basis of solid technical equipment taken over from the former Weimar Academy of Fine Arts. The graphic artist Walter Klemm, former teacher at the Bauhaus's predecessor school along with Max Thedy and Richard Engelmann, initially took over the leadership of the workshop. As Master of Craft, the well-versed lithographer Carl Zaubitzer, who held this post until the closing of the Bauhaus in Weimar, was placed at his side. At the beginning, work was apparently geared towards economical aspects, since the workshop mainly accepted printing orders and thus fulfilled the function as much of a productive operation as an artistic print shop, where the production of individual prints and larger editions of etchings, wood cuts and stone drawings (the majority from artists outside of the Bauhaus) were part of the daily work. At first glance, the workshop corresponded to Gropius's Weimar concept, according to which a renewal of art was to take place through ties with manual trades. But the Bauhaus's founder was plagued by doubts regarding the compatibility of teaching and experiment in this area of workshop work, which—and this may have been the decisive factor—had in the meantime, during the Weimar years, become one of the most financially successful workshops.

Walter Klemm soon left the Bauhaus. The painter Lyonel Feininger became Master of Form of the Graphic Print Shop in 1921. A passionate supporter of wood-carving techniques, he pushed the printing of graphic works by Masters and students of the Bauhaus, upon the initiative of Walter Gropius and with his support. Collections of prints and portfolio works of the Bauhaus Masters and representatives of the most important trends in the European artistic avant-garde were mainly produced during this time, along with numerous individual prints and postcards. The graphic art of the Bauhaus Masters was published in projects by the print shop. This included the *Twelve Wood Cuts* by Lyonel Feininger and the *Ypsilon* collection of etchings by Georg Muche of 1921. One year later, the lithography portfolio *Small Worlds* by

Wassily Kandinsky was published. This was followed in 1923 by a series of colour lithographs by Lothar Schreyer, a *Wielandslied der Edda* series of wood cuts by Gerhard Marcks, Oskar Schlemmer's *Spiel mit Köpfen* collection of lithographs, and finally the *Masters' Portfolio of the Staatliches Bauhaus*. This last work was published on the occasion of the Bauhaus Exhibition, with eight graphic works using different techniques by Lyonel Feininger, Wassily Kandinsky, Paul Klee, Gerhard Marcks, Georg Muche, and László Moholy-Nagy. Together with the exhibition catalogue, this portfolio remained the only publication of the Bauhaus publishing company founded in 1923.

The workshop's technical equipment, including a lithographic printing press, two copper printing presses and a manual printing press, allowed only the production of artistic prints. Typeset commissions such as the larger editions of brochures, posters and postcards for the 1923 Bauhaus Exhibition had to be printed elsewhere.

The apprenticeship for the three to five trainees in the Graphic Print Shop was thus limited to the learning of the graphic printing trade while fulfilling orders. Therefore the apprentices, who included Ludwig Hirschfeld-Mack, Rudolf Baschant, Gerhard Schunke, and Mordecai Bronstein, were introduced to the most common printing techniques, such as planography (lithography), intaglio (etchings, drypoint, copper engraving) and relief print (zinc etching, linocut and woodcut), particularly by Master of Craft Zaubitzer. Lyonel Feininger tried to help the students find their own artistic style through his personality and his work. In exhibitions, he presented his own artistic development. He demonstrated the methods of industrial work particularly in his woodcuts, the majority of which had been produced in the Weimar printing workshop. In addition, he introduced the students to experimental processes with different paper qualities, explaining their structure, colour and consistency. The lessons, which were always carried out with practical examples, were supplemented by the explanation of the specific uses of the different printing colours. Not only the printing students, but

also many other disciplines made use of the printing workshop's technical potential and experimented with the use of different printing techniques, artistic forms of expression and variations on diverse topics. There was a notable return to Christian motifs of the Middle Ages, as well as reflective depictions of individuals and attempts to give expression to the new man in a new time, confronted with modern architecture and technology, by employing a vocabulary of expressionist, abstract, geometric and subjective forms.

Along with the printing of graphic art by the Masters of the Bauhaus and their students, the printing workshop also produced the portfolio *New European Graphic Art* between 1921 and 1924. The first portfolio was published in 1921, with the works of the Bauhaus Masters, and was followed by portfolios of German, Italian, Russian, and French graphic art. With this incomparable and unique project of twentieth-century graphics, the Bauhaus declared its support for the newest artistic trends of the time and attempted to place itself in their milieu. At the same time, the publication of the portfolios was connected to the hope that the Bauhaus would become more well-known and that the institution's income, which at that time was logistically and politically threatened, would increase. The students had the opportunity to study in detail the works of such important German and international artists as Max Beckmann, Georg Grosz, Kurt Schwitters, Willi Baumeister, Ernst Ludwig Kirchner, Oskar Kokoschka, Erich Heckel, Marc Chagall, Mikhail Larionov, Natalia Goncharova, Georgio de Chirico, Umberto Boccioni, and Fernand Léger. The work on these large commissions also encouraged collaboration with the bookbindery workshop. There the cover papers, which had been produced in the printing workshop following designs by Paul Klee and Lyonel Feininger, were turned into corresponding portfolio covers.

Despite all these efforts and the sales of this series of portfolios as well as the graphic art of the Bauhaus Masters and students, the Graphic Print Shop did not have the expected economic effect, so they refrained from establishing a graphic printing workshop in Dessau.

The printing studio in the Bauhaus Weimar, c. 1923, photograph

Lyonel Feininger, *Gelmeroda*, 1923, wood engraving from the *Master Portfolio of the Staatliches Bauhaus in Weimar*, 1923

Gerhard Marcks, *By the Little Oven*, 1923, wood engraving from the *Master Portfolio of the Staatliches Bauhaus in Weimar*, 1923

Johannes Itten, *House of the White Man*, 1921, lithograph from the
*Master Portfolio of the Staatliches Bauhaus in Weimar*, 1921

Wassily Kandinsky, Plate 1 from the portfolio *Small Worlds*,
colour lithograph, 1922

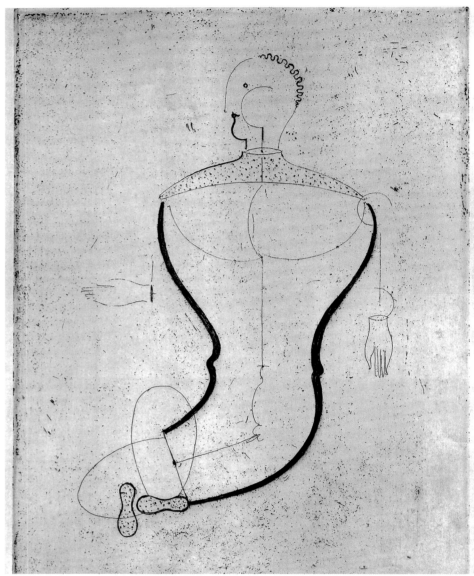

Paul Klee, *Tightrope Walker*, 1923, colour lithograph from the portfolio *Modern Art*, Munich, 1923

Oskar Schlemmer, *Abstrakte Figur nach links (Figur "S")* (Abstract figure on the left, "S" figure), 1923, lithograph

László Moholy-Nagy, *Composition*, 1923, colour lithograph from the *Master Portfolio of the Staatliche Bauhaus*, 1923

Eberhard Schrammen, Title page for *Der Austausch* (The Exchange), 1919, wood engraving

Rudolf Baschant, *Portrait of Martha Erps (Bauhaus Lady) with flower*, 1921, etching

Ludwig Hirschfeld-Mack, *Omnia mea mecum porto*, 1923, lithograph

# Typography/Printing and Advertising Workshop

Typography and advertising played a large role at the Bauhaus in Weimar. From the very beginning the school depended on presenting itself adequately to the public, and also strove to pursue new paths in this field by making it more effective and reforming communication. The early dedication of teachers and students to calligraphy and its design could thus be explained. The typographical and advertising designs of the Masters Johannes Itten, Oskar Schlemmer, and László Moholy-Nagy, and the students Joost Schmidt, Josef Albers, and Herbert Bayer, demonstrate that the Bauhaus in Weimar was already promoting advertising graphics very strongly. This was expressed in a decidedly sensitive formation of letters and text as expressions of art and life (Itten's philosophy), but also with the intention to guarantee, at the same time, clear legibility by employing capitals and *sans serif* letters (i.e. without initial or end strokes), with their combination with colour, geometric forms and signets as distinctive features. The 1923 Bauhaus Exhibition provided the opportunity and, indeed, necessity to make an impact in the typographic sector. László Moholy-Nagy in particular stood out, as he, among other things, had been commissioned to design the catalogue *Staatliches Bauhaus Weimar 1919-1923*. He seized the opportunity to introduce, on the basis of his artistic calling, elements of a contemporary, "new", "elementary typography", such as the use of Grotesque and later Futura typefaces, the inclusion of line, point, bar, raster and photography, and the emphasis of red and black to support text content. Even though it was developed according to the principles of strict objectification and disciplining of the means, the book's design showed that Moholy-Nagy, despite his intention to be clear in his message and insistent in his form, was still strongly influenced by aesthetic criteria. This is made clear by the emphasis on the spatial effect of individual letters or the optically effective organisation of planes by arranging lines of text at angles. At the same time, this type of design, which explored the expressive value of typographic means, also opened up the opportunity for a typography more oriented towards purpose. Thus Moholy-Nagy was working toward a scientifically functional design, which overcame purist aesthetics.

Moholy-Nagy's influence on the appearance of the Bauhaus was great. Along with the catalogue of the 1923 exhibition, he also left his mark on the layout of the Bauhaus books, including related advertising materials, the layout of the *Bauhaus* magazine, letterheads, and part of the business equipment of the Bauhaus, its limited company and its society of friends. In Dessau, too, Moholy's continued model remained effective.

The workshop for printing and advertising existed from 1925 to 1932. It was established in Dessau after it had been recognised in Weimar that it would be opportune to convert the printing workshop into moveable type in view of the increase in typographic commissions. It was now possible to set up a manual typesetting workshop, a platen press and a rotary printing press in the basement of the newly-constructed Bauhaus building. Junior Master Herbert Bayer was appointed head of the new workshop in Dessau. He developed this department into a workshop which, apart from developing and employing type and providing complex training in the field of advertising, also integrated aspects of mural painting and photography, a novelty at the time. He had already attracted notice in Weimar because of the murals he developed on the basis of Kandinsky's colour-shape theory for the Staatliches Bauhaus and the design of impressive, fictitious advertising structures reminiscent of the colour and form vocabulary of the Dutch artists group *De Stijl*. As head of the workshop for printing and advertising, Bayer applied himself to the basic issues of advertising and typography. At the same time, he integrated economic, technical, psychological and organisational aspects in a holistic approach, thus reacting to contemporary developments in scientific advertising. The combination of a printing and advertising workshop, new and unconventional at the time, met the requirements for an uninterrupted sequence from design to execution of a typographic product. Traditionally separate tasks such as typesetting, photography and mounting were now combined, which gave rise to the first steps in the creation of a new professional: today's graphic designer. Education with Bayer was less marked by school-like lessons than by practical work with technical instruction. Within type design, Herbert Mayer, like Josef Albers, referred to the simplest geometric elements. He took standards developed elsewhere on paper and type as a starting point for considerations which were oriented towards a complex standardisation of communication media. On this basis, the first advertising designs were produced in the Dessau workshop. This included a *Catalogue of Samples*, an advertising prospectus of selected Bauhaus products. Functional, and also advertising-technical, psychological, and linguistic criteria made up the background to the choice of type, arrangement of images and typeset design.

It was the printing and advertising workshop that initiated the type reform at the Bauhaus. Along with the consequent use of small initial letters, the changes were apparent in the design of the letterhead. Bayer tried to develop a unified appearance for the Bauhaus (he redesigned the business papers of the Bauhaus three times before 1927), but he did not succeed in the end, probably because of differing ideas within the institution. The workshop, which was now called the "Advertising Department", became one of the main workshops of the Bauhaus in 1927 and was henceforth to educate so-called "advertising experts." More than ever, commissions were sought and finally found in the field of exhibition design.

STAATLICHES BAUHAUS WEIMAR

1919 1923

WEIMAR - MÜNCHEN

BAUHAUSVERLAG

László Moholy-Nagy, Inside title page from *Staatliches Bauhaus Weimar 1919-1923*, 1923

Joost Schmidt, Poster for the Bauhaus Exhibition in Weimar, 1923

In the years between 1928 and 1930, when Hannes Meyer held the post of Bauhaus director, the school was able to acquire several design commissions for exhibitions. This also included the presentation of the stand for the Junkers Company at the 1929 exhibition *Gas and Water* in Berlin. At this time Joost Schmidt had already taken over the leadership of the workshop and had–in the spirit of Hannes Meyer–systematised and further expanded the "study of the work." It was due to his influence that the advertising means of the Bauhaus were organised and differentiated in such a manner that they could henceforth be used for the most varied advertising purposes. In the process, it turned out that the earlier conducted study of the elements of type and the education in perspective drawing, shadow construction, painting and the application of colour theory according to Wilhelm Ostwald, were necessary

prerequisites for the creative use of typographic means. The examination of optical laws of design, where elementary forms were explored at first and more complex combinations and contrasts were developped later, was initially not meant for immediate application in advertising. Its connection in meaning only becomes obvious in the collaboration of workshops on an actual project. The use of photography had already gained importance under the influence of László Moholy-Nagy, and even more under Herbert Bayer. Generally frowned upon in the field of artistic advertising until then, its value was now recognised, especially as an artistic means that was object-oriented and thus objective, and it was integrated into the design of printed matter and exhibitions, just like the elements of the plastic design field. Consequently, the newly founded photography class, whose acting head was

Josef Albers, Font templates, 1923-26

photographer Walter Peterhans, was absorbed into the advertising department along with the classes for typography and sculpture. The most important criteria for typographic practise and the revolutionary exhibition structures created by Joost Schmidt with his students in the advertising department were objective and comprehensive information, impartiality and a convincing clarity of design as a result of interdisciplinary collaboration.

Ludwig Mies van der Rohe succeeded Hannes Meyer as director in 1931/1932, and, because commissions were stagnant, Joost Schmidt again systematised the advertising course by integrating the experience of the past years in a "Design Theory" course and tying them in with elementary design exercises and aspects of perceptional psychology. Schmidt's complex claim to prepare students as completely as possible for their future work was thus necessarily lost. His working methods and the advertising department's work were viewed in an increasingly critical light within the institution, and their relevance was questioned in view of changed conditions of reception and utilisation. When the Bauhaus in Dessau was closed and the move to Berlin took place, Mies van der Rohe avoided the reintegration of the politically left-wing Joost Schmidt into the teaching staff. Temporarily, the previous head of the photography department, Walter Peterhans, became head of the advertising department.

abcdefghi
jklmnopqr
stuvwxyz

HERBERT BAYER: Abb. 1. Alfabet
„g" und „k" sind noch als
unfertig zu betrachten

Beispiel eines Zeichens
in größerem Maßstab
Präzise optische Wirkung

sturm blond

Abb. 2. Anwendung

390

Herbert Bayer, Draft of a universal font, 1926

Herbert Bayer, Design for a newspaper kiosk, 1924

Herbert Bayer, *Catalog of Patterns*, title page, 1925

**DAS BAUHAUS IN DESSAU**

Dessau, Mauerstraße 36    Fernruf 2696    Diskontogesellschaft Filiale Dessau

# KATALOG
## DER
# MUSTER

**VERTRIEB**

**durch die**

RICHTFEST BAUHAUS NEUBAU

EINLADUNG

● 4h　führung durch den bauhaus-neubau

● 5½h　richtschmaus im volks- und jugendheim bauhofstraße
anschließend tanz

sonntag
21. 3. 26

Herbert Bayer, Invitation to the topping-out ceremony for the new
Bauhaus building in Dessau, 1926

**verfolgen mit interesse** entwicklung und schaffen des bauhauses - hochschule für gestaltung - in dessau.

**durch die zeitschrift**

**bauhaus**

zeitschrift für bau und gestaltung, besteht in gesteigertem maße die möglichkeit, mit den bestrebungen dieses instituts bekannt zu werden und die geistige verbindung aufrecht zu erhalten.

der erste jahrgang der zeitschrift hat eine außerordentlich günstige aufnahme gefunden. der große „kreis der freunde des bauhauses", akademien, staatliche und städtische behörden, hoch- und tiefbauämter, gewerbe- und fachschulen, industrielle unternehmungen des bau- und ingenieurwesens, des maschinenbaues u. der verkehrstechnik, architekten u. bauunternehmungen **sind ihre leser.**

mit dem neuen jahrgang 1928 wird die zeitschrift an umfang und inhalt bedeutend erweitert, in format 210 : 297 mm (din a 4), mit vielen abbildungen auf kunstdruckpapier und in umschlag erscheinen.

der umschlag des neuen jahrganges

neben grundsätzlichen erörterungen über gestaltende arbeit bringt die zeitschrift in der hauptsache berichte mit abbildungen über die arbeitsergebnisse des bauhauses. besonderer wert wird gelegt auf mitteilungen über neuzeitliche

bauweisen, neue baumaterialien, siedlungswesen, neue wohntypen, hauseinrichtungen, gebrauchsgegenstände, mit denen werkstätten und architekturabteilung des bauhauses sich beschäftigen. auch die übrigen gebiete der gestaltung wie bühne, reklame, fotografie, malerei werden besonders behandelt.

Herbert Bayer, Pamphlet for the Bauhaus revue, 1928

László Moholy-Nagy, Pamphlet for the Bauhaus books, 1929

László Moholy-Nagy, Jacket for Bauhaus book 14, 1929

Joost Schmidt, *Creating contrasts from a given optic element*, i.e the typographical character P *(9 solutions in a square)*, 1931

Joost Schmidt, Publicity sheet for *Uher Type – Lumitype*, 1932

Was mit der Metteurmaschine alles möglich ist !

Gehrungen

kreuzende

Linien setzen

Now in the full swing of its second brilliant season...the St. Regis Roof! Again Urban's enchanting setting, that already famous fantasy of topic sky and foliage, delights patrons from the world's discriminating horizons. Again Lopez and his astounding young gentlemen sound the irresistible clarion of their dance rhythms. Again gracious St. Regis service and the choice St. Regis cuisine and the choice dinner and ... make luncheon, St. Regis Roof a

Schrägliegender Satz

UHER TYPE

500

Guilloche-Muster

Vergrössern

Joost Schmidt, Pamphlet for the city of Dessau, title page, 1930/31

Joost Schmidt and Xanti Schawinsky, Junkers stand at the exhibition
"Gas and Water", Berlin, 1929, photograph

# II

## Mural Painting Workshop

Within the history of coloured design in architecture, the mural-painting workshop of the Bauhaus took an outsider position, since its teachers often had diverse and wide-ranging ideas about which criteria should apply when building and colour are brought together. The Bauhaus largely stayed out of the contemporary verbal discussions regarding coloured design in architecture, but essentially nailed its colours to the mast with its own buildings and those of Walter Gropius. While they were predominantly white on the outside and relied on architectural quality, they often showed a varied and multicoloured spectrum on the inside.

In the spirit of the unity of all arts under the leadership of architecture, for which its foundation manifesto called, a workshop for mural painting was also set up immediately after the opening of the Staatliches Bauhaus in Weimar. Its leader was initially Weimar Court Decorative Painter Franz Heidelmann. He gave lectures on the composition of colour, on binders, pigments, additives and painting techniques. In May 1921, Heidelmann was replaced by the decorative painter Carl Schlemmer, whom Gropius assigned as Master of Craft. Johannes Itten had worked as the Master of Form in the early so-called "workshop for decorative painting" since 1920, but was replaced in the course of 1922 by Oskar Schlemmer, brother of Carl Schlemmer. Schlemmer headed the workshop for only a few months. Initial projects of the workshop referred to the colour treatment of a wooden toy produced in the woodcarving workshop and to the colouration of furniture created in the furniture workshop. The main focus from the beginning was on the colour treatment of architecture, more on the inside than on the outside. For lack of initial commissions, the school's rooms and a living room in Gropius's apartment were painted. The use of strongly coloured or earthy tones, following Johannes Itten's understanding of colour, was characteristic of these early attempts. When dealing with planes, ornaments or elements of expressionist art were sometimes employed. Walter Gropius used the workshop's potential very early on for his own building tasks, such as in Berlin's Sommerfeld House in Steglitz and in the Otte House in Zehlendorf. Here, delicate pastel tones subordinated themselves to architecture.

Following a conflict with Carl Schlemmer, Gropius replaced him in November 1922 with Heinrich Beberniss, who held the position of Master of Craft until the closing of the Bauhaus in Weimar. Only a few months earlier, Wassily Kandinsky had taken over the artistic leadership of the workshop as Master of Form, and that same year Theo van Doesburg brought his *De Stijl* influence to the Bauhaus. For van Doesburg, who never belonged to the Bauhaus, complete abstraction and limitation of artistic means to the straight line, the right angle and the three primary colours blue, yellow and red, to grey, black and white, were the most important commandments. The degree of van Doesburg's influence can be observed in the colouration and formation of many Bauhaus products. Even the design which Walter Gropius made for the furnishing and colouration of his work space designated as the director's office showed *De Stijl* elements.

In the mural-painting workshop, Wassily Kandinsky dealt with the various effects of colour in space and transferred elements of his artistic programme into the coloured mural painting of his own designs. It is evident from his murals, which were executed by students of the mural-painting workshop and displayed at an unjudged art show in Berlin in 1921, that Kandinksy understood the mural as a messenger of metaphysical ideas. Interdisciplinary issues of colourful design of architecture or colour in the city were not considered in his course.

The apprenticeship in Kandinsky's workshop was largely oriented towards the manual trades. Kandinsky tried to keep the workshop away from productive operations despite the heavily-weighing economic pressure in order to gain freedom for experimental work. The Master had structured the teaching spectrum into various topical groups. Accordingly, the painting of actual rooms, the variation of coloured and plastic treatment of walls, the testing of varied material-driven techniques (oil paint, distemper, casein paint, lime wash, sgrafitto, fresco, hot wax paint), the use of coloured materials such as wood, glass and metal, the creation of systematic patterns and the production of colour-shape tables corresponding to Kandinsky's colour-shape instruction from the preparatory course, were all planned. To this, he added the composition of colours, their psychological effects, technical use and, finally, composition. Kandinsky viewed interior design as a central concern of the

Wassily Kandinsky, Project for mural painting B presented at the *Juryfreie Kunstschau* (the jury-free art show) in Berlin, 1922

Wassily Kandinsky, Project for a mural painting presented at the *Juryfreie Kunstschau* (the jury-free art show) in Berlin, 1922

Bauhaus and thus focused on the form-changing strength of colour and its effects on the space. Some of his students tried to apply this, far from figural depictions, in their designs. Mostly pictures emerged, which were transferred to architecture without entering into an immediate relationship with it. Herbert Bayer designed murals with a theme of primary colours and the basic geometric shapes associated with them in relationship to space for the stairway of the Weimar Bauhaus building. This structure had been built as early as 1904-1911 and designed by Belgian Art Nouveau artist Henry van de Velde on the occasion of the 1923 Bauhaus Exhibition. These mural designs, with their integrated written word "secretariat", can also be interpreted as pictograms for a coloured guide system for the main Bauhaus building.

The 1923 exhibition was reason for a veritable show of achievements in the field of coloured design in architecture. Next to the already-mentioned mural by Bayer and the design work in the director's office, there was the design for a thoroughfare by the students Peter Keler and Farkas Molnar. Furthermore, the fine-tuned colouration for the interior of the exhibition structure *Haus am Horn* by Alfred Arndt and Josef Maltan and the production of murals for demonstration purposes was by mural-painting students, who in many cases also executed the designs of non-workshop members. Joost Schmidt gave artistic expression to the Weimar school's vestibule with reliefs from multicoloured plaster, stucco and glass shapes according to his own design on the

occasion of the exhibition. They were variations on the theme of penetrating elementary geometric forms. Oskar Schlemmer's reliefs and murals, which he had designed for the entrance hall, stairway and corridors of the workshop building in Weimar and executed with Josef Hartwig and Hermann Müller, represented the peak of his artistic wall design. Schlemmer's concept of mural painting also included figural depictions, true to his plastic and visual arts work. His claim was to implement his idea of a new man in visual art and in relation to space, in connection with other forms of art.

With the move of the Bauhaus from Weimar to Dessau, transformation from pictorial decorative painting to an expression of art in planes and space increased in the field of mural painting. Mural painting was understood as pure plane painting in the service of architecture. This transformation is mainly due to Hinnerk Scheper; the former Bauhaus student, who already had practical experience in the field of mural painting, took over the workshop in Dessau and completely restructured it. Scheper held a master craftsman's certificate and was thus the only Bauhaus Master to have true teaching credentials. Hence, the additional use of a Master of Craft as before was superfluous. The workshop was divided into a teaching workshop and an experimentation and execution workshop. Apprenticeship began in the third semester and ended with a Journeyman's certificate. Studies were continued in the experimentation workshop and finished with a certificate, if applicable. Poster painting was also

Herbert Bayer, *Circle*, mural for the staircase adjacent to the Bauhaus Weimar building, 1923 (reconstruction by Werner Claus, 1975/76)

Oskar Schlemmer, Overall plan of the murals in the studio building of the Staatliche Bauhaus in Weimar, 1923
© Oskar Schlemmer Archive and Theatre Estate

Peter Keler and Farkas Molnar, Colour plan for a passage in the Bauhaus Weimar, 1923

part of the teaching spectrum, as well as colour interior design and the testing of new techniques and materials. Students were accompanied from design to execution, and the associated assumption of responsibility was part of the pedagogic concept.

According to Hinnerk Scheper, interior design in colour was only to a small degree a matter of personal taste. It was, according to his understanding, subject to formal and technical laws. To him the most important function of colour in space was its psychological effect. Mural design had to be understood in immediate reference to architecture, to serve it and not to compete with it. The subdivision of a building and the functions of the individual building parts were the starting point for colouration which varied between shades of colour and tone, always seeking balance. He placed great importance on the character of materials and their surface effects, qualities he had been instructed in when he was a student in the preparatory course with László Moholy-Nagy. Scheper had had the opportunity to put his concept of colour design to the test in museum buildings and hospitals as well as in buildings by Walter Gropius, even before he became head of the Mural Painting Department. In Dessau, too, he had several opportunities to give time and attention to existing architecture and to support it in its own right by means of sensitive colouration. Among the prominent projects of Scheper and the mural painting workshop are the colouration of the new Bauhaus structure and the Masters' houses. Walter Gropius had commissioned Hinnerk Scheper to work out the colour plans for the Bauhaus building. Even though Scheper's suggestions for a part of the interior were largely implemented, those for the exterior were rejected—probably due to Gropius's intervention. Scheper also used colour as a means of orientation in the

Bauhaus classroom building: in the stairways and corridors, for example. In the offices and classrooms he also employed colour to mark individual building parts and their functions. Stronger colours like blue, yellow and red were used, as well as pastels and their varied shades, warm or cool. By employing different materials, he succeeded in increasing the spatial effect of colour. Additionally, the colour grey was given much attention in the Bauhaus building, and it was used in innumerable shades. The workshop rooms were given a neutral colouration.

The colouration of the Masters' houses was designed according to suggestions by students and Marcel Breuer, as well as to the ideas of their future inhabitants. Kandinsky, for example, employed the space-forming character of colour when designing living areas. There, the individual composition dominates opposite a uniform colour concept which integrates all living rooms. The design of the duplexes' exteriors was based on a draft by Alfred Arndt that predominantly provided for shades of white and—where building parts were to be accented—in colour. The mural painting workshop also provided drafts for the other Dessau Bauhaus buildings, which were mostly executed by students. This corresponded to the working method of "vertical brigades" introduced by Hannes Meyer, whose organisation according to the principle of self-administration contributed to an education that was practically relevant. It was also Meyer who, for economic and educational reform reasons, brought about the merging of the furniture workshop, metal workshop and mural painting departments into an "interior furnishing workshop", to which he appointed Alfred Arndt as head. Scheper, meanwhile, went to Moscow for a year. Arndt had stood out earlier with his work for the Masters' houses, particularly with the interior colour design of the Auerbach House in Jena, designed by Gropius, and other complex colour projects mainly carried out in Thuringia. His

Students spraying chromatic bars, c. 1929

colour concepts were marked by the use of light shades of blue and yellow, which were combined with white, grey and black and also very sparingly with red and brown. Being concerned with the psychological effects of colour and trying to subordinate it to architecture, Arndt was close to Scheper in his efforts.

The time after 1929 was also marked by the development of the Bauhaus wallpaper, which was put on the market by the Hanover company Rasch and earned considerable revenue for the school. The designs for this affordable standard product, which was mainly used in housing development construction, were chosen from a multitude of works which students from almost all the workshops had submitted as part of a competition. The palette included clear, strong colours as well as brownish tones. Fine structuring in the form of lines or gridlines formed hardly perceptible patterns, which in combination with a matte surface optically enlarged the space. Since the Bauhaus wallpaper was relatively heavily advertised, it was able to surpass similar wallpaper developed years earlier by the Marburg Wallpaper Factory and thus become the most successful product of the Bauhaus.

When Ludwig Mies van der Rohe took over the Bauhaus leadership, the head position in the mural painting workshop remained vacant due to budget cuts. Only in 1931 was Hinnerk Scheper able to start adjusting the Mural Painting Department to the new financial conditions. He now focused only on theory and experiment. His teaching subjects were called "Colour Theory" and "Interior Colour Design." The students got to know different colour systems, including those of Isaac Newton, Johann Wolfgang von Goethe, Philipp Otto Runge, Adolf Hölzel, Ewald Hering, and Wilhelm Ostwald. They drew colour circles, practised shading, and finally designed concrete colour plans. Practical implementation, for which the colour-tone card by "Bauman-Prase" of 1912 was used, occurred only rarely. Mies van der Rohe, trusting in the architectural quality of his buildings, preferred more muted colouring and the use of natural material colours.

After the Bauhaus had moved to Berlin and started to set up in a former telephone factory, it very quickly became clear which colour to use: white, everything white!

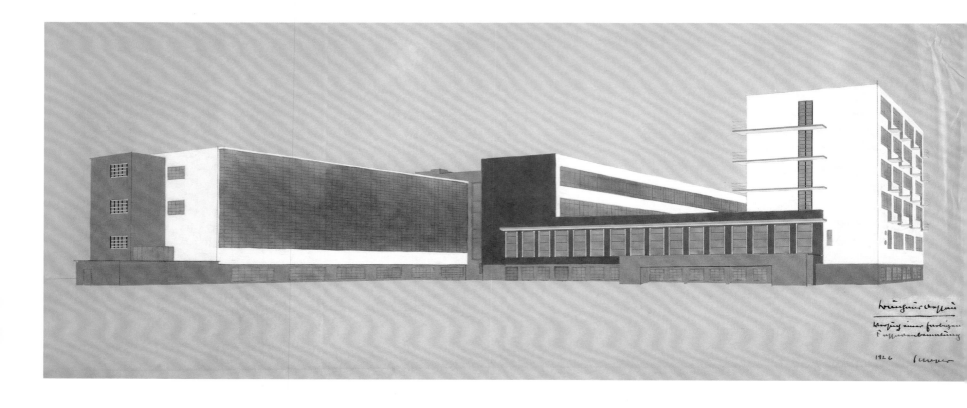

Hinnerk Scheper, Colour plan (façade) for the Bauhaus building in Dessau, 1926

Walter Gropius and Wassily Kandinsky, Stairwell of the Kandinsky House in Dessau, condition in 1999

Bauhaus Dessau, fresco studio, Bauhaus wallpaper from a book of
mock-ups, 1929/31

Hermann Fischer (Sketch), Production sample for Bauhaus frosted glass
from the Kunzendorf factories in Sorau, Niederlausitz, 1931/32

# Stone Sculpting and Woodcarving/Plastic Workshop

It was according to traditional practise at art academies that the Bauhaus in Weimar ran two workshops for sculpting. This, however, seemed hardly suitable for the implementation of the Bauhaus ideal. Oskar Schlemmer, who headed the stone sculpting and, from 1922, also the woodcarving workshop as Master of Form after Richard Engelmann, did not perceive any work opportunities apart from free artistic production for these workshops in which sculptors, stonemasons and plasterers were to be trained, and did not see how they could be brought in in connection with building, that is, with architecture. Little is known about the teaching of the Masters of Form in either workshop. In hindsight, former students could hardly recall regular lessons but rather just animated discussions. It must be assumed that the Masters of Form mainly exerted influence as examples, while the Masters of Craft sought to impart manual skills. The works which eventually emerged from the stone sculpting and woodcarving workshops were on the one hand results of training in manual trades and on the other hand the creative implementation of individual artists' ideas. Furthermore, the workshops took on service duties. Thus, sculptures in wood or stone were produced, but also candelabra, masks and plaster models for the ceramics workshop. Architectural models, too, such as for the planned buildings by Walter Gropius and Adolf Meyer, were produced in plaster, among them the models for the reconstruction of the Jena City Theatre (1921), the memorial for the March victims in the Weimar cemetery (1921/1922) and the competition design for the Chicago Tribune skyscraper (1922).

The woodcarving workshop was given a more complex task by Gropius's architectural office in 1921 with the execution of carved works on the house for the entrepreneur Sommerfeld, which was built entirely of wood according to plans by Walter Gropius and Adolf Meyer in Steglitz. The workshop was artistically directed by Johannes Itten at that time. Hans Kämpfe worked as Master of Craft, but he was replaced in 1921 by the sculptor Josef Hartwig. Doors, stairs, heating device panels and wall reliefs in the Sommerfeld house were produced according to drafts by apprentice Joost Schmidt, who, on the basis of knowledge gained from his lessons with Johannes Itten, had developed intricate combinations of geometric shapes. He rendered the client's requirements in a largely abstract form language while preserving symbolic, representational references.

A similar task came about for the stone-sculpting workshop, which had since 1921 also been headed by Josef Hartwig as Master of Craft, with the furnishing of the school building's vestibule as well as the entrance hall and the stairwell in the workshop building of the Weimar Bauhaus.

Apart from these partly architecture-related works, the design and execution of sculpted works, i.e. free sculptures, were at the centre of the work in both workshops. Their common element was the use of a clear, geometric form language which, among other things, was based on such analysis of the formal characteristics of circle, rectangle and square as was carried out in the preparatory course. Over and above that, the stylistic bandwidth included sculptures rendered either figuratively or abstractly with creation or propagation motifs, and with esoteric and spiritual meaning, simple abstracted torsos, cubist building sculptures, and neo-sculptural reliefs.

From this variety of artistic means of expression one can conclude that the students were given plenty of freedom by the Masters of Form when exploring their artistic individuality. Executed in plaster, wood or natural stone, these sculptures go back to such artists as Joost Schmidt, Lili Graeff, Kurt Schwerdtfeger, Otto Werner, Karl-Peter Röhl, Johannes Berthold, Ilse Fehling, Josef Hartwig, Theobald Emil Müller-Hummel and Oskar Schlemmer, whose experiments with wall reliefs and free sculpture stand out. The toys by Alma Buscher and the chess set by Josef Hartwig found widespread popularity. Here, too, the simple, geometrically-formed bodies, which had been cut from a single block without waste, were to provide a positive influence on children in their motivation to play with their many colours. Likewise, the chess figures developed according to strict aesthetic, mathematical and functional principles from a cube were to bring out the joy of playing in adults with their clear measure ratios and characteristic forms. Unfortunately, the chess set gained only little popularity amongst chess players, disappointing the hopes of the Bauhaus that it had a product which would help to fill its coffers.

After the move from Weimar to Dessau, sculpting workshops were not set up. The production of free art, even though tied in with romantic views of medieval craftsmanship and expressionist cults of uniqueness, was seen as anachronistic and the Bauhaus tried instead to find access to three-dimensional design which better corresponded to its precise goals. Thus, a "sculpture workshop" was established, though initially in conjunction with the theatre workshop. The workshop's profile was initially dominated by the construction of stage sets and props.

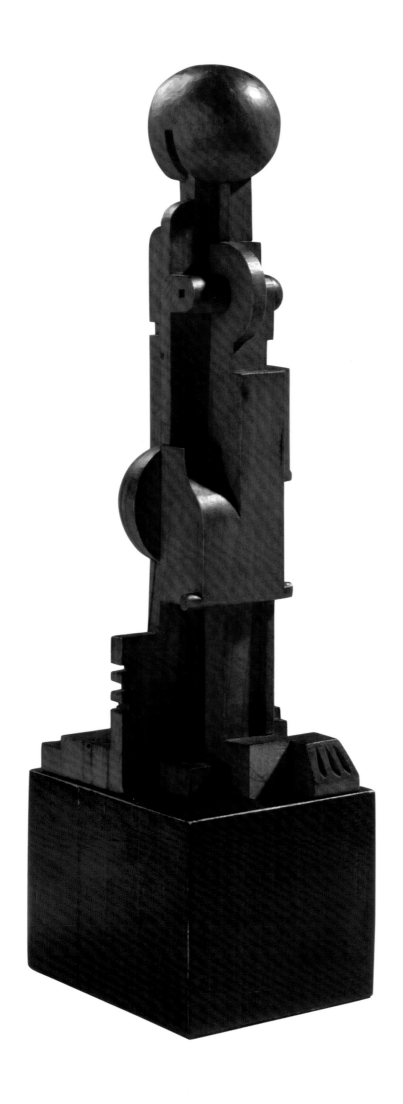

Joost Schmidt, who had ambitions for stage design, took over the leadership, but did not want to accept the reduction of his workshop's function to mere groundwork. He focused his attention on an art pedagogic orientation and tried more or less successfully to orient the themes of sculpture design according to the now-compulsory principle of technical reproducibility and to anchor them solidly in his teaching programme as well as in the workshop's profile. Joost Schmidt gave an "Elementary Sculpture Lesson" which, in addition to his teaching as part of the preparatory class, mainly went into the spatial aspect of the design process and consciously made use of photography as a modern medium. The ideas and artistic practise of László Moholy-Nagy undoubtedly had an innovative effect on this. The interaction between solid objects and space, and the movement of the solid object in space were henceforth central themes of the experimental work in the sculpture workshop. The systematic analysis by means of photography of the elementary spatial solids of cone, cube, sphere, cylinder, etc., formed the starting point for a sensitisation of spatial experience with all the senses. In balanced and concentrated perception training, contemporary aesthetic qualities were to be plumbed by means of new kinetic sculptures. Systematically run in test arrangements, it resulted in an autonomous, unmistakable profile of applied mathematics and the teaching of elementary design experience. Schmidt's complex understanding of space, which included the earthly as well as the cosmic and was oriented towards man, also played a major role. Opportunities to apply in practise what had been tested in the "laboratory" were found in model construction, in exhibition design and in theatre work. Since Joost Schmidt was also in charge of the department of publicity graphics, advertising and typography from 1928, favourable conditions existed for the optimum combination of sculpture, typographic and, especially, photographic elements. From this, Schmidt developed a complex design approach which enabled him to stage design projects that would set future standards.

The installations created by Joost Schmidt and his students of the sculpture and other departments, particularly in the field of exhibition design, must be highlighted. Stands such as those for the 1929 Gas and Water Exhibition in Berlin and the 1930 International Hygiene Exhibition in Dresden are part of this. With the assigning of the sculptures workshop to visual arts by Ludwig Mies van der Rohe in the autumn of 1930, disciplines from which Schmidt's work had distanced itself more and more, the department increasingly lost its importance, since it was more and more attached to the other workshops. Inseparably connected with Joost Schmidt, who had not been appointed to the Berlin Bauhaus, the Sculptures Department ceased to exist in Dessau.

Theodor Emil Müller-Hummel, *Man-Machine*, 1922

Sculpture Studio at the Bauhaus Weimar, 1923

Karl Peter Röhl, Sculpture in the style of a totem pole, c. 1920

Johannes Berthold, *Kronos*, 1924

Oskar Schlemmer, *Abstract Figure*, 1921/23
© Oskar Schlemmer Archive and Theatre Estate

Josef Hartwig, Bauhaus game of chess, 1924

Alma Siedhoff-Buscher, Large and small shipbuilding game, 1924

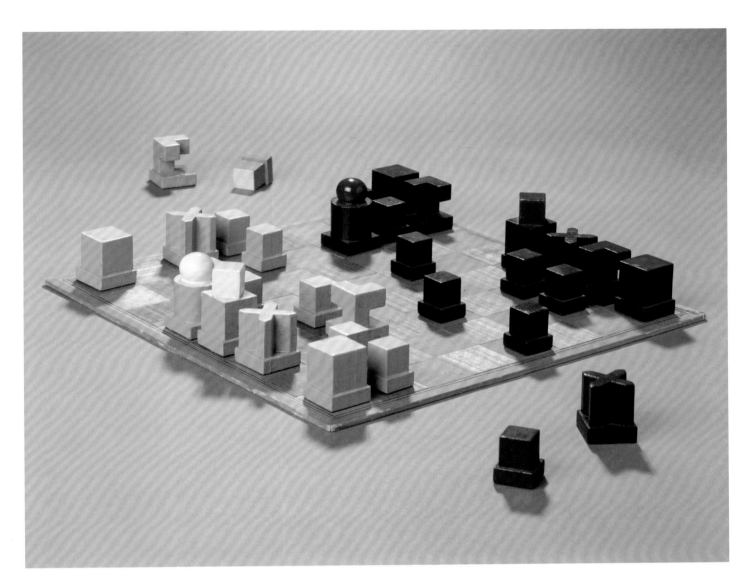

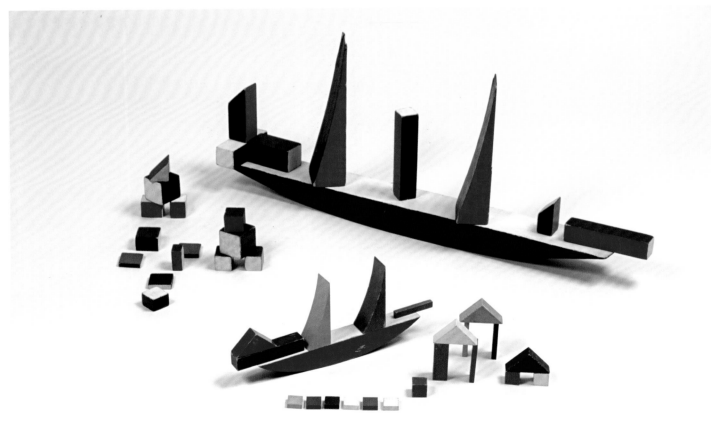

Oskar Schlemmer, Relief from the studio building of the Staatliche Bauhaus in Weimar, 1923

Joost Schmidt, Relief from the vestibule of the Bauhaus building in Weimar, 1923

Edmund Collein and Heinz Loew, Study of light sculpture, 1928

Joost Schmidt, *Parabolic Sculpture*, 1927/28 (reconstruction)

Heinz Loew, Model of a mechanical stage, 1927, reconstruction 1968

Plaster torso and technical drawing, Still life in the studio of Joost Schmidt, photograph by Heinz Loew or Joost Schmidt, 1932

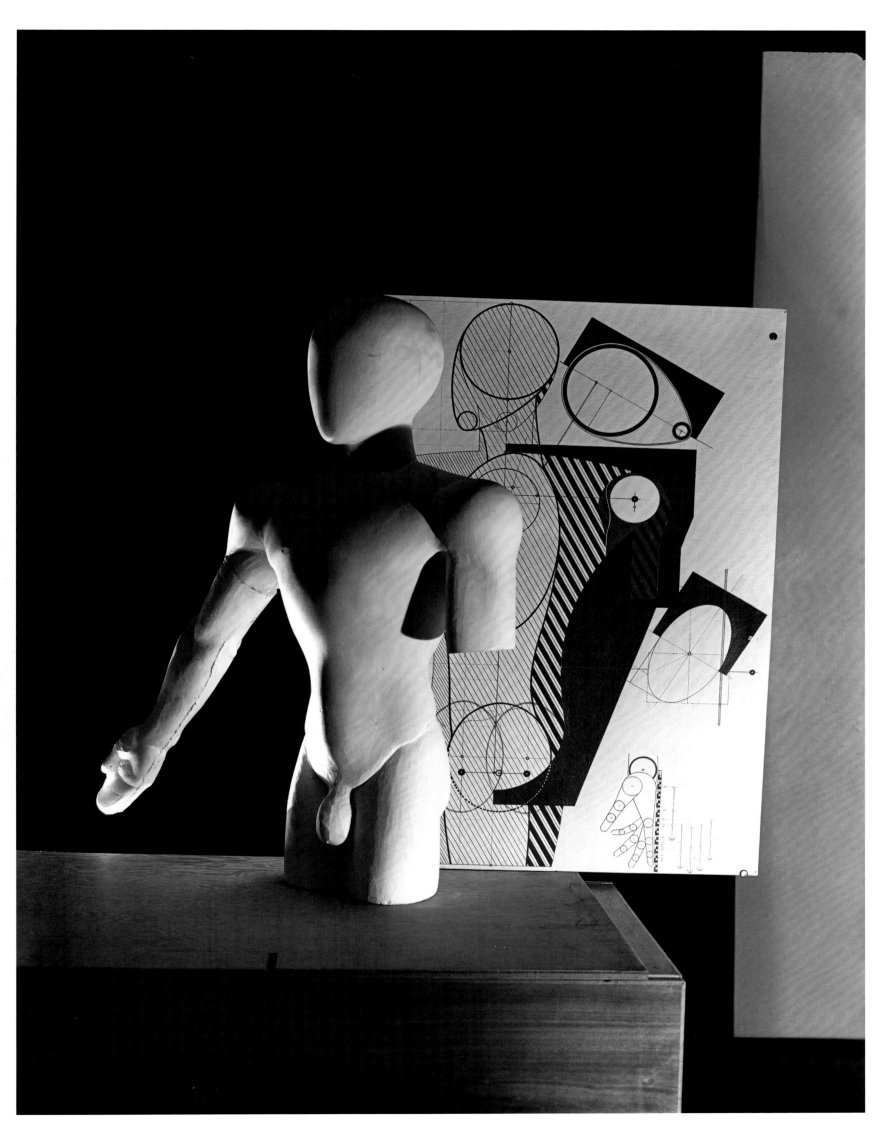

# Weaving Workshop

The textiles workshop, termed "weaving mill" at the Bauhaus, is one the of most prominent workshops and with an average of fifteen to twenty students lay well ahead of the furniture, metal and mural painting workshops in terms of numbers. Helene Börner headed the weaving workshop as Master of Craft from 1919 to 1925, providing her own looms, after she had already held the same position until 1915 at Henry van de Velde's Weimar Arts and Crafts School. The overall responsibility lay with "Masters of Form" Johannes Itten (1920/1921) and Georg Muche (1921/1927), before the Bauhaus graduates Gunta Stölzl (1925/1931), Anni Albers (1931), and Otti Berger (1931/1932) took over the responsibility for education and production in the workshop. From 1932, the architect Lilly Reich ran the furnishing as well as the textiles workshop.

The textiles workshop, into which the separate women's class had merged in 1920, also initially taught other textile techniques other than weaving, such as crocheting, knotting, cranking, embroidery, macramé, appliqué, paint and spray techniques. One of the rare pieces beyond the dominating weaving techniques was a fabric with spray technique by Felix Kube of around 1921, using templates for numbers and letters, as well as a wall hanging in felt appliqué by Ida Kerkovius. Ceiling and wall hangings as well as rugs were produced in 1921/1922 for the Sommerfeld house, among others.

Of the lavish knotted rugs of around 1923, two by Benita Koch-Otte with geometric compositions are preserved in the Weimar Bauhaus collection, while large square rugs for the Weimar director's office and the living room in the *Haus am Horn* of sixteen square metres each are preserved only as photographs. Some of the best-known non-objective geometric image compositions are tapestries by Hedwig Jungnik and Max Peiffer Watenphul of around 1921 as well as the children's room rug by Benita Koch-Otte (1923). Around 1923, Gunta Stölzl, Suse Ackermann, Martha Erps-Breuer, Anni Albers, Gertrud Arndt, and Friedrich Wilhelm Bogler used streak motifs in an inexhaustible abundance of variations, often in combination with lines and rectangular planes. Subtle colour nuances and binding variations made for the optical and haptic appeal of this textile work. The wall hanging by Benita Koch-Otte with a structure of squares in red and green tones seems like a painting of squares by Paul Klee. In this semi-tapestry, the colour nuances were created by means of weaving techniques, with warp yarns of cotton in nine colours and wool in two colours as well as weft yarns of two different partially greying cotton yarns in 24 colours and two wool yarns in four colour variations.

The students Gunta Stölzl and Benita Koch-Otte attended a dyeing class in Krefeld and subsequently established dye works at the Bauhaus. In 1924, they both acquired special knowledge in binding and material studies at a "manufacturers' class" at the Krefeld silk weaving school. The installation of a Jacquard loom and initial tests with piece goods coincided with Muche's attempts to build a production operation along with the education in order to increase the workshop's profitability. Fabrics such as piece goods with rectangular and striped structures were developed by Agnes Roghé, Hedwig Jungnik and Gunta Stölzl from 1923.

Georg Muche turned out to be a sensitive teacher, advising and encouraging his students to experiment and letting them work playfully without restricting them. Muche left the Bauhaus in 1927, as he wanted to dedicate more time to art and architecture and did not want to give theory classes in the weaving workshop. His own artistic concepts were based on intuition and obviously offered the students too little support.

Formal stimulations were—like in no other workshop—taken on from the preparatory course with Itten and Muche as well as the courses in colour and form theory by Klee and Kandinsky and the vocabulary of abstract art transferred into textiles. The formal development ran from the narrative image rug via strongly abstract, objective compositions to two-dimensionally constructive designs, for which new materials such as metal and plastic strings were tested and plastic structures developed from the bond.

The use of textiles in the context of architecture meant that at the Bauhaus in Weimar the weaving workshop needed to be reattached to industrial production processes. Decorative fabrics, wall coverings and furniture upholstery fabrics emerged next to wall hangings or rugs as individual pieces, for example in the *Haus am Horn* and Gropius's office on the occasion of the Bauhaus Exhibition in 1923.

The principle of collaboration across workshop boundaries was repeatedly practised in connection with chairs by Marcel Breuer and Gunta Stölzl from 1921, as well as a baby's cradle by Peter Keler and a jug with carrier loop by Otto Lindig in 1922.

Fashion was not a topic at the Bauhaus, not even the "type fashion" design in Germany around 1920 by the Russian avant-garde and by Lilly Reich. The few preserved garments from the textile workshop, also described in writing, indicate personal use and individual pieces of craftsmanship.

Gunta Stölzl took over the leadership of the workshop in Dessau in 1925, and after Muche's departure in 1927, the overall leadership of the textile workshop. She thus became the first woman to enter the circle of Bauhaus Masters. Stölzl organised the refurbishing of the workshop and developed a compulsory training sequence. The teaching and production operations were

Weaving workshop at the Bauhaus Weimar, c. 1923

Weaving workshop at the Bauhaus Weimar, c. 1929,
photograph: Erich Consemüller

Felix Kube, Fabric printed using a spray
technique, c. 1921

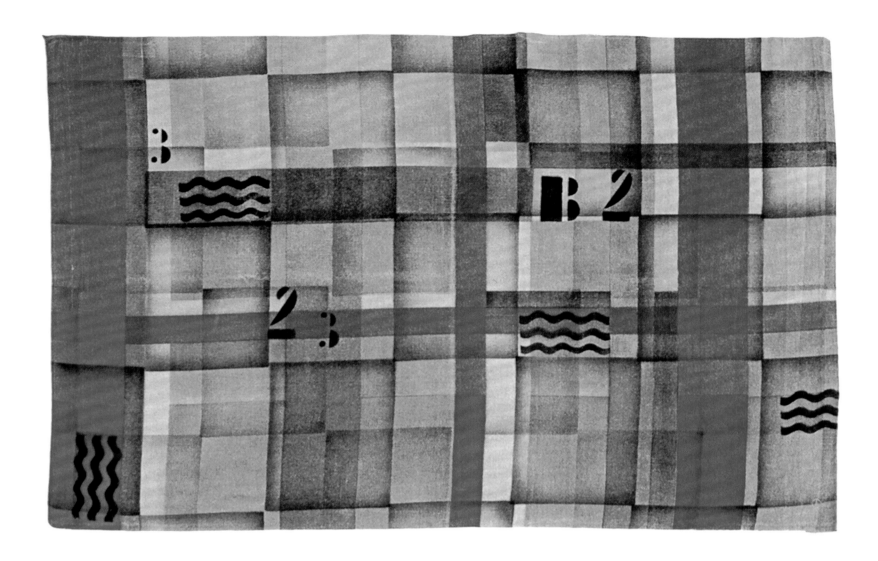

run separately. Numerous experimental weaving samples with examination of material, colour and bond were created.

The second Bauhaus director, Hannes Meyer, criticised the weaving workshop: "On the floors lay young girls' emotional complexes. Everywhere, art was strangling life."[32] He demanded a closer connection to the textile industry and suggested "external semesters", i.e. internships in industrial companies. Numerous students, such as Otti Berger, Lena Meyer-Bergner, Lisbeth Birman-Östreicher, Gertrud Preiswerk-Dirks, and Margaretha Reichardt complied with this demand.

At the Bauhaus in Dessau, various fabric types were developed: curtain fabrics, transparent drapes, wall covering and furniture fabrics. Steel thread fabric was designed for the covering of tubular steel furniture by Marcel Breuer, and produced industrially from 1928. Steel thread is an especially stable cotton yarn, treated with wax and paraffin on a special machine. Anni Albers created a tension fabric for the Federal Trade Union School in Bernau that appeared to reflect light by means of cellophane and had particular sound-insulating characteristics. For this

school's boarding area, bedside rugs made of jute and wool were developed "in systematic test work in the Bauhaus weaving workshop".[33] As early as 1927, Margaretha Reichardt had executed cellophane tension fabrics; under the directorship of Hannes Meyer several textile companies were regularly provided with sample swatches. The weaving workshop was productive and commercially very successful.

The connection to industry was established relatively late, and textile designs and prototypes could be licensed only from 1930, for example to the Berlin-based company Polytex. Transparent curtain fabrics were part of the collection, as well as table linen in various colour variations. During this time, Margaret Leischner also developed metallically shining upholstery fabrics for Mies van der Rohe made of artificial silk and cellophane. The Bauhaus weaving workshop published three sample books in 1932/1933. The first contained print fabrics, the two subsequent books woven curtain fabrics and transparent curtains (latticework tulle) with numerous colour options, as they were necessary for industrial production and commercialisation. The design of print patterns in particular

Hedwig Jungnik, Tapestry with abstract forms, 1921/23

Benita Koch-Otte, Rug of knotted wool, c. 1923

opened a new field of activity with links to applied graphics and design fundamentals, such as they were taught at the Bauhaus. At an internal invitation for print patterns at the Bauhaus in 1932, students from other workshops also participated. While Hermann Fischer developed print patterns from gridlines and coloured dots, Katja and Hajo Rose created their collection completely on a typewriter. They created a serial structure with great decorative effect made of numbers and letters. These print fabrics were produced by M. van Delden & Co. of Gronau in 1933 and were presented at the Leipzig Spring Fair at a kiosk designed by the Bauhaus. On the occasion of such exhibitions it repeatedly became clear that the Bauhaus was not the sole leader in the field of textile design. Abstract weaving with basic geometric shapes was also offered by other textile companies and weavers. The weaving workshop at the Bauhaus was innovative because the design and execution of a textile product were brought together, and thus textile design was elevated beyond pure craftsmanship.

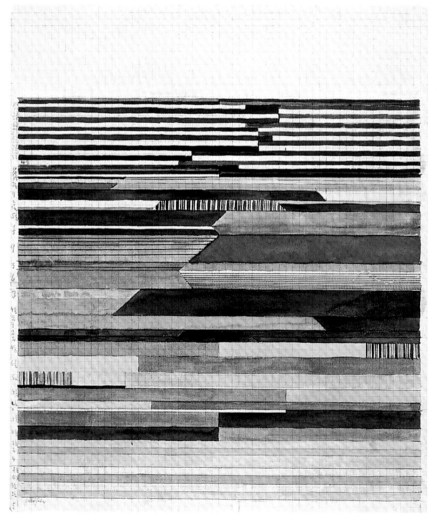

Gunta Stölzl, "Black and White" tapestry, 1923/24

Gunta Stölzl, Design for a tapestry, 1923

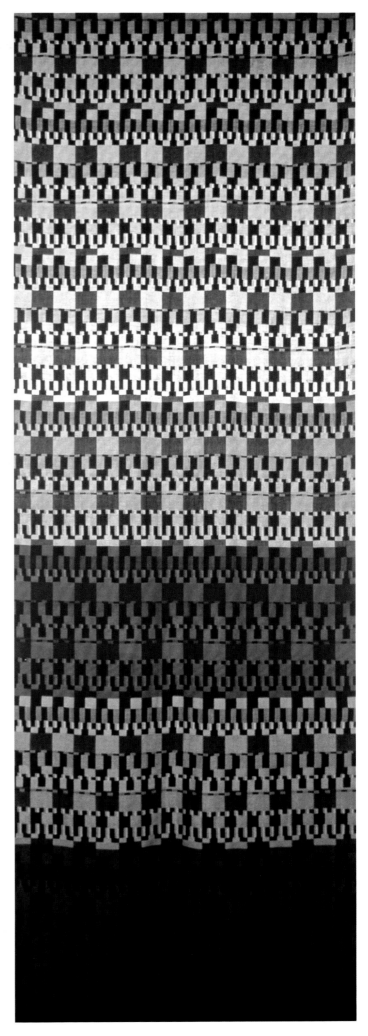

Gertrud Arndt, Tapestry, 1927

Agnes Roghé, Fabric by the metre (design), 1923/24

Gunta Stölzl, "Red-Green" slotted tapestry, 1927/28

Bauhaus dress made from fabric by Lis Volger, 1928

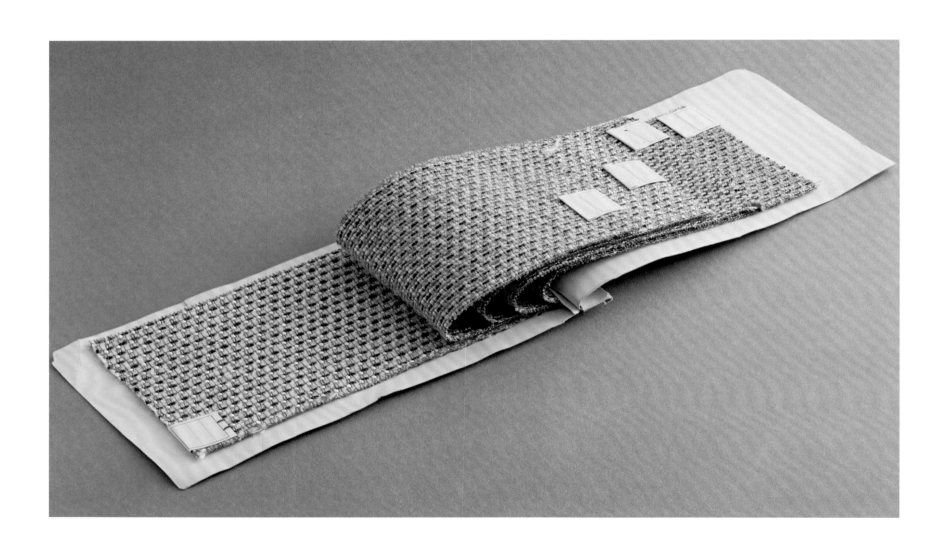

Gunta Stölzl, Bauhaus furniture fabrics, sample book, 1925-28

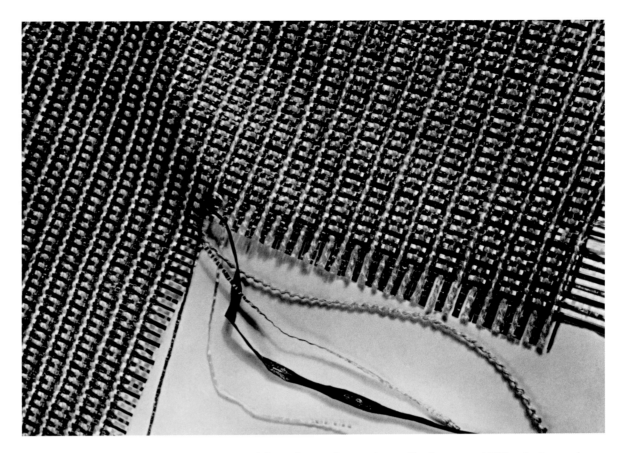

Gunta Stölzl, Wall coverings using cellophane, c. 1931, photograph:
Walter Peterhans

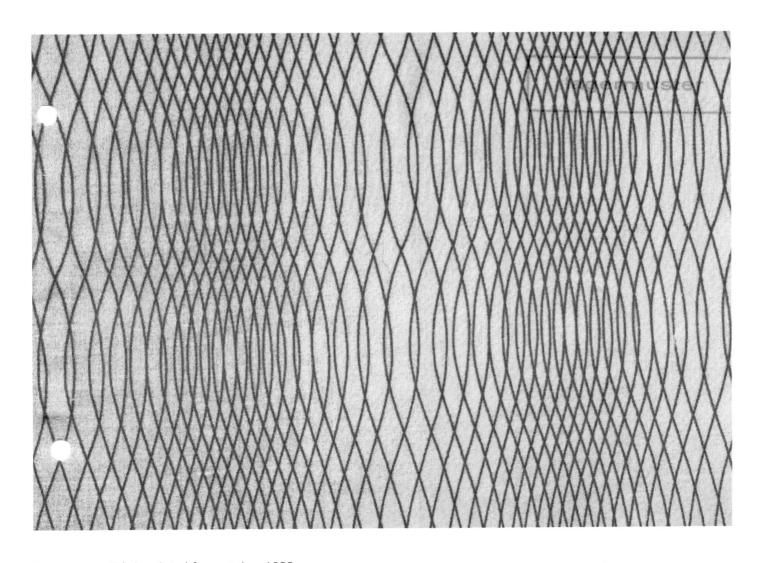

Anonymous, Fabric printed for curtains, 1932

# ‖ Carpentry/Furniture Workshop

Hardly any other workshop put its mark on the Bauhaus with such lasting effect as the carpentry workshop. Not least because of its furniture, the name *Bauhaus* became an epochal term. The developments at the Bauhaus are represented by design classics by Marcel Breuer, such as his 1922 slatted chair, a constructivist sculpture, or his functional tubular steel furniture of 1926.

Since Henry van de Velde's arts and crafts school had not included a carpentry workshop, its installation was delayed until the beginning of 1921. It was initially headed by Johannes Itten as Master of Form and Josef Zachmann as Master of Craft, before Walter Gropius took over the leadership of this workshop himself after a reorganisation of duties, supported by Reinhold Weidensee. In Dessau the first generation of graduates also took over the leadership of the Bauhaus carpentry workshop as Junior Masters, Marcel Breuer until 1928, Josef Albers until 1929 and Alfred Arndt until 1932, before Lilly Reich headed the departments as part of the building department.

In Weimar a total of thirty-one apprentices and three guests studied in the carpentry workshop in four years, among whom Erich Brendel, Marcel Breuer, Erich Consemüller, Erich Dieckmann, Hans Fricke and Felix Klee obtained a Journeyman certificate; at the Bauhaus in Dessau there were Franz Ehrlich, Ernst Gebhardt, Hans Georg Groß and Heinz Tetzner, while Peer Bücking received one of the first Bauhaus diplomas in 1929. The number of students rose from an average of eleven in Weimar to a maximum of twenty-two at the Bauhaus in Dessau in 1928.

But immediately after the foundation of the Bauhaus, the work in furniture building began with the support of the Weimar *Baugewerksschule* (Construction Trades School). The "People's Furniture with the Determann Association" of 1919, for which Walter Determann designed furniture for kitchens and dining rooms with a group of students, was one of the most interesting projects. At first glance it appeared like traditional farmhouse furniture, which corresponded to the Bauhaus programme of "We must all return to craftsmanship." Only when taking a closer look did one recognise the modern design principles of modular order as well as the functional and design variations of the basic type—the first type of furniture programme of the Bauhaus.

Thus, Determann was far ahead of such romantically expressive furniture sculptures as Johannes Itten's 1920 children's bed or the recently rediscovered "African Chair" by Marcel Breuer of 1921. This armchair with extravagant weaving by Gunta Stölzl and the carved and painted wooden frame seems like a throne or a romantic wedding chair for the designers, who were close friends.

A completely new design approach was demonstrated by the cradle by Peter Keler in 1922. It interpreted the theme of the cradle completely anew, not only with regard to form, with its blue circles, red squares and yellow triangles according to Kandinsky's design ideas, but also functionally: the triangular opening of the cradle allowed better movement of the child. A black dowel on its base made its centre of gravity very low so that the cradle could not fall over or roll away, but would straighten up by itself like a tumbler. Finally, the textile weaving inserted into its side walls allowed for natural "air conditioning."

Marcel Breuer's slatted chair of 1922/24, with stretched straps forming its seat and back, translated the Weimar *De Stijl* course by Theo van Doesburg into furniture design, and attempted at the same time to allow for modern machine production by using only a single slat cross-section.

How far furniture was integrated into the projects of Walter Gropius as a part of the unified work of architectural art could already be seen in the Sommerfeld house in Berlin with furniture by Marcel Breuer of 1921; even more so in the *Haus am Horn*, which was reconstructed in 1999; and the director's office at the Bauhaus, which Gropius carried out on occasion of the great 1923 Bauhaus Exhibition in Weimar. In the Gropius room, all furniture followed the *De Stijl* design concept of "cube in cube" and is fitted into the room to the millimetre: couch, table and club chair, desk and shelves.

The furniture designs by Erich Dieckmann, who developed his prototypes into a successfully produced type furniture programme at the Weimar Building Academy until 1930, appear less avant-garde.

The most complex furniture design of the Weimar Bauhaus is probably the game wardrobe (prototype "ti 24"), which Alma Siedhoff-Buscher had designed for the *Haus am Horn* in 1923 and produced with the assistance of Erich Brendel. She created a polyfunctional play landscape with rectangular-shaped toy blocks and cupboards which could also be used as growing seating and table elements, with a cupboard whose door acted as a puppet theatre with its window opening, and a ladder chair on wheels which could also be used as a throne or a locomotive.

Walter Determann, Draft for popular furniture: combination kitchen/living room, 1919

From 1925 Marcel Breuer developed his comprehensive collection of tubular steel furniture in rapid succession that was used to furnish the Dessau Bauhaus buildings, such as the folding chairs in the assembly hall and the stools in the dining hall. Breuer used the development of precision steel tubes for the chemical industry in furniture building. This completely new type of furniture was characterised by continuous filigree lines and spring qualities. Centuries seem to lie between Gropius's club chair of 1923 and Breuer's tubular steel chair B3 of 1926, later called the Wassily chair. But only Mart Stam succeeded in 1926 with his ingenius invention: the cantilever chair, a chair without back legs that made full use of its steel tubing's spring quality and was immediately adapted by Mies van der Rohe and Breuer.

In the area of wooden furniture, too, experiments continued in Dessau, with unit and type furniture with ever thinner material thickness. The cupboard and shelf parts of the show furniture in Dessau-Törten of 1926, for example, only have a material thickness of 10 millimetres. The end of material conservation, lightness and mobility was reached in 1929 with the "bachelor's

wardrobe" by Josef Pohl, which was made of plywood on a slat frame and could easily be moved on wheels.

Since even the industrially-produced tubular steel furniture had doubled the cost of comparable wooden furniture in 1928, the carpentry workshop increasingly experimented with wood, following Hannes Meyer's motto of "necessities, not luxuries." Light wooden furniture, sometimes foldable or stackable and thus space-saving, was presented at The People's Apartment exhibition and the travelling Bauhaus Exhibition in numerous cities in 1929. In 1928 Josef Albers developed his leaning armchair (ti 244) made of bent wood as true self-assembly furniture, which could easily be shipped in a flat-pack. Screws and connectors, spring steel and cast metal elements were integrated into the furniture design.

From 1929 Mies van der Rohe contributed furniture made of chromed band steel with leather upholstery along with his tubular steel furniture to the development of furniture design at the Bauhaus, high-quality, expensive luxury items.

The joinery workshop at the Bauhaus in Weimar, 1923

Marcel Breuer, Gunta Stölzl, "African chair", 1921

Peter Keler, Cradle, 1922

Marcel Breuer, Chair of wooden slats, 1924

Marcel Breuer, Lady's dressing table for the *Haus am Horn* in Weimar, 1923

**KINDERSPIELSCHRANK**

im Gebrauch

gesch.
**Länge 155 cm und 90 cm**
**Höhe 150 cm**
**AUSFÜHRUNG**
farbig lackiert
mit bunten herausnehmbaren Kästen
für Spielzeug und Bücher
zum Spielen, Sitzen und Fahren
mit Türausschnitt für Puppentheater

Walter Gropius, Director's office at the Bauhaus Weimar, 1923, reconstruction from 1999

Alma Siedhoff-Buscher, Toy cupboard from the *Haus am Horn* in Weimar, 1923/sample catalogue, 1925

Canteen at the Bauhaus Dessau, 1926

Bauhaus Dessau carpentry workship, Model facility for the Dessau-
Törten Estate, 1926

Marcel Breuer, Dressing table ti 60 with mirror, 1925/26

Josef Albers, Armchair ti 244, 1928

Martin Decker, Chair ti 201, 1928

Marcel Breuer (model) / Standard Möbel GmbH Berlin (production),
Club Armchair B 3, 1927/28

Anonymous / Bauhaus Dessau joinery workshop, Fold-away chair, 1929

Josef Pohl, Wardrobe on wheels for a bachelor, c. 1929          Ludwig Mies van der Rohe, Living room in the Villa Tugendhat, Brno, 1931

# Metal Workshop

"What would be the All Workshop/Without the Metal Workshop?" Thus began a self-confident birthday poem by young silversmith Wolfgang Tümpel to Walter Gropius in 1924.

The metal workshop was among the first workshops that were able to commence operations during the Bauhaus foundation year at the end of 1919. It turned out to be one of the profile-forming workshops, which allowed for an exemplary review of the changes in content and structure that took place at the Bauhaus—the development "from wine jug to lantern", as Laszlo Moholy-Nagy, being the workshop's head for many years, aptly summarised. From the silversmithing shop of the romantically expressive early years in Weimar, starting in 1923, the workshop developed into a design laboratory for the design of lighting appliances with successful contacts to industry, and in the years up to 1930 also into a workshop for metal furniture and building installations, eventually merging with the building department. Students like Josef Albers, Marianne Brandt, Hin Bredendieck, Christian Dell, Gyula Pap or Wilhelm Wagenfeld created metal objects, which today belong to the icons of twentieth century design.

Until 1922, Johannes Itten led the metal workshop, which was established with the support of the Weimar court jewellers Theodor Müller, who had already collaborated with Henry van de Velde. Paul Klee and Oskar Schlemmer temporarily led the workshop after Itten's departure in 1922/1923, before László Moholy-Nagy was identified as its congenial head until 1928. The Masters of Craft in Weimar were Naum Slutzky, Wilhelm Schabbon, Alfred Kopka, and Christian Dell.

The second Bauhaus director, Hannes Meyer, restructured the Bauhaus in 1928 and combined the metal, carpentry and mural painting workshops into a furnishing workshop, which was to collaborate closely with the Building Department. The metal workshop was run by Marianne Brandt until 1929 and by Alfred Arndt from then until 1931, before Lilly Reich took over the complete furnishing department in the course of renewed profile changes and personnel cuts by Ludwig Mies van der Rohe. In Dessau, Rudolf Schwarz and Alfred Schäfter worked as the Masters of Craft.

The number of students in the metal workshop rose from four in 1919 to nine in 1923, sank to five in Dessau in 1925 and reached its peak in 1928 with thirteen students. This meant no more than two to four students per year of study, and permanent technical exchange among all students. Concerning the number of students per workshop, the metal workshop ranked behind the weaving workshop, mural painting workshop and carpentry workshop, earning fourth place, before it merged with the Building Department in 1928. Full Journeyman certificates, mostly for silversmiths, were obtained by Martin Jahn, Gyula Pap, Hans Przyrembel, Otto Rittweger, Wolfgang Rößger, Wilhelm Wagenfeld and Richard Winkelmayer, while Marianne Brandt and Hin Bredendieck became the first recipients of the Bauhaus diploma in 1929. They were followed by students of the metal workshop/building department such as Waldemar Alder, Gerd Balzer, Josef Pohl or Helmut Schulze.

A look into the metal workshop of the Staatliches Bauhaus in 1923 still showed traditional craftsman's work stations and work benches, tools and hardly any machines. Like in an exhibition, extraordinary student works, such as the liqueur can, Gyula Pap's Journeyman's piece, a samovar by Carl Jakob Jucker and a teapot by Richard Winkelmayer, were arranged on the work benches. They documented the form design influences of the Wiener Werkstätte and Henry van de Velde, as well as the courses by Johannes Itten, the machine aesthetics of the Russian constructivists and the strict form reductions of Theo van Doesburg's De Stijl.

The sphere-shaped tin of 1920 by Naum Slutzky showed the influence of the Itten preparatory course with exercises in basic shapes and surface texture as well as the experimental manual trades orientation of the early Bauhaus. This is also documented by Slutzky's Cube Construction and an ornamental door mounting for the Itten room in 1921, which showed connecting lines to sculpture and architecture. Slutzky wrote a special Bauhaus chapter from 1921 to 1924 as head of a goldsmith's and jewellery workshop, which produced strict and formally reduced jewellery, rings, pendants and brooches.

The year 1922/1923 in the metal workshop was marked by intense work and the preparations for the great Bauhaus Exhibition in Weimar. As in the other workshops, the discussions encouraged by Kandinsky revolved around the reduction of form language to basic mathematical solids and associated primary colours. What is today often thought of as the Bauhaus style was rather a temporarily limited experiment of the year 1923, which the promoters soon dropped due to poor sales and the low acceptance of many products. Nevertheless, Marianne Brandt's collection of ash trays from 1924 still fascinates with its cigarette trays and tilting devices, hemispheres and cylinders, circular and triangular shapes, all handcrafted from bronze and nickel silver, later also from nickel-plated brass (prototype MT36). Her tea infuser pot (MT49), whose hemispheric body seems to float on a cross-shaped leg, executed in different form variations in bronze, brass, silver and tombac, but always with precious ebony handles, became an icon of the Bauhaus. Inspired by Far Eastern life practises, tea seems to have been one of the favourite drinks at the metal workshop, if the tea cans, tea pots, tea sets, tea infusers, tea warmers and samovars by Brandt, Dell, Gropius, Jucker, Knau, Pap, Przyrembel, Rittweger, Rößger, Tümpel and Wagenfeld are anything to go by.

Gyula Pap's seven-armed candelabrum with the workshop type label MT2 of 1922 and his minimalist floor lamp (MT2a, ME16) of 1923 documented in a special manner the rapid transition from the handcrafted, individual, one-of-a-kind piece to industrial design, like the programme demanded by Walter Gropius since 1922 in his appeal "Art and Technology–A New Unity". While he brilliantly played through the design theme of the hemisphere in all its parts with the moveable arms of the candelabrum, Pap's floor lamp featured electric light with a mirrored, visible light bulb as a sign of the new times and thus surpassed in its radicalism the more famous Bauhaus desk lamps (prototypes MT9/ME1 and MT8/ME 2) by Jucker and Wagenfeld. The Bauhaus desk lamp represented a special kind of teamwork at the Bauhaus with its glass version. Carl Jakob Jucker had already produced six desk lamps with glass bases and glass tubes, without finding a valid solution for the lampshade. Only the use of a frosted glass sphere by Wilhelm Wagenfeld–probably inspired by Gyula Pap's experiments with glass spheres for a samovar–led to success.

Metal workshop at the Bauhaus Weimar, 1923

Naum Slutzky, Spherical container, 1920

Wilhelm Wagenfeld, Coffee machine (MT 7), 1923/24

Gyula Pap, Candelabra with seven arms (MT 2), 1922
(version from 1923/24)

Marianne Brandt, Small teapot (MT 49), 1924

Otto Rittweger, Wolfgang Tümpel, Wilhelm Wagenfeld,
Tea infusers with stands for storage (MT 20, MT 11,
MT 59, MT 22), 1924

Josef Albers, Fruit bowl, 1923

At the Bauhaus in Dessau, "light research" became a central topic of the metal workshop. The Bauhaus building in particular inspired the creation of new lighting systems with light bulbs and soffits, such as industry provided them. The spectrum covered a ceiling lamp with a string mechanism (ME105a) by Brandt/Przyrembel for the work stations in the workshops, a wall lamp with moveable arm (ME71) and ceiling lamps with opal glass spheres (ME27, ME94, ME104a) as well as soffit lighting systems by Max Krajewsky for the assembly hall, vestibule and workshop stairway. The collaboration with the Körting & Mathiesen Company in Leipzig, which from 1928 produced KANDEM lamps in large numbers based on designs by Brandt and Bredendieck, developed particularly successfully.

The production of all metal and glass elements was carried out by machines which pressed, nickel-plated and varnished the metal reflectors and baldachins made of brass. In 1928 Marianne Brandt developed her nickel- or chrome-plated brass bowls (ME37a, ME63 and ME161), designed for reproduction using the very same industrial technology..

Wilhelm Wagenfeld, Table lamp (version in glass MT 8/ME 2), 1924

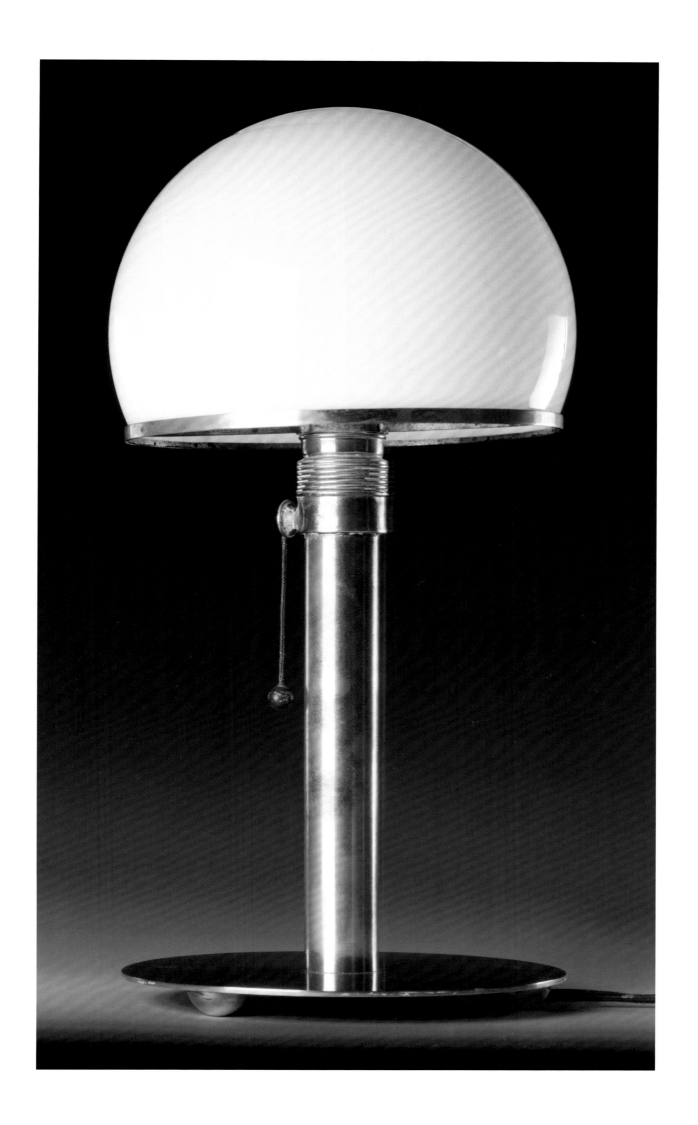

At least the same level of success was reached by the designs of Bauhaus graduate Christian Dell, whose numerous lamp designs were produced by Frankfurt companies and heavily advertised in the Frankfurt register of the magazine *The New Frankfurt*. From 1929 onwards, Hin Bredendieck and Hermann Gautel turned to the design of metal furniture, which so far had only been carried out in the carpentry workshop. They created the work stool (ME1002) from tubular steel with a shaped plywood seat and the "single spring stool" made of bent spring steel, steel base and plywood planes as well as a stool with a base of cast metal and a plywood seat. The collaboration with the Junkers factory in Dessau must also be mentioned, for which Hans Przyrembel developed an industrial-size gas water heater in 1928, Joost Schmidt assisting with the graphic design. Furthermore, the Bauhaus produced several Junkers exhibition stands. The metal workshop of the Bauhaus had established itself as a modern "laboratory for industry" with a manifold spectrum of tasks.

Bauhaus Dessau building, Vestibule with Soffitten lighting system by Max Krajewski and door handles (swing door and auditorium) by Walter Gropius in the metal workshop, 1926, photograph: Erich Consemüller

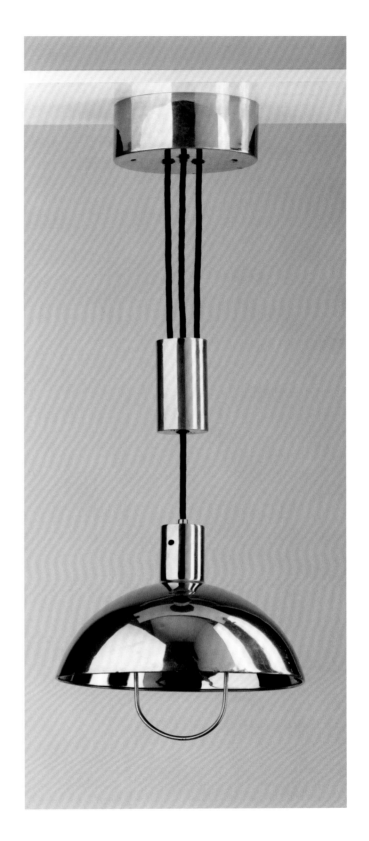

Marianne Brandt, Hans Przyrembel, Adjustable ceiling fixture (ME 105a), 1926

Marianne Brandt, Hin Bredendieck, Kandem bedside lamp (No. 702), 1928

Marianne Brandt, Platters (ME 160, ME 161), 1928

Metal workshop at the Bauhaus Dessau, c. 1928/29, photograph:
Marianne Brandt

Theatre Workshop

Building and theatre were at the centre of the Bauhaus concept that Paul Klee introduced in 1922, during the discussion on the Bauhaus study plan. He clearly elevated the newly-founded theatre class from the other study courses and gave it a central position in the teaching programme, which was focused on the development of all the students' talents. In the theatre workshop, the whole gamut of the performing arts was featured—dance, music, theatre, pantomime, performance, space, light and sound experience. Students of all workshops could participate in the theatre projects and contribute their specific technical experience. The Bauhaus stage, with its associated Bauhaus celebrations and the Bauhaus band and stage construction, became an important training ground for teamwork and the new working and living community at the Bauhaus, a living vision of *Gesamtkunstwerk*, the unified work of art.

The theatre class at the Bauhaus had no predecessors at other art academies or arts and crafts schools and had not been included in the original 1919 curriculum. Nevertheless, Lothar Schreyer was appointed to the Bauhaus in 1921 and began the establishment of a theatre workshop. He had studied theatre direction as well as law and art history, and from 1911 had worked as dramaturge and assistant producer at the Deutsche Schauspielhaus in Hamburg, before collaborating on Herwarth Walden's *Sturm* magazine in 1915 and serving as head of the expressionist *Sturm* theatre in Berlin from 1918 to 1921. Bauhaus student Hans Haffenrichter talks about Lothar Schreyer's Bauhaus theatre:

> At first, we worked on dance and movement games with masks and instruments under his instruction. We created a *Mary's Song* with the backdrop of a large wall-

hanging painted by Schreyer, a *Dance of the Wind Spirits* with rhythms played on an African calabash xylophone, and a *Lansquenet's Dance* in full costume, which we built ourselves.[34]

With the plays *Crucifixion* in 1922 and *Moon Play* in 1923, Schreyer concluded his expressionist and esoteric theatre projects at the Bauhaus and increasingly came into conflict with the new direction of the school under Gropius's guiding principle of "Art and Technology—A New Unity". Following an altercation at the rehearsals for *Moon Play*, he left the Bauhaus in March 1923.

The early theatre experiments also included Karl Peter Röhl's carved, coloured, and intricately-painted hand puppets of around 1920 and Ilse Fehling's stage construction with figurines for the *Fairy Tale of the Five Travellers* of 1922, whose masks were to be illuminated from the inside. Primitive but modern, three pairs of turned stick puppets by Eberhard Schrammen appeared around 1923. The same year, Kurt Schmidt and Toni Hergt created the marionettes for the puppet show *The Little Hunchback* with a pluralistic multitude of form types, employing materials from papier-mâché to turned elements to the use of wire for limbs or hair. The boundaries of children's play are fluid, like the hand puppets by Paul Klee for his son Felix, as well as the puppet shows *Devils and Fairies* or *Fairy Tales from the Orient*.

Oskar Schlemmer took over the theatre workshop and led it pleasantly until 1929. As early as 1921 he had begun working on his *Triadic Ballet*, which premiered in Stuttgart in 1922. This new combination of dance, mask, costume, music and pantomime, with twelve figurines and three dance sequences in twelve scenes was

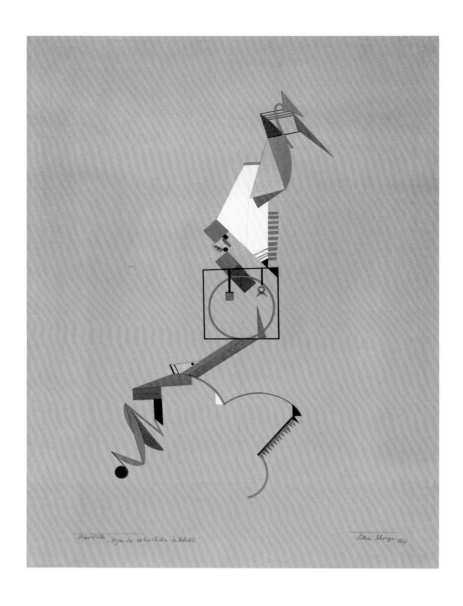

Lothar Schreyer, *Figurine of Masculine Intellect*, plate 7 from the portfolio *Birth*, 1921

also successfully presented at the Bauhaus in 1923. He summarised his experiences in 1925 in the Bauhaus book 4, *The Theatre at the Bauhaus*. As early as 1922, Schlemmer had produced the *Figurale Kabinett* on occasion of the Bauhaus carnival, a parody of belief in technology and progress. During the first weeks in his new post, Schlemmer focused on the performances on occasion of the great Bauhaus Exhibition in August 1923, thus supporting student projects such as the *Mechanical Ballet* by Kurt Schmidt, which Schmidt had been developing since the end of 1922 and preparing for performance at the Jena City Theatre together with Georg Teltscher and Friedrich Wilhelm Bogler. The programme lasted roughly half an hour, with five figurines and musical improvisations by Hans Stuckenschmidt; it showed the influence of *De Stijl*, Dada and the Futurists. It was entertaining, student-oriented fun. The *Reflective Light Play* by Kurt Schwerdtfeger was also performed, a game with abstract forms, templates, overlapping light and transparency effects, which Ludwig Hirschfeld-Mack systematically developed further into light art with colours. In 1923, Andor Weininger created his *Mechanical Stage Revue* with a stage that anticipated the stage in the Dessau Bauhaus building, while the figurines were inspired by

Schlemmer's *Triadic Ballet*. In 1924, Kurt Schmidt's *The Man on the Switchboard* followed, as well as a discussion of the theme "man and machine", where man becomes a marionette of the machine creatures he had designed.

Wassily Kandinsky had already published a stage composition entitled *Yellow Sound*, his first contribution to abstract theatre, and he published the essay "On Abstract Stage Synthesis" in 1923, before he was able to produce such a synthesis on stage in Mussorgsky's *Pictures at an Exhibition*.

In 1922 László Moholy-Nagy wrote about a "dynamically constructive power system" and designed a "kinetic constructive system" called "Building with Movement Rails for Play and Transportation," which was constructed throughout by Bauhaus graduate Stefan Sebök in 1928.

Only with the opening of the Bauhaus building in Dessau in December 1926 did the theatre workshop find suitable premises. The festival level, with the assembly hall, stage and cafeteria and its

Kurt Schmidt/Toni Hergt, Hunchback, doctor and town crier from
*The Adventures of the Little Hunchback*, 1923

potential for diverse uses, turned into ideal spatial experimenting grounds, as well as the entire building with its foyers, balconies and stairways, including the rooftop terrace of the atelier house. From 1927 the theatre reappeared in the official Bauhaus curriculum. As early as 1923 Schlemmer had demanded the examination of the basic elements of stage set creation and design: space, form, colour, sound, movement, and light. But only in Dessau was he able to begin the systematic implementation of these basic elements in the Bauhaus dances: space dance, form dance, gesture dance, hoop dance, rod dance, construction kit play, scenery dance and closet promenade. These dances as well as the associated masks, costumes and props were developed with the students, but also rehearsed with trained dancers and actors like Werner Siedhoff. In these dances, man does not appear as bearer of individual expression, but as a type of certain behaviour towards the formal stage elements. Thus, Schlemmer achieved the synthesis of man and marionette, of natural and artificial figures, into which he was able to insert a broad spectrum of expression, from weightless grace to monumental force. The Bauhaus theatre had its greatest success in 1929 during its tour to numerous German and Swiss cities.

Under the directorship of Hannes Meyer from 1928 and with new duties for Schlemmer with the "Man" and "Figure Study" courses, the Bauhaus theatre had only a modest budget. In addition, a "Young Group" had formed at the Bauhaus in 1928, which turned its attention to political theatre and current events. Working collectively, its members produced *Sketch No. 1–Three Against One* and participated with it in the Bauhaus theatre tour. Schlemmer clearly rejected political theatre at the Bauhaus; he left in 1929 and accepted an appointment in Breslau.

The theatre workshop officially had only one or two registered students at the Bauhaus in Weimar, but in Dessau by 1929 the figure had risen to nine. Only Roman Clemens received a Bauhaus diploma for theatre and free painting, which again characterises the theatre workshop as a rather semi-professional field of study for all courses.

Hannes Meyer closed the theatre in 1929 for economic reasons.

Kurt Schmidt, *Design for the Mechanical Ballet*, 1923

Kurt Schwertfeger, *Reflective games with light*, 1923, photograph

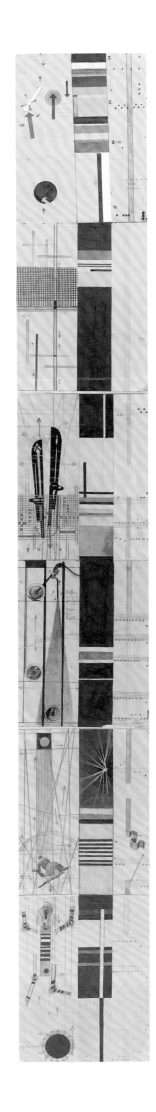

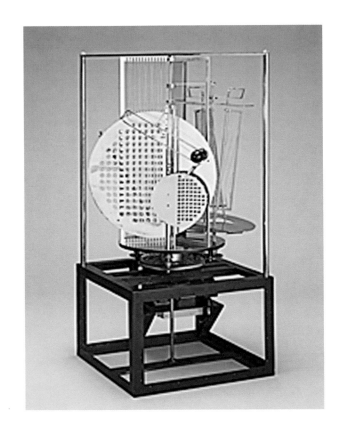

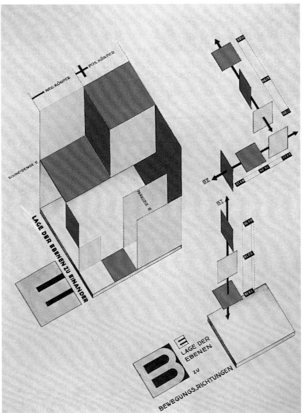

László Moholy-Nagy, Sketch of a musical score for the *Mechanical Eccentric*, 1924-25

László Moholy-Nagy, Lighting accessories from an electric stage (reproduction from 2006), 1922/30

Joost Schmidt, Mechanical stage, 1925/26

László Moholy-Nagy, *Constructive Kinetic System*, 1922/28

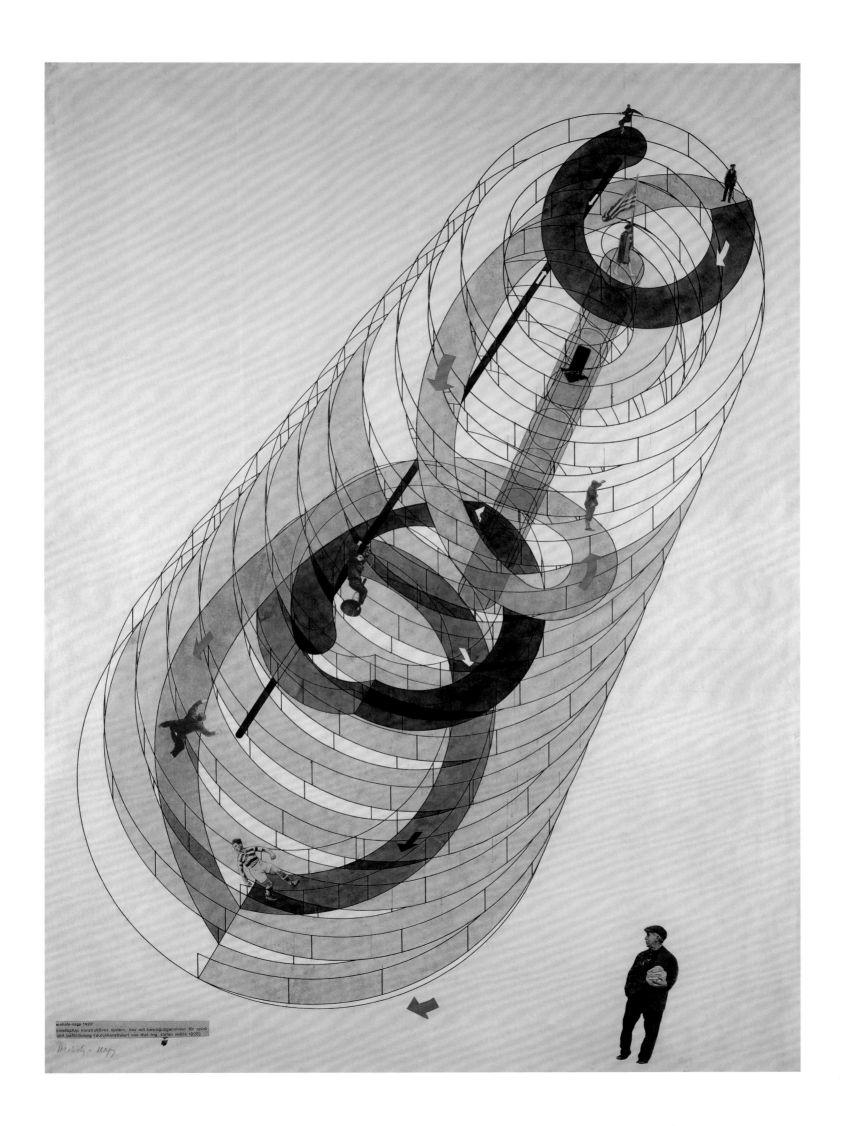

moholy-nagy 1922
kinetisches konstruktives system, bau mit bewegungsbahnen für spiel
und beförderung (durchkonstruiert von dipl.-ing. stefan sebök 1928)

moholy = nagy

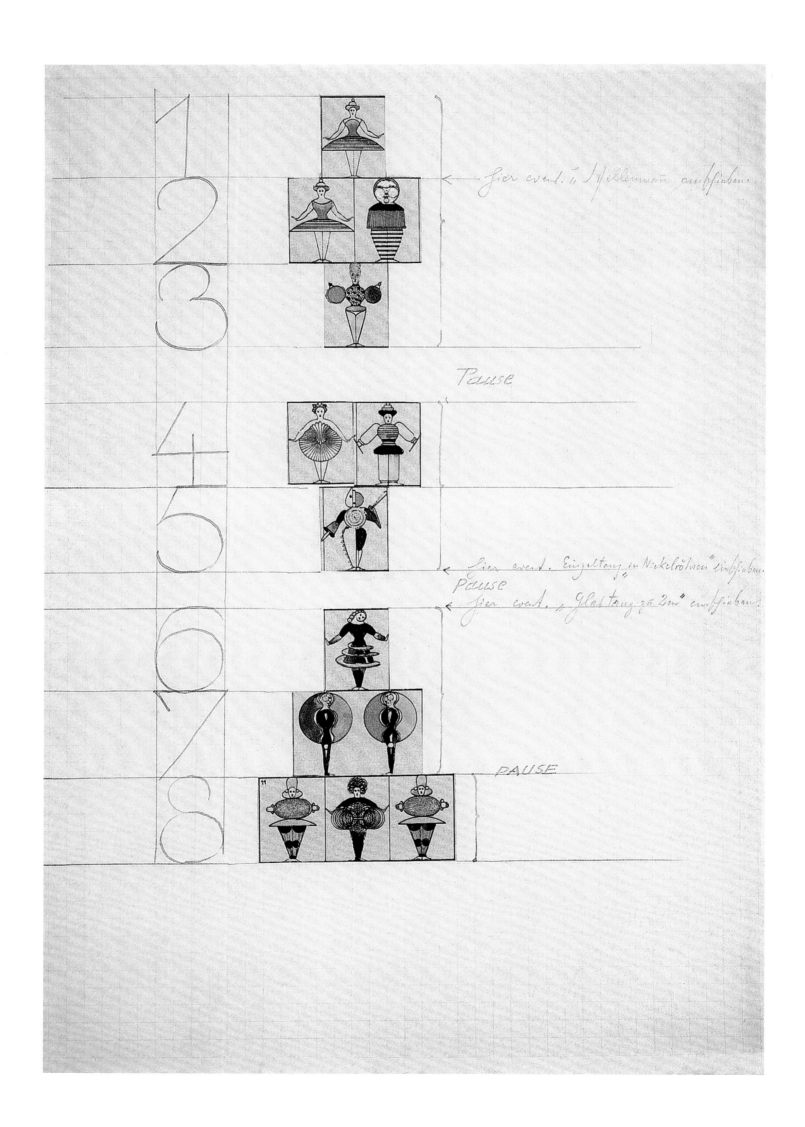

Oskar Schlemmer, Plan of figures for *The Triadic Ballet*, 1924-26
© Oskar Schlemmer Archive and Theatre Estate

The stage class in costumes from the play *The Staircase Farce* by Oskar Schlemmer, on the roof of the Bauhaus building, 1927, photograph: Erich Consemüller
© Oskar Schlemmer Archive and Theatre Estate

Oskar Schlemmer, *Hoop Dance*, 1929, dancer: Manda von Kreibig, photograph: Lux Feininger
© Oskar Schlemmer Archive and Theatre Estate

The young Bauhaus theatre in their *Bauhaus Revue* performing the *Visit of the Professor L. in the City*, 1929, photograph: Marianne Brandt

Oskar Schlemmer, Baton Dance, 1928/29, dancer: Manda von Kreibig, photograph: Lux Feininger
© Oskar Schlemmer Archive and Theatre Estate

Oskar Schlemmer / Stage workshop, *Different sequences of a dramatic gesture*, 1927, dancer: Werner Siedhoff, photograph (exposed several times): Erich Consemüller
© Oskar Schlemmer Archive and Theatre Estate

**II**

# Architecture/Building Studies/ Building Department

The architecture of the Bauhaus buildings themselves is one of the main focuses of public knowledge about the Bauhaus until this day and has gained even more importance after being included in the UNESCO World Heritage list as *The Bauhaus Sites in Weimar and Dessau* in 1996 as well as the ensuing comprehensive historic preservation efforts. From the director's office in Weimar to the *Haus am Horn* and the Bauhaus buildings, the Masters' houses in Dessau, numerous structures in the Dessau-Törten development and the Federal School of the ADGB in Bernau near Berlin, the most important pieces of architectural evidence of the Bauhaus have been historically preserved and restored and been made accessible to the general public as unified works of art. This also includes the key works of the third Bauhaus director, Ludwig Mies van der Rohe, in the Weißenhof development in Stuttgart, the Barcelona Pavilion and the Villa Tugendhat in Brno, which all date from before his time at the Bauhaus but shape the image of Bauhaus architecture until this day.

Walter Gropius and Ludwig Mies van der Rohe received important impulses for their later architectural creations in the office of Peter Behrens in Berlin from 1908 to 1910. In 1910 Gropius became a member of the *Deutscher Werkbund*, which had been founded by artists, architects and entrepreneurs in 1907, then established his own architecture practise in Berlin together with Adolf Meyer in 1910 and carried out his first main work, the Fagus Shoe Factory in Alfeld, together with Meyer in 1911. The office wing with its curtain façade over three floor levels became an icon of modern architecture. The reinforced concrete skeleton construction allowed for the design of corners made of glass, which gave the building a special transparency and elegance.

The office and factory buildings at the *Werkbund* exhibition in Cologne in 1914 became the second principal work of Gropius & Meyer. By its immediate vicinity to Henry van de Velde's theatre structure, the forward-looking architectural concept of Walter Gropius became especially apparent. While the older generation still regarded theatre building as the intellectual and cultural centre of society, Gropius symbolised the social and cultural opportunities of modern industrial society with this industrial structure. The office building with its lateral glass stairways, with the glass façade opening into the courtyard and a rooftop terrace symbolised innovative product design and modern business management. As early as 1911 Gropius had put together a photographic exhibition, combined with a lecture, on exemplary modern industrial structures for Karl Ernst Osthaus in Hagen, which was presented in Cologne in 1914. Before that, in March 1910, Gropius had presented his *Programme for the Foundation of a General Housing Construction Company with Artistically Unified Basis Ltd* to the then-head of the AEG company, Walther Rathenau,

which focused on teamwork, types, standardisation, and industrialisation as well as education in order to increase quality and efficiency and solve the housing issue, a social problem at the time. "Art and technology—a new unity" had already become Gropius's central idea in this programme, before it was to mobilise new forces in the context of the Bauhaus in 1923.[35]

In the spring of 1919, Walter Gropius underlined the central position of architecture in this new academy for design in his Bauhaus programme:

> The Bauhaus strives for the [...] reunification of all artistic disciplines [...] into a new art of building [...] The final, if distant objective of the Bauhaus is the unified work of art—the grand structure.[36]

In practise, the development of standard architectural training at the Bauhaus proved extremely difficult and could only be realised at the Dessau Bauhaus in 1927 with the appointment of Swiss architect Hannes Meyer. Starting in 1919, Gropius had organised architecture courses with the Weimar Building Trades School led by Paul Klopfer and from 1921 held seminars and lectures himself, together with Adolf Meyer, on *Spatial Studies—Practical Applied Drawing*.[37]

The Gropius architecture practise from the beginning had taken a central position in education at the Bauhaus. It arranged commissions for all Bauhaus workshops and thus gave numerous students the opportunity to implement their own ideas and designs practically while financing their studies. This also applied to the architectural projects themselves, in which the students were included at every stage, from planning and execution to model building in the sculpture workshop. For the first great post-war commission, the Sommerfeld house in Berlin, Gropius made use of this opportunity for collaboration. Inspired by the early country houses of Frank Lloyd Wright, this wooden house was erected in block construction on a limestone base and furnished with the help of the most talented students in the spirit of *Gesamtkunstwerk* under the site supervision of Fred Forbat. Joost Schmidt carried out the woodcarving work, Josef Albers made the coloured stained glass windows and Marcel Breuer designed some of the furniture.

In the spring of 1920, Gropius announced a student competition for a Bauhaus development in Weimar, for which two drafts by Walter Determann are preserved. While the first draft provided for a scattered development with wooden buildings for communal living and working, in his second draft Determann developed a complex settlement model similar to the ideal city of the eighteenth century, with surrounding walls and lighthouses on the corners. On both sides of a central axis, studio houses for

Walter Gropius, Adolf Meyer, Sommerfeld house, Berlin, 1920

the Masters, workshop buildings, student boarding houses, estate and kindergarten were grouped, as well as the main buildings for communal activities. In the centre, there was a theatre according to the Greek model, accented by a glass pyramid. City planning ideas of the English "garden city" movement were combined with Bruno Taut's architectural visions in this proposition.

In 1922 Walter Gropius founded the Bauhaus Housing Co-operative, Ltd with the young Hungarian architect Fred Forbat as planner, which was intended to construct an academic complex above the Goethe garden house with attached housing for friends of the Bauhaus. In this context, Gropius developed his "Building Blocks at Large" with functional building blocks for room cells, from which individual houses were to be industrially produced according to clients' wishes. In the age of hyper-inflation, however, of all these projects only the sample *Haus am Horn* could be carried out. This had been drafted by Georg Muche with the participation of the Gropius architecture practise

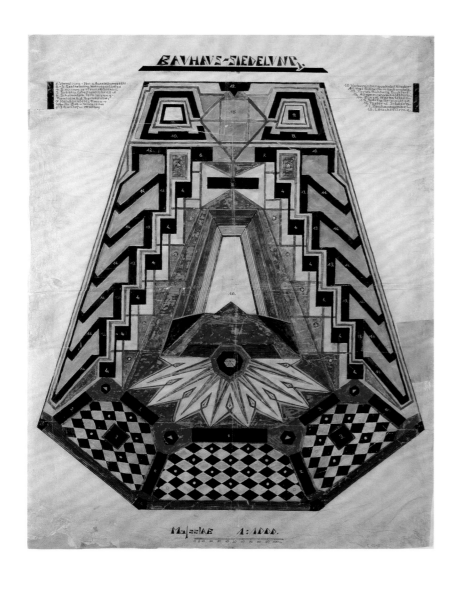

and been erected over four months on the occasion of the 1923 Bauhaus Exhibition, and furnished with the help of all the Bauhaus workshops. It was a truly experimental structure: a living experiment with individual rooms, minimised like ship's cabins to make more room for a central living room; a technological experiment with light, pre-cast concrete blocks made of industrial waste products; an ecological experiment with thermal zoning of the rooms and minimised exterior surfaces and window openings to the south-west as well as insulation materials made of peat to provide for better heat insulation; finally, a social experiment intended to lighten the load of the occupier by using easy-care materials for floors, windows, doors and wet areas as well as the most modern household technology.[38]

Almost at the same time as Walter Gropius's 1922 competition design for the Chicago Tribune Tower with its visible skeleton structure, Ludwig Mies van der Rohe developed his famous office and skyscraper projects which were unfortunately never carried out.

Mies van der Rohe designed the 20-storey office building for Berlin's Friedrichstrasse around a central utility core with stairways and elevator. The building was to be situated on a tight, triangular property in a maple leaf shape. With the prismatic sectioning of the structural masses and the hung glass façade,

Walter Determann, Draft for a Bauhaus settlement, 1920

Georg Muche / Gropius workshop, *Haus am Horn*, 1923, north-west view, condition in 1999

Ludwig Mies van der Rohe, Glass skyscaper in organic forms, 1920-21 (International Architecture Exhibition at the Bauhaus Weimar 1923)

Walter Gropius and Adolf Meyer, Sketch by Carl Fieger for the Chicago Tribune Competition, 1922

he would have achieved optimum lighting and ventilation as well as manageable and aesthetically sophisticated interior rooms. Mies van der Rohe further developed the theme with his glass skyscraper of 1922, a 30-storey building with organic forms on an irregularly-shaped property, now with two round utility cores and few interior supports.

With models for an office building made of reinforced concrete and the glass skyscraper, Mies van der Rohe was represented at the first worldwide International Architecture Exhibition of the Modern on the occasion of the 1923 Bauhaus Exhibition, which featured more than thirty architects from Germany, the U.S., France, the Netherlands, Denmark, Soviet Russia and Hungary, including Bruno Taut, Erich Mendelsohn, Le Corbusier and Frank Lloyd Wright.

In Gropius's architecture practise in Weimar, up to twelve people were employed at any one time, mainly Bauhaus graduates like Carl Fieger, Ernst Neufert, Fred Forbat, Farkas Molnár, Marcel Breuer, Joost Schmidt, Emil Lange, Erich Brendel and Heinz Nösselt. A small group of architecture enthusiasts including Muche, Breuer and Molnár had formed a loose "working association" for modern housing architecture in 1923/1924, whose designs were presented in publications and exhibitions. Muche designed a town apartment building with gardens on each level, a skyscraper with a reinforced concrete skeleton, and an assembly house with a steel skeleton. In 1924, Breuer developed a multi-level apartment building for a competition of the magazine *Bauwelt*, and a series of small metal houses starting in 1925, while Molnár already stood out with the single-family house *The Red Cube* in 1923 and a year later the design of a U-theatre.

Tied in with the offer from the magistrate of the city of Dessau to take over the Bauhaus at the beginning of 1925 was a commission to build its own school building, which was to include the reconstruction of the Professional Trades School. Carrying on the idea of the central square in the Weimar Bauhaus estate with a three-winged asymmetrical building complex with two street bridges, Gropius developed the design for the Bauhaus building in Dessau, supported by Fieger and Neufert. At the intersection of two roads in a city construction development area a few yards west of Dessau railway station, Gropius designed an expressive model of "New Building." Easily recognisable building shapes were attributed to the five functional areas: the glass cube of the workshop wing as the productive centre, the neighbouring "festival level" of the main foyer, assembly hall, stage and dining room with adjacent studio house as tall objects, the bridge for the directorate and the building department as well as the connecting trade school wing with its own entrance. The asymmetrical building complex

invited one to drive through or walk around it, seeing the architecture of a modern metropolitan city with the dynamics of automobiles and aircraft, enabling a completely new experience of space and time.

The festival level with its single room concept and the different variation options with hard doors, folding doors and curtains, and the workshop wing with its concrete frame construction into which light-separating walls could be inserted or removed according to the workshops' needs, appear definitely programmatic. The housing cells in the studio house on the east side, on the other hand, are marked by characteristic small balconies on an exposed structure façade. The trade school wing on the north side represents a very compact school structure with central corridor and even lighting by bands of windows. In March 1925, Gropius began the design; one year later the topping-out ceremony was held, and on 4th December 1926 the building was officially opened with a celebration and numerous international guests. Again, all the workshops assisted with the furnishing: colour design by Hinnerk Scheper and László Moholy-Nagy, furniture by Marcel Breuer, lights by Marianne Brandt and Max Krajewsky.

In the Dessau Bauhaus building, a modern lifestyle was spatially organised, promoting communal living and working, communal eating, all forms of fine arts and sporting activities.

During the National Socialist era, the building—after demolition requests by the Nazi Party leadership—served as a Junkers factory and a Nazi *Gau* (administrative district) leader school, and also housed the building staff of Albert Speer. Following war damage, it was provisionally repaired in 1945 and housed several schools before it was taken into stock and renovated in 1964/1965; in 1975/1976 the first serious preservation efforts took place to restore it. The development of a scientific and cultural centre with its own Bauhaus collection began in 1976, and today the building presents itself as the Foundation Bauhaus Dessau, presenting rich educational, research and cultural opportunities. From 1996 to 2006 the building was again subject to a thorough renovation according to current preservation standards.

Parallel to the Bauhaus building, Gropius was also able to design, under a commission of the city of Dessau, the houses of the Bauhaus Masters, three duplexes as well as the director's house as the main building. Construction began in September 1925, and in August 1926 Gropius, Moholy-Nagy, Feininger, Muche, Schlemmer, Kandinsky and Klee moved in with their families. The buildings were embedded in existing woods, and the gardens with their recreational areas were divided from the green areas on the roadside only by an almost-invisible chain

Walter Gropius, Bauhaus Dessau building, south-west view, 1925/26, condition in 2005

link fence. The almost identical floor plans of the duplexes, which were placed at 90° angles and mirrored, had generous studios on the upper floor facing north, with three adjacent bedrooms. The living rooms, dining rooms and kitchens on the ground floor faced the garden. Balconies and rooftop terraces with showers invited sunbathing and athletic activity. The wings facing west were topped with a second storey with guest rooms. The buildings' functionality, especially that of the director's house, was publicly presented and recorded on film. While the exterior façade was executed in primary colours and black-and-white scales according to a uniform plan by Alfred Arndt, the interior stunned with the Bauhaus Masters' individual colour design, which has been largely reconstructed over recent years.

According to plans by Gropius, the ensemble of the Bauhaus housing development in the southern Törten suburb of Dessau comprised 314 single-family town houses in five types, with the Konsum building as its centre, the steel house by Georg Muche and Richard Paulick as well as the house by Carl Fieger. Beginning in 1928, Hannes Meyer worked on an expansion

plan of the settlement towards the south with almost one thousand housing units in a mixed development of three to four-storey balcony access houses and single-storey town houses. By 1930 only the three-storey balcony access houses had been built.

Gropius used the three building stages in the Törten settlement for extensive construction and technological experiments. Thanks to a smooth, continuous production system, the first building stage with sixty town houses could be turned over in the spring of 1927 after a six-month construction period, the first two buildings (already in place at the time of the opening of the Bauhaus building in December 1926) with show-apartments furnished by the Bauhaus workshops. The Reich Research Association for Economy in Building and Housing subsidised the project from 1927 onwards and enabled the comprehensive use of building machines to prefabricate building elements at the construction site and for installation.

Georg Muche and Richard Paulick erected their steel house on a concrete slab without a basement. The load-bearing steel skeleton was clad with steel sheets on the outside, and waste concrete blocks were used on the inside. The cover strips appeared like a design element from the outside, while the porthole-shaped windows associated the house with ship-building.

Among the visionary projects of Walter Gropius was the Total Theatre for Erwin Piscator of 1927, which he worked on with Hungarian Bauhaus graduate Stefan Sebök. On an elliptic floor plan, the theatre could be used either as a traditional proscenium stage, an amphitheatre, or a round arena simply by turning a floor disc in the middle, which allowed for varying spatial relationships between actors and audience. All walls and ceilings were able to serve as projection surfaces for slides and films, using projection equipment which could be lowered from the ceiling.

The famous architecture critic Adolf Behne called the Unemployment Office in Dessau, with its successful unity of form, function and structure, Walter Gropius's best building; Gropius had won the invitational competition against Hugo Häring and Bruno Taut and supervised the construction in 1928/1929. Based on a semicircular floor plan, the numerous visitors could be directed throughout the building without getting in each others' way, while the building's great depth was evenly lit by shed roofs and dropped glass ceilings. The iron skeleton structure with adjacent administration wing made of reinforced concrete was clad with yellow bricks. The interior furnishing was carried out by the Bauhaus workshops.

Bauhaus Dessau building, Auditorium with chairs by Marcel Breuer and lighting by Max Krajewski, 1926, condition in 2005

Walter Gropius, Masters' houses in Dessau, 1925/26, condition in 2005

Georg Muche/Richard Paulick, Steel house in Dessau-Törten, 1926, condition in 2005

Walter Gropius, Cooperative in Dessau-Törten, 1928

Walter Gropius, House number 17 at the German Werkbund Exhibition The Apartment, Stuttgart, Weißenhof estate, 1927

Walter Gropius, Drawing by Carl Fieger, Total Theatre project for Erwin Piscator, 1927

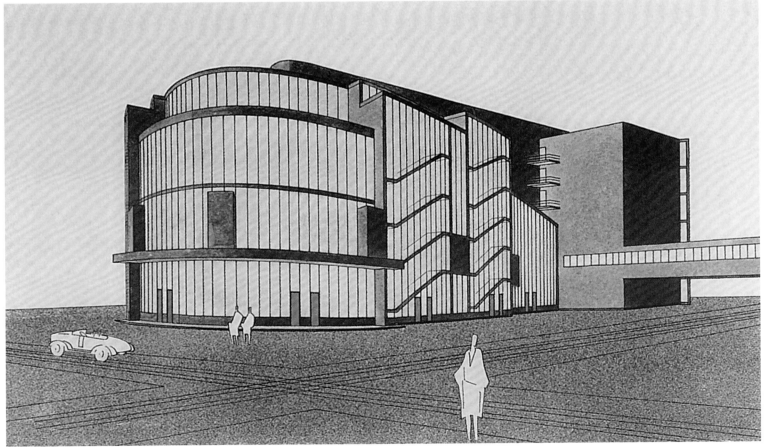

After the Freidorf communal settlement near Basel with 150 housing units and a community house, erected from 1919 to 1924, Hannes Meyer consequently turned towards the modern in 1926, one year before joining the Dessau Bauhaus, with his new office partner Hans Wittwer. Along with the competition design for the Peter School in Basel—which with its rooftop terraces seems to have landed on a square in the old town like a UFO from another world—Meyer and Wittwer participated in the international competition for the League of Nations Palace in Geneva. Their work, which received third prize among 377 participants, implemented the tender requirements in the best forward-looking manner with two independent, but connected, building parts: the hall building for 3,000 delegates in an oval shape for optimum viewing and acoustic conditions, and the secretariat complex as a flat structure from which a 24-storey double high-rise building soars upwards with 500 offices and attached radio masts as symbols of modern global communications. The authors promoted their project, which resembles an early version of the UN headquarters in New York, with its quick orientation, short vertical connections, best-possible incidence of light and best transportation with adjacent railway and underground parking.[39]

The main architectural work of Hannes Meyers with Hans Wittwer is undoubtedly the Federal School of the ADGB (General German Federation of Labour Unions) in Bernau near Berlin, which was built from 1928 to 1930. Meyer won the invitational competition against Max Berg, Erich Mendelsohn and Max Taut, among others. On the basis of a social organisation form of study and seminar groups for 120 course

participants, he created a functionally varied building complex with a close connection to the existing natural space with a pine forest and watercourse. The community centre with assembly hall and dining room is adjacent to the five staggered boarding structures connected by glass corridors, which end at the seminar building and the sports hall. Perpendicular to this, six single-family town houses for teachers and other staff are grouped together. The existing pond was expanded, connected to a swimming pool and surrounded by a jogging path. The sports facilities were completed by a sports field of Olympic standards. This union school was thus not only able to serve the political education of its members, but also to enable a new, collective lifestyle with intellectual exchange, cultural and sports activities. Brick façade and reinforced concrete structures, in combination with light steel construction from the connection corridor to the windows, as well as visible installation lines, determine the objectively precise appearance of this architecture, in which hygienic aspects like light, air and ease of care receive special consideration. The students of the building department at the Bauhaus, Hermann Bunzel, Arieh Sharon and Lotte Beese, participated in the planning stage; other Bauhaus students like Konrad Püschel helped with construction supervision. The Bauhaus weaving workshop developed a wall covering for the assembly hall, and the carpentry workshop made the desks for the rooms in the boarding facility.

The study and organisational plan of the Bauhaus by Hannes Meyer of 1928 provided for nine semesters of education for architects: a one-semester preparatory course with Albers, Kandinsky and Klee, then two semesters of construction fundamentals in design and scientific disciplines including workshop work, three semesters of construction studies with special studies in statics, building construction, building material studies and psychology and three semesters of building office and construction practise. The larger number of teachers in construction studies–Hannes Meyer, Hans Wittwer, Ludwig Hilbersheimer, Anton Brenner and Mart Stam as well as in the engineering disciplines and subsidiary subjects with Friedrich Engemann, Alcar Rudelt, Wilhelm Müller, Friedrich Köhn, Carl Fieger, etc.–speaks for the professionalism and quality of the education, which was even further increased by guest lecturers. The scientifically based and practically oriented education was at the centre of all efforts and proved a good investment for an entire study group in the construction of the balcony access houses in Törten.

The German Pavilion at the International Exposition in Barcelona in 1929 was the basis for Ludwig Mies van der Rohe's world fame. It was Germany's first participation in a World Exposition after the First World War and was to serve as self-promotion of a new, democratic state. This pavilion stood on a pedestal like a small temple and defined a flowing space, a unified work of art of meditative character with its noble walls of green marble and yellow onyx as well as the roof floating on eight chrome-plated cross supports, with reflective water surfaces and a sculpture by Georg Kolbe. The building provided the greatest possible contrast to the adjacent exhibition structures in historical styles, particularly the Spanish Village with its "copies" of important Spanish buildings from all over the country. This tension can be felt again today, after a copy of the Barcelona pavilion was erected in its former location. At the same time, Mies van der Rohe's most famous villa, the Tugendhat House in Brno, was created. Here, Mies van der Rohe made use of the sloping site and the park-like property with a view of the old town in a congenial manner, with a two-storied estate with upper-level development and generous living area on the ground floor, as well as sinkable glass walls that did away with the separation between the interior and exterior. Again, cross-shaped steel supports clad in chrome-plated sheet metal appear almost dematerialised and enable a flowing space.

Mies van der Rohe radically restructured the education at the Bauhaus after his assumption of office in 1930, drastically reducing workshop work and focusing the studies on building and furnishing, supported by Lilly Reich, into a more academic course of studies without direct connections to practise or even real construction efforts. The architectural ideas and quality criteria of Mies van der Rohe became the benchmark for student designs, and not the development of individual design ideas. Along with the systematic design studies by Ludwig Hilberseimer, however, the students still worked on free projects like the *Bauwelt* competition

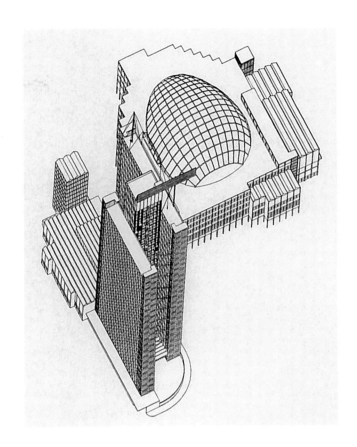

Walter Gropius, Employment agency in the city of Dessau, view, 1927-29

Hannes Meyer and Hans Wittwer, Design presented to the competition for the Palace of Nations in Geneva, axonometric projection, 1927

Hannes Meyer, Syndicate school of the ADGB in Bernau, aerial view by Junkers, 1928-30

Hannes Meyer, Hans Wittwer, and the students from the Architecture Department of the Bauhaus Dessau, Sketch for the competition for the ADGB Federation School (Allgemeiner Deutscher Gewerkschaftsbund) in Bernau, plate 3, 1928

Heiner Knaub, *The Garden as an Extension of the Living Space*, study dossier for the course with Hannes Meyer, 1930

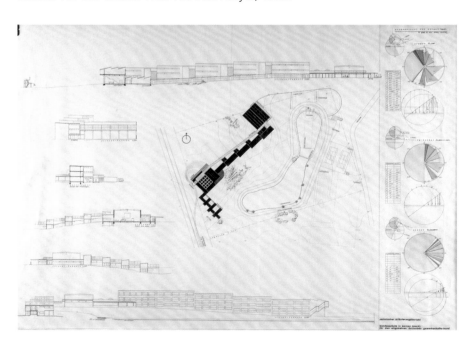

Architecture department at the Bauhaus Dessau under Hannes Meyer,
Arcade houses in Dessau-Törten, 1929-30, condition in 2005

Architecture department at the Bauhaus Dessau under Hannes Meyer,
Plan of the Dessau-Törten Estate, 1930

Reinhold Rossig, *Sketch of a socialist city*, work for the course with
Ludwig Hilberseimer, 1931

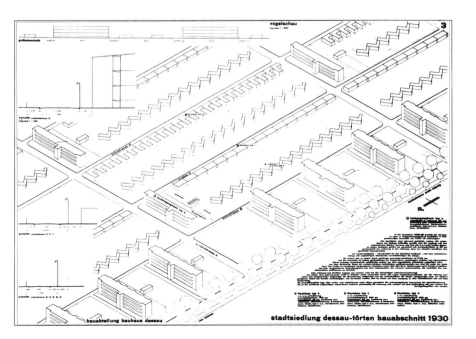

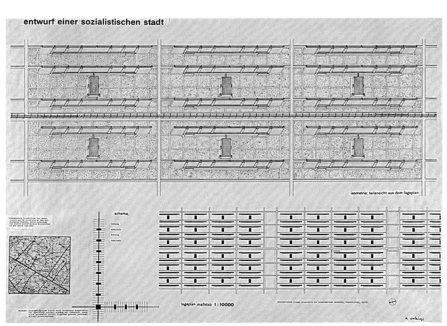

Ludwig Mies van der Rohe, German pavilion for the International Exhibition in Barcelona, 1929, condition in 2005

*The Growing House* in 1931/1932, the competition for the theatre in Kharkiv by Arieh Sharon, Wilhelm Heß, Pius Pahl and Waldemar Hüsing or the designs for the People's House and the State Printing House in Belgrade by Selman Selmanagic. Many projects which deal with contemporary city development ideas are credited to the students' own initiatives, like the *Design for a Socialist City* of 1931 by Reinhold Rossig with Russian architectural ideas of linear cities, or the seminar paper *Junkers Builds for Its Workers* by eight students in 1932, which addresses positions of the CIAM (Congrès Internationaux d'Architecture Moderne) and the Russian constructivists, such as communal boarding houses and complex infrastructure for training, education, sports and recreation.

The Bauhaus architects contributed decisively to the development of New Building in Germany and elsewhere in Europe with their international network as members of architectural organisations and associations.

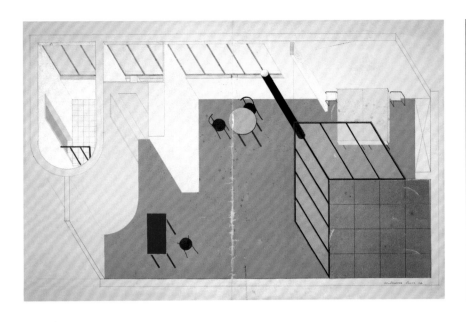

Wilhelm Heß, Plan of a studio apartment in the Junkers city in Dessau, isometry with interior and colour, study for the course with Ludwig Mies van der Rohe, 1932

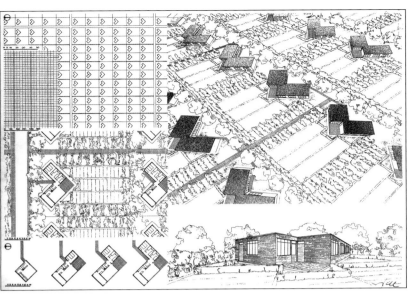

Pius Pahl, Large single-storey detached houses, plan, draft made under Hilberseimer, 1931-32

Ludwig Mies van der Rohe, Villa Tugendhat in Brno, Czech Republic, 1931, condition in 2005

# Photography/Photo Workshop

In contrast to other design areas, photography at the Bauhaus always had a marginal role in spite of the fact that every other person at the school was a photographer, and one would suspect that particularly under the banner of "Art and Technology–A New Unity" formulated in 1923, photography would have played an integrative role. Only in 1929, when the school had already existed for ten years, did photography became a permanent subject and was integrated into one of the Bauhaus departments as a workshop.

Photography at the Bauhaus appears less original than one would generally assume, in light of the historical context. For example, its contribution to the development of "New Seeing" and "New Objectivity", two trends which were generally subsumed into the term "New Photography", can more or less be reduced to the achievements of extraordinary personalities like László Moholy-Nagy and Walter Peterhans.

Nevertheless, photography at the Bauhaus contributed to the fact that this form seemed a suitable medium to let the aesthetic penetrate into everyday life and to play a part in the formation of a new mass culture in various areas of application.

The photography created at the Bauhaus showed an extraordinarily diverse spectrum of influences and concepts, just like the fine arts practised there. This was due to the general creative availability, freedom and the promotion of individualism by the various pedagogic approaches at the Bauhaus. This palette ranged from portraits, life and work documentations, exercises from lessons, still lifes and compositions via object, architecture, product photographs or stage photography to essay and milieu photographs and the specific use of photography in collage/montage.

Characteristic of this first phase (1919 to 1923) in the development of the medium of photography at the Bauhaus was the dominance of object photographs, in which products of the Bauhaus, exercise results created in the courses as well as individual works of art, were depicted in an isolated and largely neutral manner. The reasoning behind this method of depiction, in which the object dominates over independent photographic values, may have been committed to a practical application aspect, i.e. photography of a functional assignment in each phase. The resulting photographs were meant for individual documentation purposes and for the purpose of publicising the achievements of the Bauhaus in books, lectures and magazines. These photographs were produced by the Weimar craftsman photographers Otto Eckner and Louis Held, externally commissioned, but also by Lucia Moholy and students like Franz Singer, Fritz Lafeldt and Kurt Schmidt. The original photo-documentation of the Weimar Bauhaus compiled from this is happily preserved.

This corresponded to an understanding of photography that was propounded by Walter Gropius. In his opinion, it was primarily meant to be an instrument for the most neutral reproduction of reality, and the bearer of objective information. In the early Weimar phase of the Bauhaus, photography did not have a real chance of being accepted and applied as an independent artistic genre. This definitely contemporary, generally negative and ignorant attitude towards photography was an expression of the expressionist spirit which ruled the Bauhaus in its early development phase, according to which manual trades and intellectual momentum were favoured over the machine and aesthetic ones.

This aspect of photographic documentation was also subsequently (until 1927) the one that was most evident. The objects were shown as ensembles or "in their functional logic". This made it apparent that the creative achievements of photography and the photographer were increasing, not least in response to developments in technology. The works of Lucia Moholy and Erich Consemüller are to be seen primarily in this context. Walter Gropius commissioned them to photograph products from almost all areas of the Bauhaus, which resulted in the creation of an incomparable documentation of Bauhaus work. The photographs of Lucia Moholy, in particular, were able to impressively convey the architecture of the Bauhaus and the products of the workshops. They were distributed in an incomparable manner by reproduction in books, newspapers, magazines and postcard prints, and thus shaped the perception of the Dessau architecture by Walter Gropius. Erich Consemüller, student in the carpentry workshop and employee in the Gropius building office, took over the task of photographing all non-documented objects and buildings of the Bauhaus after Lucia Moholy. This happened around 1927, and as a result, a new series of more than three hundred photographs was created. Consemüller's architectural photography, to which a certain proximity to the Cologne architecture photographer Hugo Schmölz and especially to the pioneer of the newly objective photography, Albert Renger-Patzsch, is rightly attributed, was different from Lucia Moholy's particularly in the field of image composition. Yet in his work the objective depiction of the object also dominates, however occasionally in connection with a restrained inclination to monumentalise. Lux Feininger saw the architecture of Walter Gropius with completely different eyes. He was one of the "most inspired among all photographers in the Bauhaus community."[40]

The self-taught photographer László Moholy-Nagy was the one to decidedly influence the development of photography at the Bauhaus from 1923 onwards, and to contribute to the fact that the art steadily gained importance as an independent means of expression. In the centre of his own individually creative vision was a fascination with light, which culminated in the well-known intellectual and controversial Light-Space-Modulator. From 1925

Moholy-Nagy turned towards camera photography after he had applied his "Painting with Light" ideals, supported by his wife Lucia, to drive the photogram into a non-object state. More than his own experimental achievement and more than his universalistic teaching, his example was of great influence; he had, however, never learned photography at the Bauhaus. Moholy-Nagy's achievements were among the best created at the Bauhaus in the area of photography. Yet his contribution was not simply to be equalled with photography at the Bauhaus. Moholy-Nagy succeeded around 1927, when "the actual creative dealing with photography" began in the full breadth of individual achievements.[41]

The photography of this time made especially clear the influences of so-called "New Seeing" and "New Objectivity." This was demonstrated in the focus on the object to be depicted as a creative photographic element as opposed to the formerly valid, strictly documentary interest in depiction. The photographs not only pointed to the only partially-depicted object or situation, but increasingly also to themselves. Perception aspects and the

questioning of them were pronouncedly discussed by means of photography. Discernibility and interpretability gave way to conscious efforts of alienation. Here, these extreme perspectives, abstract image structures, distortions, crooked lines, shadows, etc. appeared, which today are regarded as the archetypes, as it were, of photography of the 1920s and 1930s and "under the label 'Bauhaus style' entered into the history of photography".[42]

A part of this development phase of photography at the Bauhaus was largely represented by the works of Moholy-Nagy. Imitations by individual students were seen with Moholy's works or were in exceptional cases sometimes equally well-done. Among such imitations was the undoubtedly impressive portrait photography of Hajo Rose and, in particular, the photographs, photograms and collages by Marianne Brandt. In them an independent, creative quality became apparent in the specifically diverging space-time concept, the special, exposed relationship to simultaneity as a means of expanding perception, and the ambiguity of experience, which contrasted the teacher's model and those of some other contemporaries (the Berlin Dadaists, for example) in terms of content with a pointed orientation towards the relationship of the sexes.

With Moholy-Nagy's departure, a great phase of experimental photography began at the Bauhaus in 1927/1928, during which many of his ideas were interpreted. The vehement use of the photographic medium for advertising and marketing fell into this time period.

The broad spectrum and richness of the photographs created at the Bauhaus during this time were due to the carefree attitude to the now increasingly available medium. This is where the many shots and amateur photographs that were created more for personal photo albums than for later museum presentations finally belong. Already, Lucia Moholy recognised that the intrinsic value of these photographs consisted of a specifically sensual form of world learning ("learning to see").

## The Photography Workshop

The year 1929 is regarded as a final break within the developmental spectrum of photography at the Bauhaus. The

Lucia Moholy, Silver coffee and tea service with alcohol-fuelled warmer by Marianne Brandt, 1924

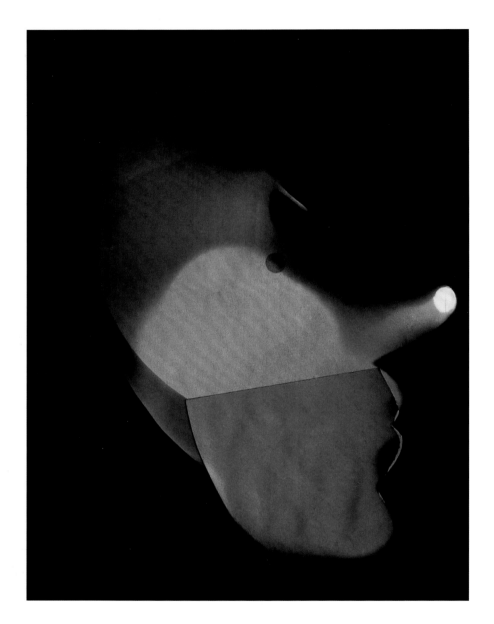

László Moholy-Nagy, Untitled, self-portrait in profile, photogram, 1922

Marianne Brandt, *Montage I* (with photogram), 1924

Paul Citroen, *Big City (Metropolis)*, 1923

László Moholy-Nagy, *Photoplastic*, 1925, photocollage

Anonymous (Gertrud Arndt?), *Portrait of Otti Berger and the studio building of the Bauhaus*, c. 1930

Fritz Heinze, Plate of printing characters, 1930

Walter Funkat, *Glass spheres*, 1929

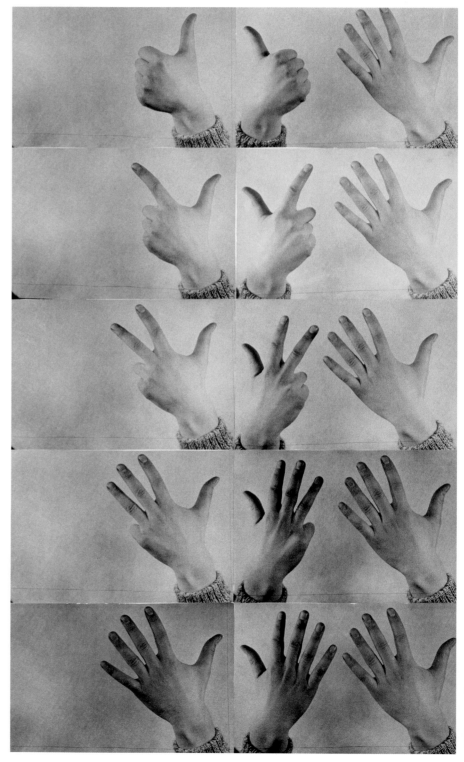

Hajo Rose, *High-jumper from the Prellerhaus* (Bauhaus Studio Building), 1930

Kurt Kranz, *Number Sign Series*, 1930/31

Walter Peterhans, *Dead Hare*, c. 1929

With Walter Peterhans as a representative of "New Objectivity", new photo-technical as well as photo-aesthetic aspects were added to the previously described spectrum and turned into the decisive momentum. The "fashioning of light" (Moholy-Nagy) was henceforth contrasted with the "magic of precision and detail" (Peterhans). The material and its technical processing possibilities during the development process were as much a challenge for Peterhans as the testing of optical effects and the depicting of three-dimensionality through a two-dimensional medium.

The resulting photographs by Walter Peterhans and some of his students were often produced surreally, largely as still lifes, rich in nuances, yet otherwise quiet and reserved. Here, we encounter evidence of a photography course built on a scientific basis in the student works from the areas of still life photography, object photography and portrait, which thus can only conditionally be regarded as free experiments of artistic photography. The photographs by Roman Clemens, Kurt Kranz, Walter Funkat, Herbert Schürmann, Eugen Batz, Werner David Feist and others were based on the intention to comprehend, in the spirit of Peterhans' "learning to see", and to depict the substance of things, the materials and specifics of surface composition as true composition and texture studies. They did not always have a meaning beyond that, which happened in many cases in Peterhans' photographs. Even the pure still life photographs, like those by Werner David Feist, Iwao Yamawaki, Albert Hennig and Fritz Heinze, were very suggestive and sometimes effective studies of material and light in close-up, direct top view or in motion. A fixed *Dingwelt* ("thing world") was presented in a "new light" (in every sense of the word) and thus relieved of its banality; that is, of the limits of the "independent existence [of things] beyond us" believed by Peterhans.[46] Portraiture, too, initially seemed to be less about an in-depth psychological exploration of the portrayed person's personality than about the testing and training of an effective use of light and the most vivid bringing-out of the physiognomy.

carefree attitude towards dealing with the medium was disciplined when photography was introduced as a subject. This phase was mainly determined by the work of photographer Walter Peterhans, who was given the subject and the photography workshop by Hannes Meyer, who himself created remarkable photographs.

With the establishment of a photography course initially assigned to the advertising department at a time when most design schools in Germany already had regular photography classes, departments and a certain form of photography education, the Bauhaus was not necessarily a pioneer in the field. The photography in the "Photography Class", which, together with the classes for typography, advertising graphics and the special class for plastics was part of the advertising workshop, print workshop and Photo Department, began in the 1929 winter semester with Walter Peterhans.[43] According to one author, "His basic course in this subject comprised a refined product photography with rich detail in surface depiction and nuances of minimal shades in the two-dimensional depiction also of voluminous objects."[44] Henceforth the photography department increasingly gained sovereignty by a process of insisting on the independence of photography as a discipline that did not only serve other disciplines and which was not always free of conflict. In 1930 the subject was shown as an autonomous teaching area in the curriculum while in 1931 a full-year course was considered necessary. The equipment in the photography department now included "four equipped dark rooms, an enlarger, a travel camera model 4, 13x18, a Stella photograph apparatus model 3, 13x18, a number of spotlights and optical instruments."[45]

The urge to go beyond the paper format into three-dimensional space or the "bottomless" floating of objects in an image plane that appeared open towards the back is significant in experimental photography at the Bauhaus under the influence of László Moholy-Nagy as well as Walter Peterhans. Elsewhere called "floating syndrome" and "floating", "weightlessness" or "removed from earthly certainty" and ascribed with a social equivalent, the means of photography here, similar to other creative fields at the Bauhaus, were used to work out a new concept of space.[47] It implied Gropius's intention to bring all creative achievements into unified relationships, adequate to anticipatory social developments.

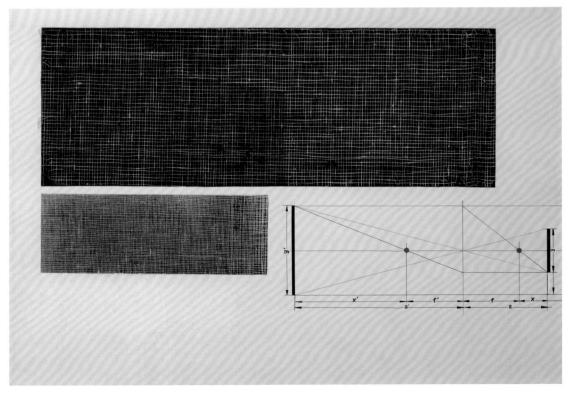

Walter Peterhans, *Champagne glass*,
1928-32

Herbert Schürmann, *Rose on glass and
grating*, 1933

Theo Ballmer, Study from the course with
Walter Peterhans, c. 1929

# Fine Arts

Until 1927 the Bauhaus was not a place for education in the fine arts, yet the educators appointed by Walter Gropius were predominantly painters. His idea of the unity of all arts under the leadership of architecture had as a consequence, however, that the results of artistic production were spatially integrated as before. Rather, it was recognised that knowledge of basics and laws in artistic design was vital, and was to be applied in a specific manner to the creative process of building through the release of creative forces. "Numerous impulses, which still unused await their realisation by the world of works, came from modern painting, which was breaking through its old boundaries," Walter Gropius wrote in 1923.

It was mainly abstract art which contributed with its systematically employed analysis of the fact that artistic means were recognised and depicted in their own right, then made available for creative work. It was based on the conviction that abstract colours and forms had an autonomous expressive force and that they were immediately and universally legible. This school of thought united a broad crisis in the avant-garde of the early twentieth century among which were also the artist-teachers of the Bauhaus. On the basis of this, the development of a formal vocabulary which could be flexibly transferred to various other areas relevant to practise, or the development of specific design principles, seemed possible, which in turn complied with the programmatic orientation of the Bauhaus school. "Painting is regarded as a force contributing to organisation," wrote Wassily Kandinsky in 1926 in the first *Bauhaus* magazine.

Lyonel Feininger, Johannes Itten, Georg Muche, Paul Klee, Oskar Schlemmer, Lothar Schreyer, Wassily Kandinsky, Gerhard Marcks and eventually László Moholy-Nagy as well as Josef Albers initially provided the formal artistic portion of training at the Bauhaus, alongside the material manual trades courses, which were provided by the master craftsmen. The new type of designer recommended by Walter Gropius was to be educated in this manner, which united both skills of the manual trade as well as the formal artistic ones. This alone marked the status attributed to art at the Bauhaus. Yet the relationship of the Bauhaus to free art remained ambivalent and the integration of painting in particular remained open.

The initial years after the school's foundation were marked by controversies which dealt with the status and role of "free", i.e. not immediately purposeful, art, like graphics, sculpture and painting within the overall make-up and the educational programme of the school. Initially, this led to the break with the professors taken from the former Weimar Fine Arts Academy, Engelmann, Fröhlich, Klemm and Thedy, who were not prepared to question their old, bourgeois nineteenth-century model of art with its traditional concept of depiction and thus their understanding of a "higher fine art." On the other hand, the disassociation of some Masters such as Johannes

Itten, Georg Muche, Lyonel Feininger, Lothar Schreyer and Gerhard Marcks, and students like Johannes Driesch, Johannes Berthold, Hans Haffenrichter, Werner Drewes, Max Peiffer Watenphul and others can be noted. Itten, who had laid the foundations for the work of the school regarding content in education and workshop practise, pleaded for a strengthened education in the arts, and saw the future of the school in the education and training of creative human beings, far from external influences like economy or industry. Johannes Itten, in the end, left the Bauhaus because of a controversy with Walter Gropius over this exact issue, bringing on an educational concept which no longer focused on the individual human being but on the creation of products.

With the installation of the so-called "Seminar for Free Sculpting and Painting Design" in the 1927/1928 winter semester and the establishment of "Free Painting Classes" by Paul Klee and Wassily Kandinsky in 1929, which institutionalised the specialist training in free fine arts in Dessau, a new phase of arguments began. When the Masters of Form were replaced in the workshops by so-called Junior Masters and were responsible only for matters of basic artistic education and the pure practise of art, the role of avant-garde art seemed to be poised between teaching, experiment and an ethically aesthetic social utopia.

An increasing insistence on function with progressive technological advances in workshop production and intensive visual arts production now opposed each other at the Bauhaus. Under Hannes Meyer, this contradiction was heightened with the increase of the theoretical portions of the classes and the social orientation of Bauhaus work. Building and fine arts finally went their separate ways in 1930, after the painters had been forced into the periphery. The previously held notion of the unification of all arts into a unity of a modern, more humane society began to disintegrate.

Nevertheless, the importance of fine artists at the Bauhaus was outstanding, despite all contradictions regarding their status. It was they who contributed the most to the formation of a new pedagogy for art, architecture and design by making a contribution to the elementary nature of the artistic potential of expression and the formation of a new space concept. Their work was often influenced in a special way by the programmatic orientation of the school. The teaching role furthermore gave these artists the opportunity to examine and state more precisely their own chosen path of artistic development. This also included the subliminal questioning of previous understandings of form. Thus Georg Muche, Gerhard Marcks and Oskar Schlemmer, for example, altered their previously abstract geometric rendering to favour more figural objectivity. Concerning quality and quantity, the works of the artists created during their service at the Bauhaus generally took on an exceptional position within the entirety of their respective *oeuvres*. Many pictures by Bauhaus artists, like

The Bauhaus Masters (l-r): Lyonel Feininger, Wassily Kandinsky, Oskar Schlemmer, Georg Muche and Paul Klee in Paul Klee's studio at the Bauhaus Weimar, 1925

those by Paul Klee and Wassily Kandinsky, became highly-organised opposite worlds to the reality of those years, which were experienced as chaotic. Some of their students, for example Josef Albers, Max Bill, Fritz Winter and Herbert Bayer, created works in the area of fine arts which today are also considered important autonomous contributions to twentieth century art.

If one attempts to obtain an overview of the fine art created at the Bauhaus, it is obvious that a uniform term for "Bauhaus art" is out of the question. The topic concerns not only the works of already famous artists like Johannes Itten, Lyonel Feininger, Wassily Kandinsky, Paul Klee and Oskar Schlemmer, but also the artistic work of students. Ernst Kállai, for a while the editor of the *Bauhaus* magazine and critical companion of Bauhaus work, noted at the end of the 1920s on the one hand the "objectivity solely determined by purpose and construction and standardised for mass production", and on the other hand the metaphysics marked by "dream, vision, bare confessions of the soul or paradox magic".[48]

An abstract geometric art did not dominate over the objective factual renderings. Rather, the fine arts at the Bauhaus in the end mirrored the broad spectrum of those artistic trends that had dominated the first half of the last century in Europe. Thus futuristic and late expressionist trends, partially influenced by Dadaism, can be found, like those documented in the works of Itten, Feininger, Marcks and their students Hans Haffenrichter, Lou Scheper, Walter Born, Max Peiffer Watenphul, Petra Petitpierre and Hajo Rose. Johannes Berthold, Werner Gilles and Kurt Schmidt with their mystical, esoteric and cosmic visions were also under the influence of expressionism, like almost the entire Bauhaus graphics portfolio edition. Lyonel Feininger was also close to expressionism. He was the first artist to be

appointed to the Staatliche Bauhaus in Weimar by Walter Gropius, where he became one of the most important integrative figures, despite his lack of teaching experience. He was a member of the school for a longer period of time than almost any other artist colleague. Feininger's position at the Bauhaus was unique. The fact that later in Dessau he was a member of the school as a teacher solely to radiate "atmosphere" without ever having to teach is yet another indicator of the openness and the unconventional intellectual climate of the institution, the visionary actions of its director and the high esteem in which the artist was held. Feininger influenced students and other Masters through his personality, his special aura and of course his works of art, which embodied their own type of image. Crystalline differentiation and a formal abstraction preserving a connection to the object as well as a pronounced and nuanced colouration marked his transcendentally excessive views on architecture. In Dessau particularly, Feininger offered the Bauhaus students the opportunity for a once-a-week consultation in his studio, where he explained his works. Convinced that art was not teachable, he tried to influence his students more through conversation than through formal lecturing. Bauhaus students like Hermann Klumpp, Werner Drewes, Wilhelm Imkamp, Franz Ehrlich, Erich Borchert or Hermann Röseler made use of this and seem to have profited from it on a human as well as an artistic level.

The works of Gerhard Marcks, Oskar Schlemmer, Johannes Driesch, Georg-Adams Teltscher and Kurt Schwerdtfeger integrate figural renderings in an individual manner. Schlemmer largely developed his own form language with his stereometric, de-individualised figures in unrealisticly heightened architectural rooms, which, with its endeavour to show the connections of being beyond things, was reminiscent of Italian *Pittura metafisica*. The landscapes by Johannes Itten and the still lifes by Georg Muche from around 1922 are also figural and objective.

During this time a strong influence from the Dutch artist movement *De Stijl* became apparent through Theo van Doesburg, who with his geometric elementarisation found expression in Karl Peter Röhl, Peter Keler, Werner Graeff and others. These works were characterised by an objectification of the non-objective. Objectification in abstraction is also a trait of these works that were created as an expression of the manifold individual treatment of Soviet Russian constructivist trends, and which found expression in the particularly complex design of an interdisciplinary concept by László Moholy-Nagy. While this, as we know, had far-reaching consequences for the development of the Bauhaus in general, which became clear in the change of course shortened to the slogan "Art and Technology—a new unity", its effects also appeared in detail, and in particular found expression in the area of photomontage/photo collage, documented, for example, in the works of Marianne Brandt, Franz Ehrlich and Erich Krause.

Johannes Itten, *Child Picture*, 1921/22

Lyonel Feininger, *Dröbsdorf*, 1927

Lyonel Feininger, *Row of Illuminated Houses*, 1929

Paul Klee and Wassily Kandinsky were the most important painters of the Bauhaus. In fact, they crucially shaped the Bauhaus students as well as the general appearance of the institution with their teaching and no less with their works. Klee and Kandinsky were already widely recognised and successful painters before they were appointed as teachers at the Bauhaus. Their art is based on the principle of abstraction. Wassily Kandinsky in particular is considered a pioneer of abstract painting who was able to theoretically substantiate this specific world view. During their tenure at the Bauhaus the work of both artists was created in more or less close interaction with their teaching. Paul Klee, who sought to transport content via signs and symbols in search of an absolute form for his pictures, tested aspects of his systematically constructed theory in practical painting. However, he considered spontaneity and free intuition of utmost importance. Uninhibited intuition united with scientific recognition was also considered an objective necessity for the creative artistic process by Wassily Kandinsky. Mystic intuition, following an "inner sound", eventually decided the choice of form which avoided a relationship to the conventional object as well as to any outward appearances. He, like his painter colleague Paul Klee, understood the creation of art

Paul Klee, *Magic Trick, 297 (Omega 7)*, 1927

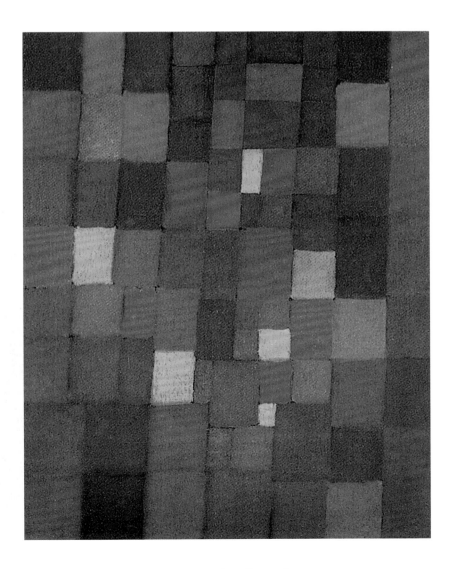

Paul Klee, *Architecture Image: Red, Yellow, Blue*, 1923

Wassily Kandinsky, *Grey and Pink*, 1924

Wassily Kandinsky, *Three Sounds*, 1926

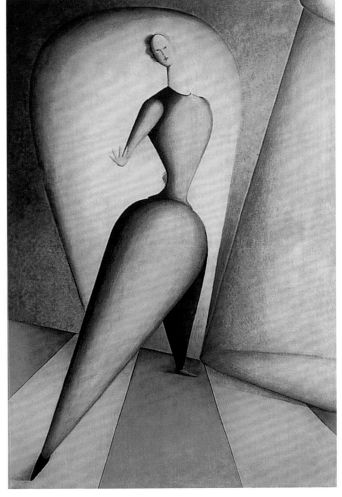

Oskar Schlemmer, *The Bauhaus Staircase*, 1932
© Oskar Schlemmer Archive and Theatre Estate

Oskar Schlemmer, *The Gesture (Dancer)*, 1922
© Oskar Schlemmer Archive and Theatre Estate

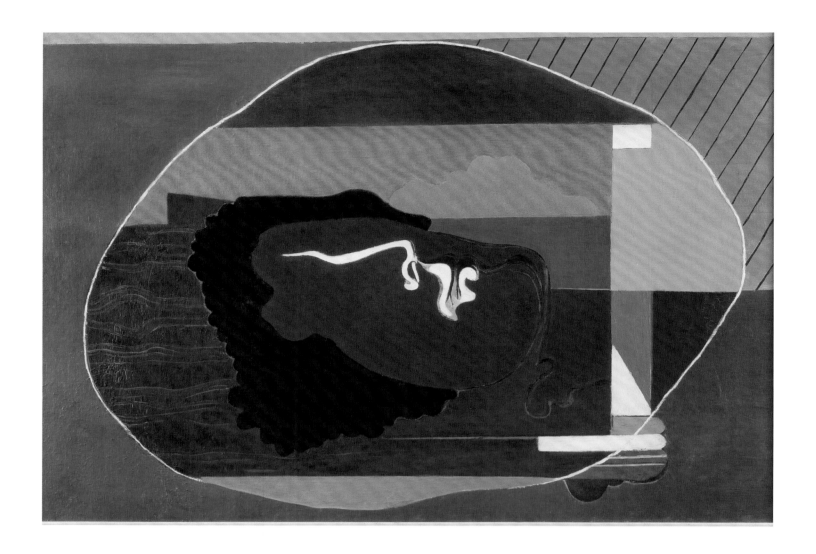

proportionate to the "becoming" in nature. Wassily Kandinsky's work and personality immediately radiated to his students such as Otto Hofmann, August Agatz, Wilhelm Imkamp, Karl Klode, Werner Drewes, Erich Krause and Hans Thiemann, while Fritz Kuhr, Fritz Winter, Herbert Bayer, Richard Oelze, Hans Thiemann, Friedl Dicker, Hajo Rose, Reinhold Rossig, Margaret Leiteritz and Eugen Batz transformed Paul Klee's form world into imaginative as well as socially critical creations.

This led to the moulding of approaches to socially critical and revolutionary art with occasional individual transformations of surrealism in Reinhold Rossig, Erich Borchert, Max Gebhardt, Carl Marx, August Agatz, Albert Hennig and Werner Kubsch. A pluralism of styles, as shown by the group's approach, thus marked in contrast to the general idea the varied spectrum of the Bauhaus fine arts works often created as compensation for workshop production as well as in an act of creative, holistic finding of oneself. In this sector, too, variety and variability as well as the pursuit of different paths may be seen as an indicator of creative freedom and availability.

Georg Muche, *Black Mask*, 1922

Georg Muche, *The Great Picture XX / Nocturnal Hour*, 1915

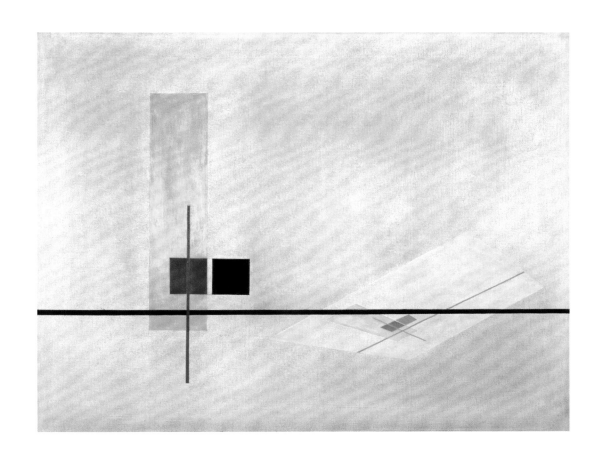

László Moholy-Nagy, *Construction Z 1*, 1922/23

László Moholy-Nagy, *Composition A 119*, 1927

Franz Skala, *The Dream*, 1919

Karl Peter Röhl, *Composition with Centres of Light*, 1920

Max Peiffer Watenphul, *Portrait of Margaret Willers*, 1922

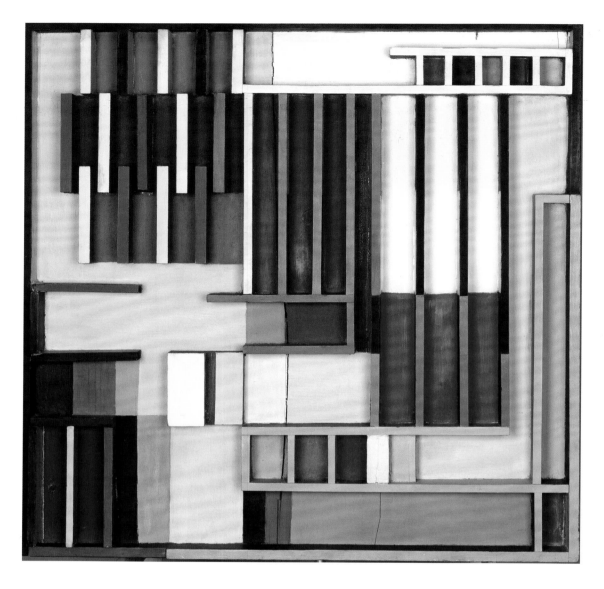

Kurt Schmidt, *Constructive wood relief*, 1923

Karl Peter Röhl, *Composition N.B. STYL*, 1923

Reinhold Rossig, *Man and Environment*, 1931

Eugen Batz, *Angular*, from the painting class with Paul Klee, 1930

# Life and Work

The open atmosphere of life at the Bauhaus, which demanded and promoted creativity, was always at the forefront of their memories when members of the Bauhaus community were asked what shaped them the most at the Bauhaus. Gropius's slogans of "freedom to individuality" and "favouring the creative" as well as "avoidance of all things stiff" from the 1919 *Bauhaus Manifesto* worked like an elixir at the time. The new way of thinking conveyed by the teachers, the use of varied methods to develop creative skills through experiment, theoretical training and practical application all contributed to the Bauhaus's exposed position in relation to other art schools. For teachers and students, it was often difficult and tiring at the same time to force the existing, sometimes conflicting forces at the Bauhaus into unity. During the early years particularly, there were representatives of the most diverse ideologies, religious orientations, and world views, often coupled with corresponding individual artistic programmes and visions, which were an expression of the general cultural situation of the time. At the Bauhaus, representatives of the most different youth movements in reform, pedagogic and artistically avant-garde circles as well as supporters of the *Deutscher Werkbund* and politically left or right-wing forces were gathered together. While at first the constructivists deemed themselves confirmed in the wake of the general, yet only short-lived, economic prosperity, the increasingly extreme political, social and economic tensions in Germany can be seen as the background for the increasingly left-wing politicisation of parts of the student body at the Bauhaus under Hannes Meyer in 1927.

From 1919 to 1933, 1,287 students from twenty-nine countries passed through the Bauhaus. Twenty percent of them were foreigners, and about one third were female. The proportion of foreigners was above average. The influence of foreign students on life at the Bauhaus had stimulating effects, and the international, inter-religious, cosmopolitan spectrum shaped the atmosphere at the school. There were, however, no equal rights for women, despite the relatively high proportion of female students, particularly during the Weimar years. Women were predominantly directed towards work in the weaving workshop. Only through extraordinary achievements and perseverance and against manifold difficulties were Marianne Brandt, Gunta Stölzl and Alma Siedhoff-Buscher, for example, able to be successful as autonomous designers for some time. The majority of Bauhaus students came from a middle-class background and disposed of a higher education. Their average age was twenty-four.[49] Many of them were consciously aware that they were part of something special. In their endeavour to fight conventions and help the breakthrough of new ideas and ideals they believed that they had to express their individuality by provocative deviation from social norms.

In Weimar there were two dominant groups. The supporters of the Mazdaznan philosophy of life propagated by Johannes Itten were concerned with a "physical and spiritual cleansing". They saw their path to self-knowledge in meditation. A special breathing technique, vegetarian food, a shaved head and wide habit-like clothing designed by Itten were some of their outer signs. The constructivists of the KURI group, on the other hand, preferred everything related to the world of technology. They appeared in suits and with exactly the same short hairstyle. In Dessau it could no longer be determined who belonged to which group, as the Bauhaus students there preferred longer or bobbed hair and tracksuits. One of the identifying signs of the Bauhaus community was the so-called Bauhaus whistle, for which a Hungarian folk song had been adapted and used as an identifier. Ten teachers and all Junior Masters married Bauhaus students, the most prominent example being Hannes Meyer's marriage to Lena Bergner. The unusually free interaction also led to the fact that there were a relatively large number of marital relationships among students and not a few children produced from these. The number of students per semester varied depending on political events, economic conditions and the institution's inherent dynamics. The highest number of students was reached in the 1919/1920 winter semester, when 245 students studied at the Bauhaus, about the average for German art schools at the time. In its endeavour also to support less well-off talents, the Bauhaus's fee policy with low rates, grants and free tuition was deliberately socially oriented. Nevertheless, many students were forced to end their studies for financial reasons. Some left the Bauhaus because they were dissatisfied with the education offered. On the basis of its status as an academy, which the Bauhaus had obtained in Dessau in 1926, a total of one hundred and thirty-three diplomas were issued from 1929, most of them in the construction department, the construction furnishing department and the weaving department.

The Bauhaus students' life was mainly shaped by a largely collective manner of learning, working and living. The principle conveyed in theory and in practise in the workshops was to analyse conditions and things, to question their purpose and consequently to reinvent them, allowing for an awareness of the noticeably heightened feeling of being alive. Work and play were equal when concerned with the fullest development of the student's natural talents. The student-teacher relationship was usually a partnership shaped by give and take, which went beyond a method of individual education, since it also referred to the practical organisation in the world outside. There were a multitude of opportunities to acquire additional knowledge and experiences beyond basic and specialist knowledge by means of interdisciplinary and non-dogmatic instruction. These included lectures, evening classes, interdisciplinary class visits, joint travel, theatre visits, work in the workshops for companies as well as the

Paula Stockmar, Johannes Itten in the Bauhaus costume designed by him, c. 1921

personal contact with teachers outside lectures and seminars. A never-ending interest in information, communication, discussion, heated debates in the cafeteria and the exchange with many areas of social life were part of the intellectual and cultural life of the institution in Weimar, as well as in Dessau and Berlin.

Nevertheless there were also violent friction, intrigues, envy and arguments. Ernst Kallai even mentioned a secret and open "opposition of most construction and workshop employees" in Dessau and attributed it to the rejection of a suppressed artistic drive.[50] The production of art was seen as antiquated at the time, the production of items for daily use for the fulfillment of social needs being the focus of interest.

In Weimar particularly, the social need of many students was great. Walter Gropius organised free lunches and tried to get financial support for the students. There had been a student council since the Bauhaus's foundation, which provided relief for the students' needs and also made sure that the students received their share of the products co-designed by them. Most students lived in furnished rooms on sub-tenancy. Only a few were granted housing in a studio building owned by the Bauhaus, a building erected in 1870, commissioned by the painter Luis Preller. To alleviate the housing shortage, work rooms were converted into living rooms and bedrooms. This was still the case even in Dessau, where beds were set up in the basement of the studio wing, for which the Weimar term of *Preller House* carried on. Here, too, only a few privileged students were granted living quarters in one of the beloved studios. Most students rented furnished rooms in *Gründerzeit* apartments or in nearby suburban developments.

The heads of the teaching team had comparatively exclusive housing in the Masters' houses developed by Walter Gropius, while the Junior Masters were assigned "the social service for students" in the *Preller House*. Gropius had developed the idea of communal living and working as early as 1919 with his idea of a lodge-like artists' community, and he tried to realise it with the Bauhaus building and the Masters' houses. Emphasising practical life over artistic work, he sought in this way to "join together related artistic natures on a friendly basis" to form a "sincere community not only in an artistic but also in a human sense".[51]

Only in Dessau was it possible to realise the postulated claim of a combination of experimental teaching and an ideal living community of designers, at least for some of the students and teachers, and thus to set an example of the imagined model society. The studio building *Preller House* played a special role in this. Gropius was concerned with its construction, since he deemed it necessary to give those working on a joint effort the opportunity for personal withdrawal into themselves. Comparatively comfortable, i.e. equipped and furnished with bathrooms, kitchens, food elevator, exercise room and electric laundry facilities, it consisted of twenty-eight live-in studios which were assigned on a semester basis by the Council of Masters according to merit and against payment of a monthly rent. The rooftop terrace and the studio front with its small protruding balconies were considered much used communication centres and were sometimes–to Gropius's great dismay–also used for balancing and climbing acts. When the influence on the students' way of life at the Bauhaus was drastically reduced under Mies van der Rohe, the *Preller House*, too, was reconstructed for space reasons, but also in order to reduce the opportunities for political meetings. The studios were left out. The unique Weimar atmosphere of learning, living, celebrating and working, which had been kept alive in Dessau, becoming thus a piece of Bauhaus identity, was lost. In Berlin, the Bauhaus students often lived in sub-let apartments, several of them together. The high cost of living prevented many Bauhaus students from making the move from Dessau to Berlin.

Rudolf Lutz, Sketch for a poster for Itten: *Our Game*, *Our Festival*, *Our Work*, 1919

Rudolf Baschant, Card for the kite festival, 1922

Farkas Molnár, Georg and El Muche with the *Haus am Horn*, 1923

Bauhaus Festival in Ilmschlößchen, 1924

Lucia Moholy, Bauhaus Band, 1925/26

The manifold private relationships and friendships among the Bauhaus students were of special integrative importance, and were cultivated in family celebrations, recreational joys, sports activities (such as the joint swimming in the Dessau rivers of Elbe and Mulde) and joint travelling. On the one hand, this furthered strong unity and on the other hand, it fostered a special way of interaction that was marked by a special sense of irony. The "cultivation of friendly interaction between Masters and students outside of work; and poetry, music, theatre, lectures, costume festivals, the creation of a ceremonious merriment at these gatherings" had already been formulated in the programme of 1919. The Bauhaus celebrations were both famed and infamous, and expressed liveliness and enjoyment. Here, two essential components of life at the Bauhaus were united—working together and celebrating together. Apart from Christmas celebrations, which took the form of a Scandinavian Yuletide festival, festivals were determined by the seasons, and it was primarily the thematically oriented events which eventually came to the attention of the public in Dessau. The Bauhaus band,

Hajo Rose, Michiko Yamawaki at the loom, 1930/32

Edmund Collein, Gropius construction workshop, 1927/28

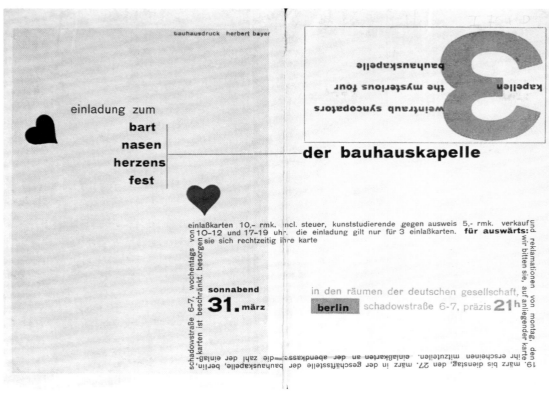

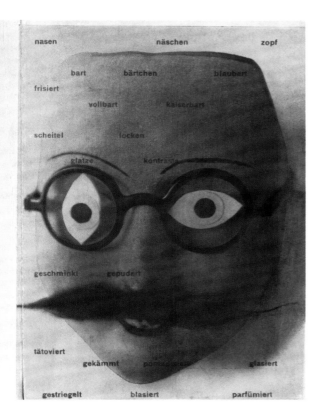

founded in 1924, whose repertoire included jazz, folk music and contemporary rhythms, gave the theme festivals, which were enjoyed by teachers and students alike, a special tone. Two of the most outstanding festivals were on 6th December 1926, on the occasion of the opening of the new school building, and the *Metallic Festival* of 9th February 1929 in Dessau. The self-designed costumes were given great attention:

> Kandinsky loved to show up as an antenna. Itten came as an amorphous monster, Feininger as two right-angled triangles. Moholy-Nagy as a segment perforated by a cross, Gropius as Le Corbusier, Muche as an unkempt apostle and Klee as the song of the blue tree...[52]

One of the last glittering Bauhaus festivals took place in February 1933, but even before this masked ball, which had 700 participants, the Bauhaus had stopped celebrating for itself: it was now selling its festivals like one its products.

Irene Bayer, Members of the Bauhaus at Elbe beach near Dessau, 1925

Erich Consemüller, Katt Both, 1927

Erich Consemüller, Marcel Breuer accompanied by his "harem" (l-r: Martha Erps, Katt Both, Ruth Hollos), 1927

Herbert Bayer, Invitation to the Beard, Nose and Heart Festival of the Bauhaus band at the German Society, Berlin, 1928

Franz Ehrlich, Invitation to the Bauhaus Carnival on March 1st, 1930

# Effect and Reaction

The Bauhaus's worldwide effect and the reaction to it has touched the areas of design, architecture, fine arts and pedagogy from the time of its foundation until today. Even during the school's existence, its ideas, principles and methods had effects beyond the Germany's borders.

The radicalism with which the Bauhaus raised pressing issues of the industrial society and provided exemplary solutions led to it becoming a synonym for the "modern." Depending on the onlooker's point of view, it became either a positive–often idealised–or negative–often demonised–point of reference. Even today, the spiritual as well as material reactions to Bauhaus achievements play a major role in discussions of the future of culture and society. Innumerable books, articles and exhibitions, as well as the continued commercial success of Bauhaus products, which have become "design classics", have contributed to the dissemination of Bauhaus ideas. This also includes the creation of the simple term "Bauhaus style."

The Bauhaus was already being internationally discussed on the occasion of its exhibition in 1923. It saw itself as a part of, and a mediator for, the movement of cultural modernity, and communicated with varied artistic and philosophical groups and movements. The Bauhaus was represented at all important congresses and exhibitions. Walter Gropius belonged to the elite of modern architects who participated in the Weissenhof development in Stuttgart beginning in 1927, which had been organised like an exhibition by the *Deutscher Werkbund*. He and other architects of the Bauhaus were integrated into the work of the CIAM (International Congresses for New Building), which beginning in 1928 posed important questions of architectural and city development. The effects of the Bauhaus were disseminated by means of public relations work geared towards the media, the production and sale of its products, the presentation of the artistic works of its members and, of course, the exemplary teaching methods and education principles.

Reaction to the Bauhaus in the area of art pedagogy had already commenced in the 1920s, when, approximately ten years after the school's foundation, parts of the pedagogic concepts of the Bauhaus were being integrated into various other schools in their arts and crafts education programmes. Reservations of art teachers regarding the Bauhaus and its art education methods led to the fact that reference was often only made to the material practise of the Bauhaus and less to its design theories. The teaching of Bauhaus ideas in German and international art schools, such as the Essen Folkwang School, the Hamburg State Art School and the Stettin Arts and Crafts School was carried on by former Bauhaus teachers and students. Gerhard Marcks joined the Burg Giebichenstein Halle Arts and Crafts School in 1925; Oskar Schlemmer taught at the Breslau Academy from 1929; and Paul Klee taught at the Dusseldorf Art Academy from 1931. These were educational institutions which sought to implement reform concepts in arts and crafts education parallel to the Bauhaus with the establishment of preparatory classes, teaching and production workshops as well as classes for special design areas. The Weimar Construction Academy, the direct successor of the Bauhaus, had Bauhaus students like Ernst Neufert, Erich Dieckmann and Wilhelm Wagenfeld on its teaching staff. The school called The Path, founded at the same time as the Bauhaus in Dresden and later with a branch in Berlin run by Bauhaus students, also expressly dedicated itself to a general creative education and activity in applied areas, as did the private Reimann School, also located in Berlin, and one of the most important private art schools of the Weimar Republic. With the intention of practising a unified art education in his spirit in connection with subjects like architecture, photography and advertising, a very specific variant of the Bauhaus emerged in 1926 with the private art school opened by Johannes Itten. The Bauhaus student Sandor Bortnik founded the Workshop (Mühely), also called the Hungarian Bauhaus, in the same year. Two years later, an arts and crafts school was created in Bratislava called the Bratislavsky Bauhaus, which in its basic orientation also showed parallels to the original Bauhaus. The schools closest to the methods and education profile of the Bauhaus were the Higher Artistic-Technical Workshops (Vkhutemas) in Moscow, which were renamed Vkhutein in 1927 and to which direct contacts existed from 1928.

## Bauhaus and the Third Reich

The National Socialists attacked the Bauhaus and denounced it as "un-German" and "Bolshevik." They brought about the final closure of the school in 1933 and thus caused the end of a democratic development oriented on holistic education. Many former Bauhaus students were persecuted, incarcerated and annihilated due to their aesthetic and political convictions. While their abstract artistic work in particular was considered "degenerate", many of their buildings with flat roofs were denounced as "un-German" and called "desert architecture." Nevertheless, there was also a continuity of Bauhaus designs in the Third Reich. Depending on expediency, modern design approaches were integrated into the cultural concept of the National Socialists, and particularly in the areas of commercial art and industrial construction, some freedom remained. Not a few Bauhaus students were thus able to continue working in their profession. This chapter of Janus-faced modernisation split the Bauhaus students remaining in Germany into victims, accomplices, "internal emigrants", and resistance fighters.

## The Bauhaus and the United States

Largely removed from all far-reaching social and cultural visions, The International Style Exhibition in 1932 at New York's Museum of Modern Art, as well as the book of the same title by Henry-Russell Hitchcock and Philip Johnson, increased and broadened the international concept of "the modern" as a style. Continued work, especially in Bauhaus pedagogy, was possible with the emigration of many Bauhaus teachers and students to the U.S., where they found a favourable reception. Thoughts, methods and principles of the Bauhaus were spread by individual strategies and attempts at integration with existing education systems. The interest in the establishment of a new Bauhaus-like education operation had already faded by 1938, since the Bauhaus was by then considered antiquated, but there was interest in its teaching methods and their implementation.[53] Josef Albers taught at Black Mountain College in North Carolina beginning in 1933, and from 1950 at Yale University in New Haven, Connecticut. Walter Gropius went to London in 1934, and from there followed a call to become an architecture professor at Harvard University in Cambridge, Massachusetts in 1937. Marcel Breuer, Ludwig Mies van der Rohe, Ludwig Hilberseimer, Walter Peterhans and Herbert Bayer also emigrated to the United States. They all influenced American art and culture. In 1937, the foundation of the "New Bauhaus" in Chicago by László Moholy-Nagy took place, but it was later continued under a different name and annexed to the Illinois Institute of Technology in 1946. Unlike any other Bauhaus student, Moholy-Nagy tried to take over the

Bauhaus model as a whole. Exposed to free market conditions and confronted with the special American circumstances (autonomy of art, design and architecture), his enterprise was doomed to failure. The Museum of Modern Art hosted a great Bauhaus Exhibition in 1938, whose catalogue represents the first comprehensive publication on the topic and continues to shape the American view of the Bauhaus with its focus on the directorship of Walter Gropius. Gropius and Ludwig Mies van der Rohe became the most influential architects in the United States for a generation because of their work and their teaching.

## The Bauhaus and the Soviet Union

Hannes Meyer and a group of his Bauhaus students tried to contribute to the establishment of a truly socialist society in the Soviet Union. They worked on city planning and architectural projects in Moscow and other regions until the mid 1930s. They eventually fell victim to the increasingly powerful Stalinist repression machinery, which was able to suppress not only its own but also imported avant-garde concepts in favour of the doctrine of socialist realism, and at the same time push the political persecution of immigrants. Thus, members of the Hannes Meyer camp were displaced into Stalin's camps and murdered. Meyer himself, who had also fallen into political disfavour, eventually returned to Switzerland in 1936.

## The Bauhaus and the Federal Republic of Germany

In post-war Germany, the Bauhaus initially enjoyed a growing reputation. This process continued in different ways with the split into the two new German states in 1949. In both East and West Germany, Bauhaus students exerted important influence on design, architecture and design pedagogy, working in art and architecture schools or practising their respective professions. While the Bauhaus was initially reduced to its most important artists in the west and mystically transfigured, rather than fully examined, a process of differentiated examination began with the *Ulm Hochschule für Gestaltung* (HfG, Ulm Academy for Design) founded at the beginning of the 1950s, in which the former Bauhaus student Max Bill played a great part. He became the first director of the Ulm school, which existed until 1968. Other Bauhaus students worked in the fields of architecture, product design, visual communication and information. Like the Bauhaus, the HfG was led by a holistic concept, which contained democratic aims and focused in particular on the cultural, social and economic conditions of design. The pedagogic concept of the HfG, whose teaching ceased as a result of both controversial discussion about its orientation concerning content and cuts of financial subsidies, can still be seen as a model, especially in the education of designers.

Then, based on the initiative of Hans M. Wingler, the Bauhaus Archive was founded in 1960, an institution which was the first to dedicate itself to the research into the Bauhaus and the preservation of its factual evidence. Located in Berlin since 1971, it was given a new building designed by Walter Gropius in 1978.

## Bauhaus and the GDR (German Democratic Republic)

It was initially possible, in the Soviet occupation zone in Germany, for a broad spectrum of design directions to form. Former Bauhaus students were again the protagonists in many places with the revival or re-establishment of architecture and design schools. In almost all cases, there was a conscious attempt to make a connection to the Bauhaus. Hermann Henselmann, together with Peter Keler, Gustav Hassenpflug and others,

dared to suggest a new approach to an academy for building and fine arts in Weimar. In Dessau, Hubert Hoffmann was the very first to try to reopen the Bauhaus with a planning association which he started. His plans were centred on Hannes Meyer, expanded by a biological, ecological approach. Attempts at beginnings in Dresden and Berlin-Weissensee were associated with the likes of Mart Stam and Marianne Brandt.

But soon, often before the foundation of the GDR itself, these developments came to an end largely because they collided with a political system struggling for self-assertion in general, and with the Stalinist orientated concept of social realism in particular. The peak was the so-called "formalism debate", which started in 1951, in which the Bauhaus was condemned as an expression of late bourgeois ideology and thus detrimental to socialism. Nevertheless, there were opportunities in furniture design, and also in other areas—mainly industrial construction, trade-fair design, and the construction of embassy-like trade representations in Western countries—to continue along the modern way in the spirit of the Bauhaus.

The contemplation of industrial construction styles from the beginning of the 1950s seemed to have reopened some freedom for design:

> Forces of production strength development pushed the decorative style, which had been prescribed in a decree, aside. Despite, or even because of the intellectually unprocessed about-face from bigoted historicism to the evenly bigoted technicism of large slab building, the regime of desperate over-ideologisation remained.[54]

Experience from the "left-wing functionalism" of the 1920s, in which industrial social housing construction had had remarkable results, was not used. The beginning of a differentiated theoretical examination of the Bauhaus started only in 1962 with the German translation of an essay by the Soviet author Pazitnov, "The Creative Heritage of the Bauhaus." This was followed by exhibitions, magazine essays and book publications. From the mid–1970s the GDR pushed for Bauhaus research that was especially carried out by the Academy for Architecture and Building in Weimar, which organised five international Bauhaus conferences.

The ceremonial reopening of the preserved and reconstructed Bauhaus building on 4th December 1976 was not only an outer sign of a new level in the official appreciation of the Bauhaus heritage, it was also the result of many years of constant, if not powerful, pressure by different designers and scientists, not least by former Bauhaus students. With the Dessau Bauhaus, a place of conservation of the Bauhaus heritage and creative examination of design issues in environmental design was established in 1976, whose results disappeared into the reality of the GDR without lasting effects. Bauhaus's reception in the GDR was marked by a divergence from a socio-theoretical approach despite latent political commissioning.

## Bauhaus in Reunified Germany

Understanding of the Bauhaus since German reunification continues in the areas of museum and university research into its history, the preservation and teaching of its factual evidence, in the area of design as well as in the interconnection of political and economic goals. The basis for this process is the conviction that—in the opinion of the Bauhaus researcher and university lecturer Rainer Wick—the historic Bauhaus still disposes of a number of approaches which deserve our attention even in the digital age at the beginning of the twenty-first century.[55]

While the art of the Bauhaus students is scattered around the world in great museums and private collections, large public Bauhaus collections are located, for example, in Cambridge, Massachusetts, Tokyo, Milan and Paris, as well as in a number of public collections and museums in the Federal Republic of Germany, which focus expressly on the Bauhaus and its history, led by the Bauhaus Archive Museum of Design in Berlin. The inventory collected in this research and exhibition institution is unique in its scope and quality. In order to ensure a modern museum and archive operation in the future, the expansion of the Gropius building, which is bursting at the seams, with an investor building is planned.

The Bauhaus Museum of the Weimar Classic Foundation art collections are among the largest Bauhaus collections in the world. Since 1995, the museum has presented the history of the Weimar Bauhaus in a permanent exhibition opposite the German National Theatre. In Weimar too, consideration is being given to integrating the local Bauhaus collection into a new museum building.

The highest form of social recognition of the ideas and achievements of the Bauhaus took place in 1996, when the Bauhaus sites in Weimar and Dessau were included in the UNESCO World Heritage List. As a place of learning, research and experimental design, a public foundation was established at the Dessau Bauhaus building, which concerns itself with the expansion of a collection of preservation, research and teaching of the Bauhaus heritage. Furthermore, the Foundation Bauhaus Dessau, with its interdisciplinary work that includes research, teaching and design, is currently concerned with the city in particular, its contradictions and its cultural power in the conflict between population growth, globalisation and technological revolution.

With a similarly complex claim, the Academy for Architecture and Building in Weimar, which since 1996 has been called "Bauhaus-University Weimar", is trying to assert itself by endeavouring to contribute to the respective areas of art and science of construction, conception and design of present and future living spaces. Love of experimentation, openness, creativity, proximity to industrial practise and internationality are elementary reference points in its historic heritage for this Thuringian institution at its current location, as well as in the rooms of the former Bauhaus itself.

The *Zentrum für Kunst und Medientechnologie* (ZKM, Centre for Art and Media Technology), founded in 1988 in Karlsruhe also as a public foundation, is considered one of the most demanding and ambitious German enterprises that more or less expressly refer to the traditions of the Bauhaus as a "Bauhaus of the Present." Being a unique cultural institution, the ZKM in its work endeavours to respond to the rapid development of information technologies and the changing social structures that unite research and production, exhibitions and events, teaching and documentation. By applying the traditional arts to media technology and electronic production methods, it sees a new artistic and pedagogic project in the education sector.

The Bauhaus Europe can be listed as one of the last controversial projects, which seeks to express its ambitious goals in a largely content-free, apparently solely conceptual application. Located in Aachen, a city rich in tradition, the Bauhaus Europe, which is still in the developmental stages, is dedicated to the European integration process. As a European cultural centre, it is supposed to give further encouragement to European thought and take on cultural, political and educational tasks.

The Bauhaus does not only belong to Europe, it belongs to the whole world!

## Bauhaus: A Creative Method

The Bauhaus was simultaneously marked by socio-utopian visions and manifold attempts to implement a school for design in practise. A series of issues and problems of the early 1920s are currently reappearing in discussions on reforms in the education and university systems.

The Bauhaus—with its 150 to 200 students, its teachers, avant-garde artists as "Masters of Form" and master craftsmen, with as many as 50% foreign teaching staff among the Masters of Form and an average of 25% foreign students, with up to 50% female students, with first-years aged between 16 and 40 whose educational backgrounds ranged from middle school to post-graduate—formed a unique sociological basis for dynamic life and work processes in continuous dialogue and constant change.

Equal opportunities and free access for all talented young people were guaranteed through the preparatory course as a trial semester. Academic acceptance obstacles such as proof of high school or academy graduation were abolished and economic obstacles were at least cushioned by grants and scholarships. Sex, race, religion and nationality were no obstacles for acceptance into the Bauhaus community; on the contrary, the varied experience of its students made the study process more fertile.

The preparatory course taught mental and sensitivity training as well as creative play. All the senses were trained as well as the ability to concentrate. Detailed observation and precise analysis of the environment or the design exercise were part of the methods of training from the first semester: creativity training by today's standards.

The workshop training from the first day (Albers's preparatory course workshop since 1923) and the practical work in an architecture firm or at a construction site formed a completely new foundation for academic pedagogy, which previously had only been successfully employed in arts and crafts schools. Any artistic, scientific, technical-technological, economic or sociological, psychological or philosophical instruction was closely connected to the solving of projects in the workshop. In Weimar, the workshops were staffed with avant-garde artists with a love of experimentation as Masters of Form and rather straight-laced, traditional Masters of Craft. This dual system carried potential for conflict as well as creativity, as the students had to find their own way. The Bauhaus was probably also the first school in which communal work—teamwork—was programmed and starting in 1919 became a reality amongst the students. In practical design exercises and projects the students were able to work with each other.

Bauhaus pedagogy meant the opportunity for a training of all talents and the shaping of individual personalities. Along with the specialist training for designers or architects, the basics of fine and applied arts were also taught, as well as the performing arts. In this sense, the theatre workshop led by Oskar Schlemmer played a special role as a semi-professional cross-section workshop, the Bauhaus celebrations also being a most significant training ground for cross-disciplinary collaboration. The Bauhaus band became a well-known German jazz band. Playing, sports, dance and evening lectures completed the living and working community, which was also always a supportive society in times of trouble. The many marriages and lifelong friendships among Bauhaus students speak for the success of the social model.

In order to understand the Bauhaus and its successes, it is recommended that the reader turns away from traditional concepts of style or the comprehension of the Bauhaus style as an unintentional consequence, negating the creative methods of the Bauhaus with its creativity training, teamwork and workshop work, with its internationalism and permanent discourse. The Bauhaus was not characterised by preconceived schools of thought or style requirements, but by a high degree of individualism and pluralism.

# NOTES

1. Walter Gropius, Vorschläge zur Gründung einer Lehranstalt als künstlerische Beratungsstelle für Industrie, Gewerbe und Handwerk, 1916. Main Archive of the Free State of Thuringia in Weimar, File Hochschule für bildende Kunst 100, pp.22-29.

2. Walter Gropius, *Programm des Staatlichen Bauhauses in Weimar*, 1919. The Foundation of Weimar Classics, Inv. Nr. DK 1/87.

3. Main Archive of the Free State of Thuringia, Weimar, File Bauhaus 57, pp.2-75.

4. See manuscript dated March 10, 1910, Bauhaus Archive Berlin, Gropius Estate, in: Hartmut Probst, Christian Schädlich: Walter Gropius, Volume 3: *Selected Writings*, Berlin 1987, pp.18-25

5. Prof. Dr. Heine in: *Anhalter Anzeiger* dated 30.06.1932.

6. Bauhaus Dessau, Semester Plan 1927.

7. Walter Gropius, Grundsätze der Bauhausproduktion. In: Neue Erziehung (Jena), 7, 1925, Nr. 6, p.656.

8. The City of Dessau and Surroundings, Dessau 1926, p.6.

9. Letter by Hannes Meyer to Walter Gropius dated 01.03.1927, in: Meyer-Bergner, Lena (ed.): *Hannes Meyer, Bauen und Gesellschaft*, Dresden 1980, p.42.

10. Meyer, Hannes: Speaches given to Students on the occasion of his appointment of Director of the Bauhaus. Cited according to: Winkler, Klaus-Jürgen: Der Direktorenwechsel von 1928 und die Rolle Hannes Meyers am Bauhaus. In: Thesis- Wissenschaftliche Zeitschrift der Bauhaus-Universität Weimar, 4/5. Issue 1999, p.82.

11. See Nerdinger, Winfried: Zwischen Kunst und Wissenschaft: Positionen des Funktionalismus der Zwanziger Jahre, in: T. Valena and U. Winko (Eds.): *Prager Architektur und die europäische Moderne*, Berlin 2006, pp.121/122.

12. Meyer, Hannes: Mein Hinauswurf aus dem Bauhaus. Offener Brief an den Oberbürgermeister Hesse, in: *Das Tagebuch*, Berlin, 11 (1930), 33, p.1308 onwards.

13. Der Fall Bauhaus. In: *Stein Holz Eisen*. *44*.1930. Issue 19 of 10.06.1930 p.418.

14. See Bauhaus Diary, Entry dated 10.02.1932, in: Hahn, Peter (ed.): *bauhaus berlin*, Weingarten 1985, p.96.

15. Das Steglitzer „Bauhaus", in: *Steglitzer Anzeiger*. October 1932, cited according to: Hahn, Peter (ed.): *bauhaus berlin*, Weingarten 1985, p.93.

16. Ibid.

17. Johannes Itten; *Mein Vorkurs am Bauhaus. Gestaltungs- und Formenlehre*, Ravensburg 1963.

18. Albers lecture, presumably 1930, Bauhaus Archive Berlin.

19. Hannes Beckmann, Die Gründerjahre, in: Eckhard Neumann (ed.): *Bauhaus und Bauhäusler*, Cologne 1985, pp.275-277.

20. Wulf Herzogenrath, Stefan Kraus (eds.): *Erich Consemüller. Fotografien Bauhaus-Dessau*, Munich 1989, Fig. 155.

21. Petition by the Journeymen and Apprentices dated 10.20.1922, Main Archive of the Free State of Thuringia in Weimar, Bauhaus File 12, p.235.

22. Stasny, Peter: Von der Vorlehre zur Formlehre. Der Unterricht von Paul Klee, Wassily Kandinsky und Ludwig Hirschfeld-Mack, in: *Das frühe Bauhaus und Johannes Itten*, Weimar 1994, p.187.

23. Ostwald, Wilhelm: *Die Harmonie der Farben*, Leipzig 1921, p.1.

24. See Wick, Rainer K.: *Bauhaus-Pädagogik*, Cologne 1982, p.212.

25. Ibid.

26. Schlemmer, Oskar: Analysen eines Bildes und anderer Dinge, in: *Bauhaus*, Issue 4, 1929, p.6.

27. Klee, Paul: *Beiträge zur bildnerischen Formlehre*, 1921/22, published with transcription and preface by Jürgen Glaesemer, Basel-Stuttgart 1979, pp.155 and 158.

28. See Stasny, Peter: Von der Vorlehre zur Formlehre. Der Unterricht von Paul Klee, Wassily Kandinsky und Ludwig Hirschfeld-Mack, in: *Das frühe Bauhaus und Johannes Itten*, Weimar 1994, pp.182/183.

29. See Wick, Rainer K.: *Bauhaus-Pädagogik*, Cologne 1994, p.279.

30. Schlemmer, Oskar: Unterrichtsgebiete der Mensch, in: *Zeitschrift bauhaus*, Nr. 2/3, 1928, p. 23.

31. Wick, Rainer K., *ibid*. p.308.

32. Hannes Meyer, Mein Hinauswurf aus dem Bauhaus, 1930. In: Hannes Meyer, *Bauen und Gesellschaft*, Dresden 1980, pp.67-73.

33. See Klaus-Jürgen Winkler: *Der Architekt Hannes Meyer. Anschauungen und Werk*, Berlin, 1989, pp.91-106

34. Eckard Neumann, *Bauhaus und Bauhäusler*, Cologne 1985, p.50 onwards.

35. Walter Gropius, Programm zur Gründung einer allgemeinen Hausbaugesellschaft auf künstlerisch einheitlicher Grundlage m.b.H., in: Hartmut Probst, Christian Schädlich: *Walter Gropius*, Volume 3: Selected Writings, Berlin,1987, pp.18-25.

36. Walter Gropius, *Programm und Manifest des Bauhauses*, Weimar 1919, Classic Foundation Weimar, Inv.-Nr. DK 1/87

37. See Klaus-Jürgen Winkler: *Baulehre und Entwerfen am Bauhaus 1919-1933*, Weimar 2003

38. See Adolf Meyer: *Ein Versuchshaus des Bauhauses in Weimar*, Munich 1925 (Bauhaus books 3) and Bernd Rudolf (Ed.): *Haus am Horn*. Rekonstruktion einer Utopie, Weimar, 2000.

39. See Klaus-Jürgen Winkler: *Der Architekt Hannes Meyer. Anschauungen und Werk*, Berlin, 1989, pp.61-72.

40. Fiedler, Jeannine: T. Lux Feininger: „Ich bin Maler und nicht Fotograf!", in: Fiedler, Jeannine and Feierabend, Peter (eds.): *Fotografie am Bauhaus. Überblick über eine Periode der Fotografie im 20. Jahrhundert* Berlin, 1990, p.45.

41. Glüher, Gerhard: *Licht-Bild-Medium. Untersuchungen zur Fotografie am Bauhaus*, Berlin, 1994, p.59.

42. Glüher, ibid., p.60 and Wick, Rainer K.: Mythos Bauhaus-Fotografie, in: *Das Neue Sehen*, Munich 1991, p.22.

43. Meyer, Hannes: *Junge Menschen kommt ans Bauhaus*, Dessau, 1929, no page.

44. Sachsse, Rolf: *Bild und Bau. Zur Nutzung technischer Medien beim Entwerfen von Architektur*, Wiesbaden, 1997, p.145.

45. Meeting Transcript dated 5 March 1930 and manuscript of Notice for Students at the Bauhaus – Dessau, approx. 1930, Foundation Bauhaus Dessau Archive.

46. Peterhans, Walter: Zum gegenwärtigen Stand der Photographie, in: *RED*, Issue 5, Prague, 1930, pp.138-141.

47. Wick, Rainer K.: Mythos Bauhaus-Fotografie, in: *Das Neue Sehen*, Munich, 1991, p.15.

48. Kállai, Ernst: Zehn Jahre Bauhaus, in : Die Weltbühne, 26 (1930) 4. Cited according to: Kállai, Ernst: *Vision und Formgesetz*, Dresden, 1980, p.138.

49. For statistical data see: See Dietzsch, Folke: *Die Studierenden am Bauhaus*, Dissertation, *Hochschule für Architektur und Bauwesen Weimar*, 1991.

50. Kallai, Ernst: 10 Jahre Bauhaus, in: *Die Weltbühne*, Vol. 26, 1930, Nr. 4.

51. Gropius, Walter: Response to a Survey of the Working Council for Art, in: *Ja! Stimmen des Arbeitsrates für Kunst in Berlin*, 1919.

52. Molnar, Farkas: Das Leben im Bauhaus, in: *Wechselwirkungen*, Marburg 1986, p.274.

53. See Grawe, Daniela Diana: *Die Mitglieder des Bauhauses in Nordamerika*, Dissertation, Hochschule der Künste Berlin 1998.

54. Hüter, Karl Heinz: Das Bauhaus in der DDR – Schwierigkeiten einer Rezeption, in: Gillen, Eckhardt and Haarmann, Rainer (eds.): *Kunst in der DDR*, Cologne, 1990, p.436.

55. Wick, Rainer K.: Bauhaus. *Kunstschule der Moderne*, Ostfildern-Ruit, 2000, p.8.

# Chronology

## Bauhaus 1919

Walter Gropius becomes director of the Academy of Fine Art, which includes the former School of Arts and Crafts in Weimar. This Staatliche Bauhaus Weimar is an institution operated by the Free State of Saxony-Weimar-Eisenach. Walter Gropius issues a manifesto and programme which reads:

> The Bauhaus is committed to forging all forms of artistic creation into a single whole, to bringing back together all artistic disciplines–sculpture, painting, arts and crafts, and manual trades–and making them integral components of a new art of building.

Gropius moves his office from Berlin to Weimar. The first Bauhaus signet is created following a design by Bauhaus student Karl Peter Röhl. The first meeting of the Council of Masters is attended by the professors from the former Academy of Arts (Max Thedy, Walther Klemm, Otto Fröhlich, Richard Engelmann). Lyonel Feininger, Johannes Itten and Gerhard Marcks are appointed. The criticism Walter Gropius levels at the first exhibition of students' work raises tensions with some of the students and the old Academy staff. The Bauhaus brings together workshops and classes in: stone sculpture, painting (Johannes Itten), graphics and printing (Walther Klemm), drawing, anatomy, bookbinding (Otto Dorfner) and weaving (Helene Börner). These are joined in December by a gold, silver and coppersmiths' workshop (a private venture run by Naum Slutzky). Johannes Itten starts teaching the trial semester, later to become the *Vorkurs*, the preparatory course, an integral part of the curriculum from 1921. Gertrud Granow launches her course on harmonisation theory. Adherents of the German National Party among the students and the people of Weimar condemn what they see as Spartacist and Bolshevist influences at the Bauhaus.
The Bauhaus has 101 female and 106 male students.

## Politics 1919

Spartacus revolt in Berlin. Assassination of Liebknecht and Luxemburg. Elections to the National Assembly: Conservative Parties 44, National Liberals 22, other Liberals 75, Centrists 91, Social Democrats 163, Independent Social democrats 22, others 4 seats.
1 Dollar = 8.50 Marks (1913: 1 Dollar = 4.20 Marks). The National Assembly is convened in response to the street fighting in Berlin and Weimar. The Social Democrat Friedrich Ebert is elected President. The Scheidemann administration disbands workers' and soldiers' councils. A general strike is put down in Berlin and other cities. Bavarian Soviet Republic. 1 Dollar = 13.50 Marks. The Treaty of Versailles is signed. Weimar Constitution.

## Science, Technology, Arts 1919

Science and Technology: First address relayed by PA system in Berlin. German airmail gets underway between Berlin and Weimar. Hugo Junkers' F13, the world's first all-metal plane, takes to the air in Dessau. Literature: *Demian* by Hermann Hesse, *The Last Days of Mankind* by Karl Kraus. Theatre and Music: Max Reinhardt stages *Oresteia* (Aeschylus). Mary Wigman develops expressive dance. Film: Robert Wiene *The Cabinet of Dr. Caligari*. Arts: Le Corbusier and Amédée Ozenfant found the magazine *L' Esprit Nouveau* in Paris. Painting: major futurist exhibition in Milan. Architecture: Auguste and Gustave Perret design Esders clothing factory, Paris.

## Bauhaus 1920

The painter Georg Muche, from the circle of the Berlin gallery *Der Sturm* is appointed. He joins as Master of Form in woodcarving and bookbinding. German National Party members in Weimar publish a polemic against the Bauhaus. The Bauhaus responds with a brochure of its own, including a message of support by the Thuringian Minister of Culture. Walter Gropius turns down leading Dadaist Johannes Baader's offer to join the Bauhaus. First Bauhaus evenings, including a lecture by Else Lasker-Schüler, a paper by Bruno Taut and concerts. For a short while the Bauhaus has its own department of architecture (headed by Adolf Meyer). Establishment of a copper and silver smithy (later metal workshop), a stone and wood-sculpting workshop, a decorative painting workshop (later mural painting) and a carpenter's shop. According to the conceptual combination of art and manual trades, the workshops are led by a craftsman as Master of Craft and an artist as Master of Form. Max Krehan (Master of Craft) and Gerhard Marcks (Master of Form) set up a pottery workshop in Dornburg. Classes begin in October. Johannes Itten teaches the preparatory course which is henceforth obligatory for all students, and also teaches material and design studies to develop creativity. Lyonel Feininger's works exhibited at the Museum of Arts and Crafts in Weimar, Paul Klee's works at the Kunstverein in Jena. Theo van Doesburg visits the Bauhaus.
The school has 62 female and 81 male students.

## Politics 1920

1 Dollar = 49.80 Marks. The Treaty of Versailles comes into force (territorial losses, occupation, reparations). Fighting between the red Ruhr Army and the German *Reichswehr*. Militant right-wing Kapp-Lüttwitz *Putsch* against the government in Berlin and other cities foiled by general strike by the unions. Reichstag elections: conservative parties 71, national liberals 65, other liberals 39, centrists 90, social democrats 102, independent social democrats 81, communists 2, others 9 seats. League of Nations established.

## Science, Technology, Arts 1920

Science and Technology: *Notgemeinschaft der deutschen Wissenschaft* founded, death of sociologist Max Weber, spectral analysis produces first findings on stellar atmosphere. Literature: *The Theory of the Novel* by Gyorgy Lukacs, Knut Hamsun awarded Nobel Prize for Literature. Theatre and Music: *The Dead City* by Erich Korngold, *Concord Sonata* by Charles Ives. Film: Fred Niblo *The Mark of Zorro*, *The Golem* by Paul Wegener. Arts: Vkhutemas (abbreviation for Higher Artistic-Technical Workshops, from 1927 Academy) founded in Moscow. Teachers at this school (comparable to the Bauhaus) include Kazimir Malevich, Wassily Kandinsky, Alexander Rodchenko, Vladimir Tatlin and El Lissitzky. Art: *Realistic Manifesto* by Naum Gabo and Antoine Pevsner. Dada demonstration in Cologne. Architecture: Vladimir Tatlin's *Monument to the Third International* (project), Moscow.

## Bauhaus 1921

Paul Klee and Oskar Schlemmer are appointed. The constitution of the Staatliches Bauhaus at Weimar is published, which will remain in force, after a revision, from 1923 to 1925. The teachers are called Masters, the students apprentices and Journeymen. The Bauhaus now incorporates the following workshops and Masters of Form: stone sculpture (Schlemmer), woodcarving (Muche), carpentry (Gropius), pottery (Marcks), gold, silver and copper smithies (Itten), mural painting and stained glass painting (Itten), weaving (Muche), graphic printing (Feininger), bookbinding (Klee). Gropius's architectural practise (Walter Gropius, Adolf Meyer, and Carl Fieger) designs and builds a residence for the Berlin entrepreneur Adolf

Sommerfeld in Berlin-Dahlem. Almost all Bauhaus workshops participate in the interior furnishing. Walter Gropius designs the Memorial to the Victims of the Right-Wing *Putsch* of March 1920, which is erected at the Weimar cemetery. The State Academy of Fine Arts is re-established by professors defecting from the Bauhaus. Walter Gropius is commissioned to convert the Municipal Theatre in Jena. Paul Klee starts his classes, which he calls "practical training in composition". Johannes Itten attends a congress of the Zoroastrian Mazdaznan sect in Leipzig and introduces this esoteric doctrine of salvation (founded by the German-Russian Ottoman Zar-Adusht Otto Hanish in the US) at the Bauhaus in collaboration with Georg Muche. Gropius delivers lectures on the theory of space and practical technical drawing, supplemented by seminars from Adolf Meyer. The expressionist artist Lothar Schreyer becomes head of the theatre workshop. The Council of Masters resolves to publish the Bauhaus prints. The *Dragon Festival* is celebrated in the autumn. Tuition fees are 120 Marks per semester, twelve students are relieved of school fees for the winter semester.
The Bauhaus has 44 female and 64 male students.

## Politics 1921

German-Soviet economic agreement. Government of social democrats, German democrats and centrists. Walter Rathenau (German Democratic Party, AEG general manager) becomes Minister of Reconstruction. Hyperinflation begins:
1 Dollar = 88 Marks. Separate German-American peace treaty.
1 Dollar = 209 Marks.

## Science. Technology. Arts. 1921

Science and Technology: Albert Einstein awarded Nobel Prize for Physics, invention of coal liquefaction, insulin discovered. Literature: Jaroslav Hasek *The Good Soldier Schweik*. André Gide *Fruits of the Earth*. Theatre and Music: *Murderer: the Women's Hope* by Paul Hindemith and Oskar Kokoschka. Arturo Toscanini becomes Director of La Scale in Milan. Film: Charlie Chaplin *The Kid*. Hans Richter *Rhythmus 21*. Fritz Lang *Between Two Worlds*. Painting: Pablo Picasso *Three Musicians*. Francis Picabia *l'Oeil cacodylate*. Architecture: Erich Mendelsohn Einstein-Tower, Potsdam.

## Bauhaus 1922

Oskar Schlemmer designs a new Bauhaus signet. Johannes Itten resigns as head of the metal and furniture workshop. Theo von Doesburg launches his *De Stijl* course in Weimar, attracting a group of Bauhaus Masters and students. Adolf Meyer, previously office manager in Walter Gropius's architecture practise, becomes extraordinary Master of Architecture. Exhibition of works by Bauhaus apprentices and Journeymen. Institution of the Bauhaus housing co-operative, designed to forge a single community of everyone at the Bauhaus. The government of Thuringia calls for the work of the Bauhaus to be presented at an exhibition of achievement. All energies are directed to this event, which finally takes place in 1923. The Council of Masters decides in the autumn to display a show-house at the exhibition with all interior decorations in order to demonstrate the collaboration of all workshops. Inauguration of the Monument to the Victims of the March 1920 *Putsch* at Weimar cemetery. Architecture exhibition at the Bauhaus: works by Walter Gropius and Adolf Meyer. Wassily Kandinsky is appointed. He heads the mural painting workshop and begins his design classes called "Colour." The conflict between Gropius, who demands an opening of the Bauhaus to external commissions, and Itten, who rejects this in principle and favours the autonomous artist, intensifies and touches on the institution's very existence. Gropius's architecture practise enters the *Chicago Tribune* competition. Lantern and midsummer celebrations. The Bauhaus Masters display their works at the first Thuringian Exhibition of Art in Weimar. Oskar Schlemmer's *Triadic Ballet* is premiered in Stuttgart. The municipal theatre redesigned by Walter Gropius opens in Jena. Congress of the Constructivist International in Weimar (Theo van Doesburg, Max Burchartz, László Moholy-Nagy et al.). Works by Klee, Kandinsky and Feininger are installed in several rooms at the Schlossmuseum in Weimar. A group of Bauhaus students favouring constructivism join together to form KURI (German acronym for "constructive, utilitarian, rational and international"). Bauhaus Exhibition in Calcutta, India.
The Bauhaus has 48 female and 71 male students.

## Politics 1922

1 Dollar = 186.75 Marks. Treaty of Rapallo between Soviet Russia and Germany (waiving of reparations, institution of normal diplomatic and trade relations). Foreign Minister Walter Rathenau is assassinated. National Socialist Party (NDSAP) banned in Prussia, Saxony, Thuringia and elsewhere.
1 Dollar = 1,298.37 Marks.
1 Dollar = 7,500 Marks.

## Science, Technology, Arts 1922

Science and Technology: Niels Bohr explains the periodic system of the elements, vitamin E discovered. Literature: *Drums in the Night* by Bertolt Brecht, *Ulysses* by James Joyce. Theatre and Music: Arnold Schönberg develops twelve-tone music, Louis Armstrong makes his first recordings in Chicago. Film: *Nosferatu* by Friedrich Wilhelm Murnau, *Cops* by Buster Keaton. First talkie. Arts: First monumental mural in Mexico, Man Ray invents the rayograph, *The Art of the Insane* by Hans Prinzhorn. Architecture: Ludwig Mies van der Rohe designs a Berlin office block in reinforced concrete (project). Le Corbusier *Ville Contemporaine* (project), Paris.

## Bauhaus 1923

A majority of Bauhaus members rejects Lothar Schreyer's play *Mondspiel*. He leaves the Bauhaus, Oskar Schlemmer heads the Bauhaus Theatre (together with the stone sculpture and woodcarving workshops). Itten departs for new pastures and is succeeded by László Moholy-Nagy, who takes over the *Vorkurs* and the metal workshop in October. Josef Albers heads the study of materials and the stained glass workshop. Walter Gropius delivers a paper on the *Unity of Art, Technology and Science* in Hanover. German Nationalist members of the Thuringian parliament criticise the organisation and management of the Bauhaus. The Education Minister speaks in its defence. Bauhaus Exhibition in Weimar with several displays (including international architecture, with works by Le Corbusier, Ludwig Mies van der Rohe, J. J. P. Oud and others), wall designs in the Bauhaus building (Herbert Bayer, Joost Schmidt, Oskar Schlemmer), publications (*Staatliches Bauhaus Weimar 1919-1923*) and special events including the *Mechanical Ballet* by Kurt Schmidt and Georg Teltscher in Jena. The pinnacle of achievement is the *Haus am Horn* (idea and design by Georg Muche, assisted by Adolf Meyer) with furniture and objects by Marcel Breuer, Erich Dieckmann, Benita Otte, Gyula Pap and others. Walter Gropius opens the Exhibition with a paper entitled "Art and Technology—A New Unity". He seeks to separate the production workshops from teaching. Classes by Paul Klee and Wassily Kandinsky accompany the two-semester preparatory course. The army searches Walter Gropius's home in response to an anonymous political tip-off.
The Bauhaus has 41 female and 73 male students.

## Politics 1923

French troops occupy the Ruhr, passive civil resistance.
1 Dollar = 21,000 Marks

1 Dollar = 78,250 Marks.
1 Dollar = 1,100,000 Marks.
60% of Germans jobless. General strike. Stresemann administration (grand coalition). Postwar crisis reaches a climax.
1 Dollar = 2 trillion Marks. The Rentenmark is introduced on the basis of land ownership: 1 Rentenmark = 1,000 billion paper Marks.
Communist revolts in Saxony, Thuringia and Hamburg. Workers' government of independent social democrats and communists in Thuringia overthrown by the army. Hitler-Ludendorff *Putsch* put down in Munich. NDSAP banned throughout Germany. Marx (centrist) administration. Dawes Plan stabilises German currency.

## Science, Technology, Arts 1923

Science and Technology: Madsen develops whooping cough vaccine, wireless photo-telegraphy between Italy and United States, Henry Ford's autobiography *My Life and Work* appears in German translation. German public radio goes on air. Electronic image transmission. Literature: Rainer Maria Rilke *Duinese Elegies, Sonnets to Orpheus*. Film: James P. Johnson *The Charleston*. Harold Lloyd *Safety Last*. Arts: Marcel Duchamp *The Large Glass, or the Bride Stripped Bare by her Bachelors, Even*. El Lissitzky Proun Room in Berlin. Architecture: Le Corbusier *Vers Une Architecture*. Erich Mendelsohn hat factory, Luckenwalde.

## Bauhaus 1924

Conservative forces in the Thuringian government demand the closure of the Bauhaus. Marcel Breuer, Georg Muche and Farkas Molnár pen a memorandum on the institution of an architecture department. The Bauhaus is represented at the building exhibition in Stuttgart. By way of precaution, the provincial government terminates the Masters' and the director's employment contracts with effect from 31st December 1925, after it is concluded that the Bauhaus is unprofitable. The Landtag budget committee debates the Bauhaus and slashes its budget from 146,000 to 50,000 Marks. Plans are made to transform the Bauhaus into a limited company. The Bauhaus band is founded. Bauhaus Festival celebrating five years of existence. Hendrik P. Berlage, Peter Behrens, Marc Chagall, Albert Einstein, Oskar Kokoschka, Arnold Schönberg and others join together to form the Society of Friends of the Bauhaus. The Bauhaus Director and Masters write an open letter stating the Bauhaus is to be abolished with effect from 1st April 1925.
At this time the Bauhaus has 45 female and 82 male students.

## Politics 1924

Reichstag elections: extreme right 32, conservative parties 95, national liberals 45, other liberals 28, centrists 81, social democrats 100, communists 62, others 29 seats. Allied conference in London adopts Dawes plan and resolves to withdraw occupying French troops from the Ruhr. The Reichsmark replaces the Rentenmark. Reichstag endorses Dawes plan. Industrial output rises to 71.9% of 1913 level. Reichstag elections: extreme right 14, conservative parties 103, national liberals 51, other liberals 32, centrists 88, social democrats 131, communists 45, others 29 seats.

## Science, Technology, Arts 1924

Science and Technology: *Australopithecus* remains found, ten millionth car by Ford, rotary printer invented. Literature: Thomas Mann *The Magic Mountain*. Theatre and Music: Arthur Honegger *Pacific 231*. George Gershwin *Rhapsody in Blue*. Film: Fritz Lang *Nibelungen*. Buster Keaton *The Navigator*. Arts: André Breton *Manifeste du Surréalisme*. Otto Dix *War*. Architecture: Schröder House by Gerrit Rietveld, Utrecht. Fritz Höger Chilehaus, Hamburg.

## Bauhaus 1925

Several cities want to take on the Bauhaus. Klee, Muche and Feininger hold talks with Dessau Mayor, Fritz Hesse, on the relocation of the Bauhaus to Dessau. Dessau City Council resolves to take over the Bauhaus, in spite of opposition from the right-wing. Farewell celebration in Weimar. The fiscal committee of Dessau Council approves the erection of the Bauhaus building (design: Walter Gropius). Relocation from Weimar to Dessau. Official start of classes in Dessau on 1st April. All Masters of Form except Gerhard Marcks move to Dessau. Former students, now Junior Masters, take over the workshops and thus the role of Masters of Form: Josef Albers (preparatory class), Herbert Bayer (typography), Marcel Breuer (furniture), Hinnerk Scheper (mural painting), Joost Schmidt (sculpture), Gunta Stölzl (weaving). The pottery, stained glass painting, woodcarving and stone sculpting workshops are not continued in Dessau. The posts of Masters of Craft and master craftsmen continue to be staffed in order to be able to train apprentices. Classes are held at the Municipal School of Arts, Crafts and Manual Trades pending completion of the Bauhaus building, while the workshops are based in storerooms at a mail order firm. The first of the series of Bauhaus books appears with works by Walter Gropius, Paul Klee, Adolf Meyer, Oskar Schlemmer, Piet Mondrian, Theo van Doesburg and László Moholy-Nagy. Visits to industry and landscapes are part and parcel of teaching at the Bauhaus. The Bauhaus in Dessau switches to the lower case in all its writings and adheres to DIN standards. At talks in Weimar Gropius secures the rights of ownership for the Dessau Bauhaus of all items produced in the Bauhaus workshops up to 1st April 1925. 165 selected workshop items (design objects) are donated to the Staatlichen Kunstsammlungen in Weimar. Bauhaus Ltd is incorporated to market the products developed by the Bauhaus. Some Dessau citizens form an association to oppose the Bauhaus. Topping-out ceremony for the Masters' houses.
The Bauhaus has 28 female and 73 male students.

## Politics 1925

Death of the president of the German Reich, Friedrich Ebert, Paul von Hindenburg succeeds him. National Socialist Party (NDSAP) re-founded with 270,000 members. Locarno Conference, a move to safeguard peace in Europe. The annual number of owner-occupied and rented dwellings completed as detached, semi-detached or multi-family houses in non-perimeter block developments rises from 106,502 in 1925 to 317,682 in 1929. Growing urbanisation: 26.8% of Germans live in cities with more than 100,000 inhabitants in 1925, 30.4% in 1933.

## Science, Technology, Arts 1925

Werner Heisenberg and others develop quantum mechanics. Television technology begins in Germany. Literature: *Manhattan Transfer* by John Dos Passos, *Inquisiciones* by Jorge Luis Borges. Theatre and Music: *Wozzeck* by Alban Berg, George Balanchine takes over the Ballets Russes in Paris. Film: *The Gold Rush* by Charlie Chaplin, *Battleship Potemkin* by Sergey Eisenstein. Art: International Arts and Crafts Exhibition in Paris (Art Deco), *New Objectivity* exhibition in Mannheim. First exhibition of surrealist paintings in Paris, Paul Klee participates. Architecture: Pessac Housing Project near Bordeaux by Le Corbusier and Pierre Jeanneret; Soviet Pavilion in Paris by Konstantin Melnikov.

## Bauhaus 1926

The workshops are subdivided into teaching and productive sections. Topping-out ceremony for the Bauhaus building, followed by celebration (Festival in White) at the community and youth centre. Students move into the studio building. The workshops move to the Bauhaus building and the new constitution is issued: "It is the purpose of the Bauhaus… to:

(1) shape the intellectual, craft and technical abilities of creatively talented human beings to equip them for design work, particularly construction, and (2) perform practical experiments, notably in housing construction and interiors, and to develop models for industry and the manual trades."

The Bauhaus is an Institute for Design. Study courses now lead to the Bauhaus diploma. The Bauhaus building is inaugurated in the presence of more than 1,000 guests from home and abroad. The first issue of the magazine *Bauhaus* appears. A grassroots association in Dessau decides to protest against the "un-German" Bauhaus (including a leafleting campaign to coincide with the inauguration). The first buildings of the Dessau-Törten development (design: Walter Gropius) are presented to the public. The Masters' houses designed by Gropius are completed and handed over to the future inhabitants.

The Bauhaus has 28 female and 73 male students.

## Politics 1926

German-Soviet neutrality pact (Treaty of Berlin) signed. Plebiscite on expropriation of the aristocracy defeated. Germany becomes a permanent member of the League of Nations, moves towards German-French reconciliation.

## Science, Technology, Arts 1926

Science and Technology: 16mm film developed. Roald Amundsen and Umberto Nobile fly over the North Pole in an airship. First liquid-fuel rocket. Literature: *The Castle* by Franz Kafka (posthumously), *The Seven Pillars of Wisdom* by T.E. Lawrence. Theatre and Music: Giaccomo Puccini's last opera *Turandot* premiered (posthumously) at La Scala, *First Symphony* by Dmitri Shostakovich. Film: *Nana* by Jean Renoir, *Mother* by Vsevolod Pudovkin. Arts: Classes begin at the *Staatliche Hochschule für Handwerk und Baukunst*, the Bauhaus's successor school in Weimar, headed by Otto Bartning. Max Ernst develops frottage, Adolf Loos builds a house in Paris for Tristan Tzara, a group of architects establishes *Der Ring*.

## Bauhaus 1927

The architecture department opens under the guidance of the Swiss architect Hannes Meyer. Georg Muche and Richard Paulick experimental steel house is completed in Dessau-Törten. Institution of a "Seminar for Free Sculpting and Painting" with free painting classes (Wassily Kandinsky, Paul Klee, Lyonel Feininger, Joost Schmidt). Gret Palucca dances on the Bauhaus stage. The Bauhaus Dessau participates in the German Theatre Exhibition in Magdeburg. The fourth regular meeting of the Regional Planning Association (settlements committee) for the central German industrial region is convened in the Bauhaus. The right-wing Dessau press stirs up opinion against Bauhaus Masters. Georg Muche leaves the Bauhaus. Gunta Stölzl takes over the weaving workshop. Béla Bartók gives a concert in the hall, organised by the Society of Friends of the Bauhaus. Festival of Catchwords.

The Bauhaus has 41 female and 125 male students.

## Politics 1927

1.3 million unemployed in Germany. The German economy grows back to its 1913 level. Local employment exchanges come under the Reich. Compulsory unemployment insurance introduced throughout the Reich.

## Science, Technology, Arts 1927

Science and Technology: 15 millionth car by Ford, Charles Lindbergh flies non-stop across the Atlantic, theory of chemical bonding. Literature: *Being and Time* by Martin Heidegger, *Steppenwolf* by Hermann Hesse. Theatre and Music: Josephine Baker in Paris, Erwin Piscator founds theatre in Berlin. Music: *Black and Tan Fantasy* by Duke Ellington. Film: *Metropolis* by Fritz Lang, *Berlin: Symphony of a Metropolis* by Walter Ruttmann, *Napoléon* by Abel Gance. Arts: El Lissitzky's *Cabinet of the Abstract* in Hanover, Malevich section at the Grand Berlin Art Exhibition. Architecture: Dymaxion House by Richard Buckminster Fuller, *Werkbund* Exposition, *The Apartment* in Stuttgart (*Weißenhofsiedlung*) co-ordinated by Ludwig Mies van der Rohe, Bruno Taut *A House*.

## Bauhaus 1928

Beard-Nose-Heart Festival at the Bauhaus (to mark its ninth anniversary). Walter Gropius is commissioned to build a new employment office for the city of Dessau. Official resignation of Walter Gropius. Moholy-Nagy, Herbert Bayer and Marcel Breuer leave the Bauhaus with him. Hannes Meyer is appointed Gropius's successor at the latter's suggestion. He criticises formalist tendencies at the Bauhaus and gears it to scientific principles and the "needs of the common people rather than luxuries". A group of Bauhaus members (Gunta Stölzl, Arieh Sharon and Peer Bücking) go to Moscow where they visit the Higher Art and Technical Workshops Vkhutein. Marianne Brandt steps in as head of the metal workshop until 1929. Design sales (metal lamps and later textiles) to industry. Mussorgsky's *Pictures at an Exhibition* is performed at the Dessau Friedrich Theatre with stage decor by Wassily Kandinsky. Kandinsky's painting class exhibits its works at the Anhaltische Gemäldegalerie. Oskar Schlemmer starts his "Man" course. The Bauhaus exhibits photos by its members. The Hungarian Ernst Kállai becomes editor of the magazine *Bauhaus* (until 1929). The Bauhaus Dessau is represented at the Congress of Art Educationalists in Prague. The Constructivist Naum Gabo delivers a series of papers on fundamental design issues. Bauhaus members debate modern architecture, the Bauhaus and Vkhutein (previously Vkhutemas) with El Lissitzky. Lu Märten presents a paper on historical dialectics and experimentation. The architect Mart Stam becomes a visiting lecturer (until 1929). The engineer Alcar Rudelt holds structural engineering classes at the Bauhaus (until 1933).

The Bauhaus has 46 female and 120 male students.

## Politics 1928

Reichstag elections: NDSAP 12, conservative parties 73, national liberals 45, other liberals 25, centrists 78, social democrats 153, communists 54, others 51 seats. The government decides with NSDAP support to build armoured cruiser "A."

## Science, Technology, Arts 1928

Science and Technology: Alexander Fleming discovers penicillin, first flight around the world. CFCs discovered. Literature: *Orlando* by Virginia Woolf, the *Gypsy Ballads* by Federico García Lorca. Theatre and Music: *Threepenny Opera* by Kurt Weill and Bertolt Brecht, *Bolero* by Maurice Ravel. Film: *October* by Sergey Eisenstein, first film by Walt Disney featuring Mickey Mouse, *Heir to Genghis Khan*, or *Storm over Asia* by Vsevolod Pudovkin. Art: *Dutch Interior I* by Joan Miró, *Großstadt* by Otto Dix, German edition of *Surrealism and Painting* by André Breton. Architecture and design: The so-called Budapest Bauhaus Mühely is founded. International press exhibition (*Pressa*) in Cologne with Pavilion by El Lissitzky, Institution of the Congrès Internationaux d'Architecture Moderne (CIAM) in La Sarraz, Switzerland, Rusakov Workers' Club, Moscow by Konstantin Melnikov.

## Bauhaus 1929

The *bauhaus-wanderschau* exhibition tours Basel, Essen, Mannheim, Breslau and Zurich with products from all workshops. Works of Bauhaus Masters exhibited at the Kunsthalle Basel. An exhibition of young Bauhaus painters tours Braunschweig, Krefeld, Halle an der Aaale, Erfurt

and Berlin. Kandinsky exhibtion in Paris. *Metallic Festival*. The Bauhaus Dessau is represented at the Leipzig Spring Fair. The Bauhaus Theatre travels to Berlin, Breslau, Frankfurt-am-Main, Stuttgart and Basel. Anton Brenner runs a construction studio (until summer 1930). Photographer Walter Peterhans is appointed head of the new photography workshop. Topping-out ceremony for the German Labour Unions School in Bernau near Berlin. Built by Hannes Meyer and Hans Wittwer, the school drew on the work of the building department and all workshops at the Bauhaus Dessau. Otto Neurath of Vienna delivers a paper on visual statistics and the present day. Masters' contracts extended for another five years. Design of Junkers & Co stand at the Gas and Water Exhibition in Berlin (Joost Schmidt and Bauhaus students). The metal, furniture and mural-painting workshops are merged to form the interior decoration department headed by Alfred Arndt. The *Bauhaus people's apartment* is displayed at an exhibition in the Grassi Museum, Leipzig. Oskar Schlemmer leaves the Bauhaus and takes up a post in Breslau. The Bauhaus Theatre develops into an *agitprop* theatre (until 1930). Ludwig Hilberseimer becomes lecturer in urban planning. The students become politically more extreme. The KPD (Communist Party) members among them join together to form KOSTUFRA (German acronym for Communist Students Group). 32,000 Reichsmarks in licence revenues are paid out to the students through the company Bauhaus Ltd. The workshops are represented at the World Exhibition in Barcelona.
The Bauhaus has 58 female and 143 male students.

## Politics 1929
22.8 million unemployed in Germany. Bloody May: the Berlin chief of police (SPD) attempts to enforce a ban on demonstrations on the 1st of May by force of arms (33 dead). France puts forward the idea of a United States of Europe to the League of Nations. French government overthrown. Petition for a referendum in Germany against the Young Plan (reparations of 34.5 billion Goldmarks). Black Friday on the New York Stock Exchange unleashes the Great Depression. The Reichstag rejects the Young Plan bill.

## Science, Technology, Arts 1929
Science and Technology: First International Congress on the History of Science in Paris, Edwin P. Hubble develops the idea of the expanding universe, Albert Einstein *General Field Theory*, first TV broadcast in Berlin. Literature: *The Philosophy of Symbolic Forms* by Ernst Cassirer, *Berlin Alexanderplatz* by Alfred Döblin, *Deutschland, Deutschland über alles* by Kurt Tucholsky and John Heartfield, *All Quiet on the Western Front* by Erich Maria Remarque, *The Revolt of the Masses* by José Ortega y Gasset. Theatre and Music: *Cyankali* by Friedrich Wolf, *Political Theatre* by Erwin Piscator. Film: *Un chien andalou* by Luis Buñuel and Salvador Dalí, first German talkies. Arts: Film and Photo Exhibition in Stuttgart (with Bauhaus representation), founding of the New York Museum of Modern Art, opening of the new building of the Folkwang Museum in Essen. Architecture: German Pavilion by Ludwig Mies van der Rohe at the Barcelona World Exposition, 2nd CIAM Congress, *The Apartment for the Subsistence Level* in Frankfurt-am-Main, exhibition *Home and Workroom* by the *Werkbund* in Breslau.

## Bauhaus 1930
Developed in 1929, the Bauhaus wallpaper is now available by retail and becomes the school's most successful product. Eduard Heiberg teaches architecture at the Bauhaus until the middle of the year. Visiting lecturer Karel Teige holds a course on contemporary literature and typography. Bauhaus carnival with political protests by students, Bauhaus attacked in the right-wing press. A group of students (including Hubert Hoffmann) start a study on the Dessau housing master plan which three

Bauhaus members continue, by arrangement with Walter Gropius, after graduating. The study produces forty-seven plans, which are presented at the 4th CIAM congress in 1933. Visiting lecturer Count Karlfried von Dürckheim delivers papers on design psychology (intermittently until 1932). Completion of the housing blocks with balcony access by Hannes Meyer and students of the building department in the expansion of Dessau-Törten development. Hannes Meyer is called to account for the growing politicisation of the Bauhaus and dismissed by the city of Dessau as communist-oriented students step up their activities. He leaves for Moscow with several Bauhaus students. The Bauhaus is closed. At Gropius's suggestion, Ludwig Mies van der Rohe becomes the new director. The school is re-opened with a new constitution which forbids all political student activities. All students have to renew their application to the Bauhaus at the beginning of the winter semester. Mies van der Rohe streamlines study courses and focuses more on architecture, notably the connection between the technology of building and aesthetic issues. Workshop activities are reduced. Training takes place in five departments: Building and Interior Furnishing, Advertising, Weaving, Photography and Fine Arts. The Bauhaus Theatre no longer exists. Mies van der Rohe seeks to keep the Bauhaus out of all political conflicts and expels the communist-oriented students.
The Bauhaus has 44 female and 122 male students.

## Politics 1930
First NSDAP Minister in a provincial government (Thuringia). 3.5 million jobless in Germany. Reichstag approves Young Plan. Fall of grand coalition under Müller (SPD). Minority cabinet led by Brüning. Hindenburg dissolves the Reichstag. Presidential government with emergency decrees under article 48 of the Weimar Constitution. Reichstag elections: NSDAP 107, conservative parties 41, national liberals 30, other liberals 20, centrists 87, social democrats 143, communists 77, others 72 seats. 4.4 million jobless, new emergency decrees.

## Science, Technology, Arts 1930
Science and Technology: the planet Pluto discovered, theory of metallic conductivity. First wireless telecommunications, first airmail across the Atlantic, opening of the Museum of Hygiene with the *Man of Glass* in Dresden. Literature: *The Man without Qualities* by Robert Musil. Theatre: *Rise and Fall of the Town of Mahagonny* by Bertolt Brecht and Kurt Weill, *Transatlantic* by George Antheil. Film: *The Blue Angel* by Josef von Sternberg, *Animal Crackers* by the Marx Brothers. Arts: Paul Schultze-Naumburg (NSDAP) becomes director of the Weimar State Institute for the Art of Building, Fine Arts and Manual Trades. Under his leadership, wall designs in the former Weimar Bauhaus are destroyed. *Manifesto of Concrete Art* by Theo van Doesburg, *Zapata* by Diego Rivera, *War* by Otto Dix. Architecture and Design: Exhibition of the *Société des Artistes Décorateurs Français* in Paris, the German department designed by Walter Gropius, Herbert Bayer, Marcel Breuer and László Moholy-Nagy. Chrysler Building in New York by William van Alen, 3rd CIAM meeting debates rational development planning in Brussels.

## Bauhaus 1931
Paul Klee takes up a post at the Düsseldorf Academy. The workshops and architecture department are merged to become the building and interior decoration department. First Bauhaus exhibition in the US (John Becker Gallery, New York). The *Brochure with the Large Letters* is published, emphasizing the non-political character of Bauhaus work. Gret Palucca dances in the Bauhaus assembly hall. Exhibition with works by Wassily Kandinsky. The last issue of the *Bauhaus* magazine, dedicated to Paul Klee, is published. Gunta Stölzl leaves the Bauhaus, Anni Albers stands in

as head of the weaving workshop. Council elections in Dessau. The NSDAP demands as the first point on its campaign poster that the Bauhaus be deprived of its funding and the building demolished. Bauhaus exhibition in Moscow. Bauhaus concert (with Henry Cowell and others). The Bauhaus has 53 female and 141 male students.

## Politics 1931

The Nazis become the strongest party in Dessau. 5 million unemployed in Germany. Emergency decree abolishes the right to demonstrate. Darmstädter Bank and National Bank collapse. Second Brüning cabinet. Far right Harzburg front (NSDAP, DNVP, Stahlhelm). Hitler wins support of leading German industrialists. Mass redundancies.

## Science, Technology, Arts 1931

Science and Technology: Discovery of radio waves from space, *Incompleteness Theorem* by Kurt Gödel, the airship *Graf Zeppelin* flies over the Arctic. Literature: *Castle Gripsholm* by Kurt Tucholsky, *Airman's Odyssey* by Antoine Saint-Exupéry. Theatre: Federico García Lorca founds *La Barraca* Theatre Group. Arts: *Abstraction–Création* group founded in Paris, Whitney Museum of American Art opens in New York. Film: *M* by Fritz Lang, *City Lights* by Charlie Chaplin, *Frankenstein* by James Whale. Architecture and design: German building exhibition in Berlin with participation by the Bauhaus and many former Bauhaus students, Villa Savoye at Poissy by Le Corbusier and Pierre Jeanneret, Empire State Building completed in New York. Berlin Broadcasting Centre by Hans Poelzig.

## Bauhaus 1932

Lily Reich appointed to head the weaving workshop and interior decoration department. The Dessau City Council rejects the Nazi motion to close the Bauhaus and demolish the building. Mounting political conflicts among the students. The police disperse a student assembly in the Bauhaus cafeteria. Expulsion of several students. Lyonel Feininger paintings exhibited at the Bauhaus. Oskar Schlemmer's paintings exhibited at the Bauhaus. Completion and handing over of a refreshment kiosk built for a Dessau owner close to the Masters' houses (designer: Ludwig Mies van der Rohe, site manager: Eduard Ludwig). Architect Paul Schultze-Naumburg, Prime Minister Freyberg, Council Leader Hofmann and a certain Herr Sommer (NSDAP) visit the Bauhaus in the company of Mayor Fritz Hesse. A few days later the NSDAP in Dessau initiates another motion for the closure of the Bauhaus. The students petition newspapers and the President of the Reich. Councillors led by Fritz Hesse visit the Bauhaus. The council meeting approves the NSDAP motion for the closure of the Bauhaus and the dismissal of all teaching staff with only four votes against (3 KPD, 1 Mayor Hesse) and the SPD abstaining. Mayor Hofmeister forbids the Bauhaus to use the lower case. Mies van der Rohe holds talks on the relocation of the Bauhaus to Magdeburg or Berlin. More than 900 people (on a special train from Chemnitz) visit the Bauhaus in a single day. The Dessau Bauhaus is officially closed. It moves to Berlin. Joost Schmidt, Alfred Arndt and Lyonel Feininger do not follow. Its new home is a former telephone factory in Siemensstraße in the suburb of Steglitz. In talks with the city of Dessau, Mies van der Rohe manages to secure the rights to the *Bauhaus* name and license revenues. The Bauhaus in Berlin is Ludwig Mies van der Rohe's private school.
The Bauhaus has 25 female and 90 male students.

## Politics 1932

6.1 million unemployed in Germany. Reich presidential elections: Hindenburg 18 million votes, Hitler 11 million votes, Thälmann 5 million votes. Hindenburg dismisses Chancellor Brüning. Von Papen administration (centrist) is appointed. The Socialist and Democrat Anhalt state government is overthrown and replaced by an NSDAP and DNVP government. Hindenburg dissolves the Reichstag. Lausanne conference: reparations concluded with a final payment of 3 billion Reichsmarks. Reichstag elections: NSDAP is strongest party. Hindenburg rejects Hitler as Chancellor. Reichstag dissolved. Reichstag elections: NSDAP remains strongest party. Schleicher becomes Chancellor. Armament restrictions in the Treaty of Versailles abolished.

## Science, Technology, Arts 1932

Science and Technology: Discovery of the neutron and deuterium, Piccard ascends to 16,940 metres in a hot-air balloon, *Socioeconomic Theory of Art* by Max Raphael. Literature: *Little Man, What Now* by Hans Fallada, *Brave New World* by Aldous Huxley. Theatre and Music: *Moses and Aaron* by Arnold Schönberg. Film: *Borinage* by Joris Ivens and Henri Storck, *Kuhle Wampe* by Slatan Dudow, first Venice Film Festival. Art: Surrealist exhibition in New York, major Picasso retrospective in Zurich. Architecture and design: the International Style Exhibition in New York Museum of Modern Art. Book by John-Russell Hitchcock and Philip Johnson *The International Style: Architecture since 1922*, Frank Lloyd Wright sets up the Taliesin Fellowship.

## Bauhaus 1933

Almost 700 people join in the Bauhaus carnival celebrations throughout the building. The Masters each design a department of their own. Plans for the conversion of the Bauhaus Berlin. Police search the Bauhaus on the orders of the Dessau district attorney's office, thirty-two students are detained for one to two days and an application is made for the closure of the Bauhaus. Gebr. Rasch company and Bauhaus Ltd. conclude a contract on the purchase of the rights to the name *Bauhaus Wallpaper*. Ludwig Mies van der Rohe dissolves the Bauhaus at the start of the summer semester with the Masters' consent, due to unacceptable conditions.
At the time of its closure, the Bauhaus has 5 female and 14 male students.

## Politics 1933

Schleicher resigns as Chancellor. Hindenburg names Adolf Hitler Chancellor. Communists call for a united front and a general strike. Hindenburg dissolves the Reichstag, new elections scheduled, demonstrations banned. SA, SS and *Stahlhelm* become police auxiliaries. Fire at the Reichstag. Final Reichstag elections: NSDAP 288, DNVP 53, centrists 73, social democrats 110, communists 81, German people's party 19 seats. NSDAP declares communist seats invalid and orders arrest of communist members of the Reichstag, giving Nazis an absolute parliamentary majority. Empowerment Act (government can enact legislation without the Reichstag). GESTAPO (secret police) founded. Labour unions abolished. Banned books burned in Berlin. Social democrats outlawed. Other parties dissolve themselves. Germany leaves the League of Nations. Legislation on the unity of party and state.

## Science, Technology, Arts 1933

Science and Technology: H. C. Urey isolates heavy water, land speed record of 437.91 kilometres per hour, freeways built in the United States and Germany. Literature: *Blood Wedding* by Federico García Lorca, *Man's Fate* by André Malraux. Theatre: School of American Ballet founded. Film: *The Crimes of Dr Mabuse* by Fritz Lang, *King Kong* by E. B. Schoedsack, *The Invisible Man* by James Whale. Art: Edward Hopper exhibition at Museum of Modern Art, New York, Josef Albers at Black Mountain College, USA, Francis Bacon deals with the topic of crucifixion. Architecture and design: 4th CIAM Congress, *The Functional City*, on a sea journey from Marseilles to Athens (Charter of Athens).

# Bibliography

Anna, Susanne (ed.): Das Bauhaus im Osten. Slowakische und Tschechische Avantgarde 1928-1939. Ostfildern-Ruit, 1997.

Argan, Giulio Carlo: Gropius und das Bauhaus. Reinbek, 1962.

Bauhaus: Zeitschrift für Gestaltung. Dessau 1926-1931 (quarterly).

Bauhausbücher: New series of bauhausbücher initiated by Walter Gropius and László Moholy-Nagy, bauhausbücher, Vol. 1-14, Reprints edited by Hans Maria Wingler, Gebr. Mann Verlag, Berlin. Bauhaus-Archiv, Berlin (ed.): Sammlungskatalog (Auswahl): Architektur, Design, Malerei, Grafik, Kunstpädagogik. 2. Aufl. Berlin (West), 1981.
Herbert Bayer. Das künstlerische Werk 1918-1938. Berlin (West), 1982.
Der vorbildliche Architekt: Mies van der Rohes Architekturunterricht 1930-1958 am Bauhaus und in Chicago. Berlin (West), 1987.
50 Jahre new bauhaus: Bauhausnachfolge in Chicago. Berlin (West), 1987.
Experiment Bauhaus. Das Bauhaus-Archiv, Berlin (West) zu Gast im Bauhaus Dessau. Berlin (West), 1988.
Bauhaus-Möbel. Eine Legende wird besichtigt. Berlin, 2002.

Bauhaus-Archiv Berlin und Deutsches Architekturmuseum Frankfurt-am-Main (ed.): Hannes Meyer. 1859-1954. Architekt, Urbanist, Lehrer. Berlin (West), 1989.

Bauhaus-Archiv Berlin und Droste, Magdalena/ Ludewig, Manfred (ed.): Marcel Breuer. Design. Cologne, 1992.

Bauhaus Dessau (ed.): Dimensionen. Dessau, 1993.

Bayer, Herbert/Gropius, Walter / Gropius, Ise (ed.): Bauhaus: 1919-1928. New York, NY, 1938.

Beyme, Klaus von: Das Zeitalter der Avantgarden. Kunst und Gesellschaft 1905-1955. Munich, 2005.

Bittner, Regina (ed.): Bauhausstil: Zwischen International Style und Lifestyle. Berlin, 2003.

Biundo, Christin/ Haus, Andreas (ed.): Bauhaus-Ideen 1919-1994: Bibliografie und Beiträge zur Rezeption des Bauhausgedanken. Berlin 1994.

Bothe, Rolf/Hahn, Peter/ von Travel, Christoph (ed.): Das frühe Bauhaus und Johannes Itten. Ostfildern-Ruit, 1994.

Brüning, Ute (ed.): Das A und O des Bauhauses. Bauhauswerbung: Schriftbilder Drucksachen, Ausstellungsdesign. Leipzig, 1995.

Busch-Reisinger Museum Collection (ed.): Concepts of the Bauhaus. The Busch-Reisinger Museum Collection. Cambridge, Massachusetts, 1971.

Kunstsammlungen zu Weimar/ Ceské Museum Vytvarnych Umeni v Praze/Siebenbrodt, Michael/ Procházka, Miro (ed.): Bauhaus Weimar – European Avant-garde 1919-1925, Prague,1997.

Claussen, Horst: Walter Gropius. Grundzüge seines Denkens. Hildesheim/Zürich/New York, NY, 1986.

De Michelis, Marco/ Kohlmeyer, Agnes/Fondatione Antonio Mazzotta (ed.): Bauhaus 1919-1933. Da Kandinsky a Klee, da Gropius a Mies van der Rohe. Milano, 1996.

Dearstyne, Howard: Inside the Bauhaus. London/New York, NY, 1986.

Derout, Christian/ Boissel, Jessica: Œuvres de Vassily Kandinsky (1866-1944). Paris, 1985.

Dietzsch, Folke: Die Studierenden am Bauhaus. Eine analytische Betrachtung zur strukturellen Zusammensetzung der Studierenden, zu ihren Studien und Leben am Bauhaus sowie zu ihrem späteren Wirken. Hochschule für Architektur und Bauwesen Weimar, 1991.

Diss. A: Die Bauhaus-Debatte 1953. Dokumente einer verdrängten Kontroverse.

Droste, Magdalena/ Nerdinger, Winfried/ Strohl, Hilde/ Conrads, Ulrich (ed.): Braunschweig/Wiesbaden, 1993.

Droste, Magdalena: Bauhaus 1919-1933. Cologne, 1990.

Droste, Magdalena: Bauhaus. Cologne 2006.

Droste, Magdalena/ Ludewig, Manfred (ed.): Das Bauhaus webt. Die Textilwerkstatt am Bauhaus. Berlin, 1998.

Düchting, Hajo: Farbe am Bauhaus. Berlin 1992.

Düchting, Hajo: Wie erkenne ich? Die Kunst des Bauhauses. Stuttgart, 2006.

Engelmann, Christine/ Schädlich, Christian: Die Bauhausbauten in Dessau. Berlin, 1991.

Ewig, Isabelle/ Gaejtgens, W. Thomas/ Noell, Matthias (ed.): Das Bauhaus und Frankreich 1919-1940. Berlin, 2002.

Fiedler, Jeannine (ed.): Fotografie am Bauhaus. Überblick über eine Periode der Fotografie im 20. Jahrhundert. Berlin (West), 1991.

Fiedler, Jeannine (ed.): Social Utopias of the Twenties. Bauhaus, Kibbutz and the Dream of the New Man. Wuppertal, 1995.

Fiedler, Jeannine/ Feierabend, Peter (ed.): Bauhaus. Cologne, 1999.

Fischer-Leonhardt, Dorothea: Die Gärten des Bauhauses. Gestaltungskonzepte der Moderne. Berlin 2005.

Fleischmann, Gerd (ed.): Bauhaus. Drucksachen, Typografie, Reklame. Düsseldorf, 1984.

Forgács, Éva: The Bauhaus Idea and the Bauhaus Politics. Budapest, 1995.

Form+Zweck, Fachzeitschrift für industrielle Formgestaltung (Sonderhefte Bauhaus) Berlin (Ost), 8, 1976, Nr. 6; 11, 1979, Nr. 3; 15, 1983, Nr. 2 (Bauhaus-Sonderheft)

Franciscono, Marcel: Walter Gropius and the creation of the Bauhaus in Weimar. Chicago / London, 1971.

Franciscono, Marcel: Paul Klee. His Work and Thought. Chicago/London, 1991.

Fundació "la Caixa" (ed): La Bauhaus de Festa 1919-1933. Barcelona, 2005.

Gaßner, Hubertus (ed.): Wechselwirkungen. Ungarische Avantgarde in der Weimarer Republik. Marburg, 1986.

Geelhaar, Christian: Paul Klee und das Bauhaus. Cologne, 1972.

Geelhaar, Christian (ed.): Paul Klee. Schriften, Rezensionen und Aufsätze. Cologne, 1976.

Giedion, Siegfried: Walter Gropius. Mensch und Werk. Stuttgart, 1954.

Grohn, Christian: Die „Bauhaus-Idee". Entwurf, Weiterführung, Rezeption. Berlin, 1991.

Gropius, Walter: Die neue Architektur und das Bauhaus. Grundzüge und Entwicklung einer Konzeption. Mainz/Berlin (West), 1965.

Gumbrecht, Hans Ulrich: 1926. Ein Jahr am Rand der Zeit. Frankfurt-am-Main, 2001.

Hahn, Peter (ed.): Wassily Kandinsky. Russische Zeit und Bauhausjahre. Berlin (West), 1984.

Hahn, Peter (ed.): bauhaus berlin: Auflösung Dessau 1932, Schließung Berlin 1933, Bauhäusler und Drittes Reich. Eine Dokumentation, zusammengestellt vom Bauhaus-Archiv Berlin. Weingarten, 1985.

Herzogenrath, Wulf (ed.): 50 Jahre bauhaus. Stuttgart, 1968.

Herzogenrath, Wulf: Oskar Schlemmer. Die Wandgestaltung der neuen Architektur. Munich, 1973.

Herzogenrath, Wulf/ Krauss, Stefan (ed.): bauhaus-utopien. Arbeiten auf Papier. Cologne, 1988

Herzogenrath, Wulf/ Krauss, Stefan (ed.): Erich Consemüller. Fotografien Bauhaus Dessau. Munich 1989

Herzogenrath, Wulf/ Buschhoff, Anne/ Vowinkel, Andreas (ed.): Paul Klee – Lehrer am Bauhaus. Bremen, 2004.

Hess, Hans: Lyonel Feininger. Stuttgart, 1959.

Hesse, Fritz: Von der Residenz zur Bauhausstadt. Erinnerungen an Dessau. Bad Pyrmont, 1963.

Hirdina, Karin: Pathos der Sachlichkeit. Tendenzen materialistischer Ästhetik in den zwanziger Jahren. Berlin (East)/Munich, 1981.

Hitchcock, Henry-Russell/ Johnson, Phillip: Der internationale Stil (1932). Braunschweig/Wiesbaden, 1984.

Hochmann, Elaine S: Bauhaus: crucible of modernism. New York, NY, 1997.

Hochschule für Architektur und Bauwesen Weimar Wissenschaftliche Zeitschrift
Bauhauskolloquium. Jg. 23, H. 5/6, 1976,
Bauhauskolloquium. Jg. 26, H. 4/5, 1979,
Internationales Bauhauskolloquium, Jg. 29, H. 5/6, 1983, 3.
4. Internationales Bauhauskolloquium, Jg. 33, H. 4/5/6, 1987.

Hüneke, Andreas (ed.): Oskar Schlemmer. Idealist der Form. Briefe, Tagebücher, Schriften 1912-1943. Leipzig, 1990.

Hüter, Karl-Heinz: Das Bauhaus in Weimar. Studie zur gesellschaftspolitischen Geschichte einer deutschen Kunstschule. Berlin (East) 1976.

Hyman, Isabelle: Marcel Breuer, Architect. The Career and the Buildings. New York, NY, 2001.

Isaacs, Reginald R: Walter Gropius. Der Mensch und sein Werk. Berlin (West), 1983/84.

Itten Johannes: Mein Vorkurs am Bauhaus. Ravensburg, 1963.

Jaeggi, Annemarie: Adolf Meyer. Der Zweite Mann. Ein Architekt im Schatten von Walter Gropius. Berlin, 1994.

James-Chakraborty, Kathleen (ed.): Bauhaus culture. From Weimar to the Cold War. Minneapolis/London, 2006.

Kandinsky, Nina: Kandinsky und ich. Munich, 1976.

Klee, Felix (ed.): Paul Klee. Briefe an die Familie. Band 2. 1907-1940. Cologne, 1979.

Költzsch, Georg W/ Tupitsyn, Margarita (ed.): Bauhaus Dessau – Chicago – New York. Cologne, 2000.

Kröll, Friedhelm: Bauhaus 1919-1933. Künstler zwischen Isolation und kollektiver Praxis. Düsseldorf, 1974.

Kunstmuseum Bonn (ed.): Josef Albers. Werke auf Papier. Bonn, 1989.

Lang, Lothar: Das Bauhaus 1919-1933. Idee und Wirklichkeit. Berlin (East), 1965.

Lichtenstein, Claude (ed.): Bauhaus 1919-1933. Meister- und Schülerarbeiten. Weimar, Dessau, Berlin. Zürich, 1988.

Marzona, Egidio: Joost Schmidt. Düsseldorf, 1984.

Maur, Karin von: Oskar Schlemmer. Munich, 1979.

März, Roland (ed.): Lyonel Feininger. Von Gelmeroda nach Manhattan. Retrospektive der Gemälde. Berlin, 1998.

Miller Lane, Barbara: Architecture and Politics in Germany; 1918-1945. Cambridge, Massachusetts, 1968.

Misawa Homes: Bauhaus Collection. Tokyo, 1991.

Moholy-Nagy, Sibyll: László Moholy-Nagy, Experiment in Totality. Cambridge, Massachusetts, 1950.

Möller, Werner/Mácel, Otakar: Ein Stuhl macht Geschichte. Munich, 1992.

Möller, Werner/Neumüllers, Marie/ Stiftung Bauhaus Dessau (ed.): Mart Stam—Architekt, Visionär, Gestalter. Dessau, 1998.

Muche, Georg: Blickpunkt. Sturm – Dada – Bauhaus – Gegenwart. Munich, 1961.

Müller, Ulrich: Raum, Bewegung und Zeit im Werk von Walter Gropius und Ludwig Mies van der Rohe. Berlin, 2004.

Museum Fridericianum Kassel (ed.): László Moholy-Nagy. Ostfildern-Ruit, 1991.

Nerdinger, Winfried (ed.): The Walter Gropius Archive. An Illustrated Catalogue of the Drawings, Prints, and Photographs in the Walter Gropius Archive at the Busch-Reisinger Museum, Harvard University. New York, NY/London/Cambridge, Massachusetts, 1990.

Nerdinger, Winfried (ed.): Bauhaus-Moderne und Nationalsozialismus. Zwischen Anbiederung und Verfolgung. In Zusammenarbeit mit dem Bauhaus-Archiv Berlin. Munich, 1993.

Nerdinger, Winfried: Walter Gropius. Der Architekt Walter Gropius, Zeichnungen, Pläne und Fotos aus dem Busch-Reisinger Museum der Harvard University Art Museum, Cambridge, Massachusetts, und dem Bauhaus-Archiv, Berlin (West), mit einem kritischen Werkverzeichnis. Cambridge, Massachusetts/Berlin (West), 1985.

Neumann, Eckhard (ed.): Bauhaus und Bauhäusler. Erinnerungen und Bekenntnisse. Cologne, 1985.

Paret, Paul: Experimental Photography from the Bauhaus Sculpture Workshop. Edited by Stephen Feeke, The Henry Moore Institute, Leeds, 2006.

Paul-Klee-Stiftung, Kunstmuseum Bern (ed.): Paul Klee. Catalogue Raisonné, Bd. 1-9. Bern, 1998-2001.

Poling, Clark V: Kandinsky – Unterricht am Bauhaus. Farbseminar und analytisches Zeichnen, dargestellt am Beispiel der Sammlung des Bauhaus-Archivs Berlin. Weingarten, 1982.

Prigge, Walter (ed.): Bauhaus, Brasilia, Auschwitz, Hiroshima. Weltkulturerbe des 20. Jahrhunderts. Modernität und Barbarei. Berlin, 2003.

Probst, Hartmut/ Schädlich, Christian (ed.): Walter Gropius. 3 volumes, Berlin (East), 1986-88.

Regel, Günter (ed.): Paul Klee: Kunst – Lehre. Leipzig 1995.

Riley, Terence: Ludwig Mies van der Rohe. Die Berliner Jahre 1907-1938. Munich, 2001.

Rehm, Robin: Das Bauhausgebäude in Dessau. Die ästhetischen Kategorien Zweck Form Inhalt. Berlin, 2005.

Roethel, Hans K / Benjamin, Jean K: Kandinsky. Catalogue Raisonné of Oil-Paintings. Volume One 1900-1915; Volume Two 1916-1944. London, 1982/84.

Roters, Eberhard: Maler am Bauhaus. Berlin, 1965.

Rowland, Anna: Bauhaus Source Book. Bauhaus Style and its worldwide Influence. London, 1990.

Rüden, Egon von: Zum Begriff künstlerischer Lehre bei Itten, Kandinsky, Albers und Klee. Berlin, 1999.

Sachsse, Rolf: Lucia Moholy. Düsseldorf, 1985.

Sachsse, Rolf: Lucia Moholy. Bauhausfotografin. Berlin, 1985.

Scheidig, Walther: bauhaus Weimar 1919-1924, Werkstattarbeiten. Leipzig, 1966.

Scheiffele, Walter: bauhaus, junkers, sozialdemokratie. ein kraftfeld der moderne. Berlin, 2003.

Scheper, Dirk: Oskar Schlemmer – Das Triadische Ballett und die Bauhausbühne. Berlin (West), 1988.

Scheper, Renate (ed.): Farbenfroh! Die Werkstatt für Wandmalerei am Bauhaus. Berlin, 2005.

Schlemmer, Tut (ed.): Oskar Schlemmer. Briefe und Tagebücher. Munich, 1958.

Schmidt, Diether: Bauhaus. Weimar 1919 bis 1925, Dessau 1925 bis 1932, Berlin 1931 bis 1933. Dresden, 1966.

Schnaidt, Claude: Hannes Meyer. Bauten, Projekte und Schriften. Buildings, Projects and Writings. Teufen, 1965.

Schöbe, Lutz/Thöner, Wolfgang: Stiftung Bauhaus Dessau. Die Sammlung. Ostfildern-Ruit, 1995.

Schöbe, Lutz (ed.): Bauhaus. Fotografien aus der Sammlung der Stiftung Bauhaus Dessau. Florence, 2004.

Schreyer, Lothar: Erinnerungen an Sturm und Bauhaus. Munich, 1956.

Siebenbrodt, Michael/ Constanze Hofstaetter (ed.): Karl Peter Röhl in Weimar 1912-1926. Weimar, 1997.

Siebenbrodt, Michael/ Prents, Lena (ed.): Eberhard Schrammen. Bauhäusler, Maler, Formgestalter, Fotograf. Weimar, 2003.

Siebenbrodt, Michael (ed.): Bauhaus Weimar. Entwürfe für die Zukunft. Ostfildern-Ruit, 2000.

Solomon R Guggenheim Museum, New York (ed.): Josef Albers. New York, NY, 1988.

Staatliches Bauhaus Weimar (ed.): Staatliches Bauhaus Weimar 1919-1923, Munich/Weimar, 1923.

Steckner, Cornelius: Zur Ästhetik des Bauhauses. Ein Beitrag zur Erforschung synästhetischer Grundsätze und Elementarerziehung am Bauhaus. Stuttgart, 1985.

Stiftung Bauhaus Dessau (ed.): Kentgens-Craig, Margret: Bauhaus-Architektur. Die Rezeption in Amerika 1919-1936. Frankfurt-am-Main /Cambridge, Massachusetts/ London, 1993.

Stiftung Bauhaus Dessau/ Tapetenfabrik Gebr. Rasch GmbH (ed.): Bauhaustapete. Reklame & Erfolg einer Marke. Cologne, 1995.

Stiftung Bauhaus Dessau (ed.): ... Das Bauhaus zerstört 1945. 1947 das Bauhaus stört... Der Versuch einer Neueröffnung des Bauhauses in Dessau nach dem Ende des II. Weltkrieges. Dessau, 1996.

Stiftung Bauhaus Dessau (ed.): Gunta Stölzl. Meisterin am Bauhaus Dessau. Textilien, Textilentwürfe und freie Arbeiten 1915-1983. Ostfildern-Ruit, 1997.

Stiftung Bauhaus Dessau (ed.): Das Bauhausgebäude in Dessau 1926-1999. Basel/Berlin/Boston, Massachusetts, 1998.

Stiftung Bauhaus Dessau (ed.): Bauhausobjekte. Berlin, 2004 (CD-ROM)

Stiftung Weimarer Klassik und Kunstsammlungen/ Siebenbrodt, Michael (ed.): Alma Siedhoff-Buscher. Eine neue Welt für Kinder. Weimar, 2004.

Szezon Museum of Art, Tokyo (ed.): Bauhaus 1919-1933. Tokyo, 1995.

Thöner, Wolfgang: The Bauhaus Life. Life and Work in the Masters' Houses Estate in Dessau. Original: Das Bauhaus wohnt – Leben und Arbeiten in der Meisterhaussiedlung Dessau. Leipzig, 2003.

Thöner, Wolfgang: Das Bauhaus leuchtet. Die Dessauer Bauhausbauten im Licht. Leipzig 2005.

Valena, Tomáš und Winko, Ulrich (ed.): Prager Architektur und die europäische Moderne. Berlin, 2006.

Vegesack, Alexander von/ Remmele, Mathias (ed.): Marcel Breuer – Design und Architektur. Weil am Rhein, 2003.

Vitale, Elodie: Le Bauhaus de Weimar. 1919-1925. Liège/Brussels, 1989.

Wagner, Christoph/ Gustav-Lübke-Museum Hamm (ed.): Johannes Itten—Wassily Kandinsky—Paul Klee. Das Bauhaus und die Esoterik. Hamm, 2005.

Wahl, Volker (ed.): Die Meisterratsprotokolle des Staatlichen Bauhauses Weimar 1919-1925. Weimar, 2001.

Weber, Klaus (ed.): Keramik und Bauhaus. Geschichte und Wirkungen der keramischen Werkstatt des Bauhauses. Berlin (West), 1989.

Weber, Klaus (ed.): Die Metallwerkstatt am Bauhaus. Geschichte und Wirkungen der keramischen Werkstatt des Bauhauses. Berlin, 1992.

Weber, Klaus (ed.): Punkt. Linie. Fläche. Druckgraphik am Bauhaus. Berlin, 1999.

Whitford, Frank: Bauhaus. London, 1984.

Whitford, Frank (ed.): The Bauhaus. Masters and Students by Themselves. London, 1992.

Wick, Rainer K: Bauhaus-Pädagogik. Cologne, 1982.

Wick, Rainer K: Bauhaus. Kunstschule der Moderne. Ostfildern-Ruit 2000

Wingler, Hans Maria: Das Bauhaus 1919-1933. Weimar Dessau Berlin. Bramsche/Cologne, 1962.

Winkler, Klaus-Jürgen: Die Architektur am Bauhaus in Weimar. Berlin/Munich, 1992.

Winkler, Klaus-Jürgen: Der Architekt Hannes Meyer. Anschauungen und Werk. Berlin (East), 1989.

Winkler, Klaus-Jürgen: Baulehre und Entwerfen am Bauhaus 1919-1933. Weimar, 2003.

Winkler, Klaus-Jürgen (ed.): Bauhaus-Alben 1, Weimar, 2006.

Wolfe, Tom: From Bauhaus to our House. New York, NY, 1981.

Wünsche, Konrad: Bauhaus. Versuche das Leben zu ordnen. Berlin (West), 1989.

Zimmermann, Reinhard: Die Kunsttheorie von Wassily Kandinsky. Volumes 1-2. Berlin, 2002

# Bauhaus Teachers

| | WEIMAR | | DESSAU | | BERLIN | |
|---|---|---|---|---|---|---|
| Directors | Walter Gropius | 1919-25 | Walter Gropius | 1925-28 | | |
| | | | Hannes Meyer | 1928-30 | | |
| | | | Ludwig Mies van der Rohe | 1930-32 | Ludwig Mies van der Rohe | 1932-33 |
| Masters of Form (Professors from 1926) | *Teachers taken over from the Weimar Institute of Fine Arts:* | | | | | |
| | Max Thedy | 1919-20 | | | | |
| | Otto Fröhlich | 1919-20 | | | | |
| | Richard Engelmann | 1919-20 | | | | |
| | Walther Klemm | 1919-20 | | | | |
| | *Newly appointed teachers:* | | | | | |
| | Lyonel Feininger | 1919-25 | Lyonel Feininger | 1925-32 | | |
| | Johannes Itten | 1919-23 | | | | |
| | Gerhard Marcks | 1919-25 | | | | |
| | Georg Muche | 1920-25 | Georg Muche | 1925-27 | | |
| | Paul Klee | 1920-25 | Paul Klee | 1925-31 | | |
| | Oskar Schlemmer | 1921-25 | Oskar Schlemmer | 1925-29 | | |
| | Lothar Schreyer | 1921-23 | | | | |
| | Wassily Kandinsky | 1922-25 | Wassily Kandinsky | 1925-32 | Wassily Kandinsky | 1932-33 |
| | László Moholy-Nagy | 1923-25 | László Moholy-Nagy | 1925-28 | | |
| | *Newly appointed associate teachers:* | | | | | |
| | Adolf Meyer (architecture) | 1919-25 | | | | |
| | Lothar Schreyer (Arts and Crafts) | 1921 | | | | |
| | Emil Lange (Practical Building) | 1922 | | | | |
| | Gertrud Grunow (Harmonisation Theory) | 1923-24 | | | | |
| | | | Hannes Meyer | 1927-30 | | |
| | | | Ludwig Hilberseimer | 1929-32 | Ludwig Hilberseimer | 1932-33 |
| | | | Walter Peterhans | 1929-32 | Walter Peterhans | 1932-33 |
| | | | Lilly Reich | 1932 | Lilly Reich | 1932-33 |
| Junior Masters | | | Herbert Bayer | 1925-28 | | |
| | | | Marcel Breuer | 1925-28 | | |
| | | | Gunta Stölzl | 1925-31 | | |
| | | | Joost Schmidt | 1925-32 | | |
| | | | Hinnerk Scheper | 1925-29, 1931-32 | Hinnerk Scheper | 1932-33 |
| | | | Josef Albers | 1925-32 | Josef Albers | 1932-33 |
| | | | Alfred Arndt | 1925-32 | | |
| Preparatory Course | Johannes Itten | 1919-23 | | | | |
| | Georg Muche | 1921-22 | | | | |
| | László Moholy-Nagy | 1923-25 | László Moholy-Nagy | 1925-28 | | |
| | Josef Albers | 1923-25 | Josef Albers | 1925-32 | Josef Albers | 1932-33 |
| Creative Form Theory | Paul Klee | 1921-25 | Paul Klee | 1925-31 | | |
| Form and Colour Theory | Wassily Kandinsky | 1922-25 | Wassily Kandinsky | 1925-32 | Wassily Kandinsky | 1932-33 |
| Figure Drawing | Max Thedy | 1919-21 | | | | |
| | Oskar Schlemmer | 1921-25 | Oskar Schlemmer | 1925-29 | | |
| | | | Joost Schmidt | 1929-32 | | |
| Calligraphy, Design Theory | Dora Wibiral | 1919-20 | Joost Schmidt | 1925-32 | | |
| Stone Sculpting | *Masters of Form:* | | | | | |
| | Richard Engelmann | 1919-20 | | | | |
| | Johannes Itten | 1920-22 | | | | |
| | Oskar Schlemmer | 1922-25 | | | | |
| | *Masters of Craft (Heads of Workshop):* | | | | | |
| | Karl Krull | 1919-20 | | | | |
| | Max Krause | 1920-21 | | | | |
| | Josef Hartwig | 1921-25 | | | | |
| Woodcarving | *Masters of Form:* | | | | | |
| | Richard Engelmann | 1919-20 | | | | |
| | Georg Muche | 1920-21 | | | | |
| | Johannes Itten | 1921-22 | | | | |
| | Oskar Schlemmer | 1922-25 | | | | |
| | *Masters of Craft (Heads of Workshop):* | | | | | |
| | Hans Kämpfe | 1920-21 | | | | |
| | Josef Hartwig | 1921-25 | | | | |
| Sculpting Workshop | | | Joost Schmidt | 1925-30 | | |
| Printing | *Masters of Form:* | | | | | |
| | Walter Klemm | 1919-21 | | | | |
| | Lyonel Feininger | 1921-25 | | | | |
| | *Masters of Craft (Heads of Workshop):* | | | | | |
| | Carl Zaubitzer | 1919-26 | | | | |
| Typography, Advertising | | | Herbert Bayer | 1925-28 | | |
| | | | Joost Schmidt | 1928-32 | | |
| | | | *Master of Craft (Head of Workshop):* | | | |
| | | | Willi Hauswald | 1928-30 | | |
| Bookbinding | *Masters of Form:* | | | | | |
| | Georg Muche | 1920-21 | | | | |
| | Paul Klee | 1921 | | | | |
| | Lothar Schreyer | 1921-22 | | | | |
| | *Masters of Craft (Heads of Workshop):* | | | | | |
| | Otto Dorfner | 1919-22 | | | | |
| Pottery | *Masters of Form:* | | | | | |
| | Gerhard Marcks | 1919-25 | | | | |
| | *Masters of Craft (Heads of Workshop):* | | | | | |
| | Gerhard Leibbrand | 1919-20 | | | | |
| | Leo Emmerich | 1920 | | | | |
| | Max Krehan | 1920-25 | | | | |
| | *Heads of Production Workshop:* | | | | | |
| | Theodor Bogler | 1924 | | | | |
| | Otto Lindig | 1924-25 | | | | |
| Weaving (Textile Workshop) | *Masters of Form:* | | | | | |
| | Johannes Itten | 1920-21 | Georg Muche | 1925-27 | | |
| | Georg Muche | 1921-25 | Gunta Stölzl | 1925-31 | | |
| | *Masters of Craft (Heads of Workshop):* | | Anni Albers | 1931 | | |
| | Helene Börner | 1919-25 | Otti Berger | 1931-32 | | |
| | | | Lilly Reich | 1932 | Lilly Reich | 1932-33 |
| | | | *Master of Craft (Head of Workshop):* | | | |
| | | | Gunta Stölzl | 1925-26 | | |
| | | | Kurt Warnke | 1926-32 | | |
| Furniture | *Masters of Form:* | | | | | |

| Subject | Weimar teachers | | Dessau teachers | | Berlin teachers | |
|---|---|---|---|---|---|---|
| | Johannes Itten | 1920-22 | | | | |
| | Walter Gropius | 1922-25 | Beck | 1931-1932 | | |
| | *Masters of Craft (Heads of Workshop):* | | Marcel Breuer | 1925-28 | | |
| | Vogel | 1920-21 | Josef Albers | 1928-29 | | |
| | Josef Zachmann | 1921-22 | Alfred Arndt | 1929-31 | | |
| | Anton Handik | 1922 | Lilly Reich | 1932 | Lilly Reich | 1932-33 |
| | Erich Brendel (temporarily as Journeyman) | 1922-23 | *Masters of Craft (Heads of Workshop):* | | | |
| | Reinhold Weidensee | 1923-26 | Heinrich Bökenheide | 1925-31 | | |
| | Eberhard Schrammen (atelier de tourneur) | 1922-25 | | | | |
| Metal Workshop | *Masters of Form:* | | | | | |
| | Johannes Itten | 1920-22 | | | | |
| | Paul Klee | 1922 | | | | |
| | Oskar Schlemmer | 1922-23 | László Moholy-Nagy | 1925-28 | | |
| | László Moholy-Nagy | 1923-25 | Marianne Brandt | 1928-29 | | |
| | *Masters of Craft (Heads of Workshop):* | | Alfred Arndt | 1929-31 | | |
| | Naum Slutzky | 1919-20 | Lilly Reich | 1932 | Lilly Reich | 1932-33 |
| | Wilhelm Schabbon | 1920-21 | *Masters of Craft (Heads of Workshop):* | | | |
| | Alfred Kopka | 1921 | Willi Wirths | 1925 | | |
| | Christian Dell | 1922-25 | Rudolf Schwarz | 1925-27 | | |
| | Naum Slutzky (Goldsmith's workshop) | 1921-24 | Alfred Schäfter | 1927-31 | | |
| | | | Paul Tobias | 1931-32 | | |
| Stained Glass Painting | *Masters of Form:* | | | | | |
| | Johannes Itten | 1920-22 | | | | |
| | Oskar Schlemmer | 1922 | | | | |
| | Paul Klee | 1922-25 | | | | |
| | *Masters of Craft (Heads of Workshop):* | | | | | |
| | Carl Schlemmer | 1922-25 | | | | |
| | Josef Albers (temporarily as Journeyman) | 1922-25 | | | | |
| Mural painting | *Masters of Form:* | | | | | |
| | Johannes Itten | 1920-22 | | | | |
| | Oskar Schlemmer | 1921-22 | | | | |
| | Wassily Kandinsky | 1922-25 | Hinnerk Scheper | 1925-29, 1931-32 | Hinnerk Scheper | 1932-33 |
| | *Masters of Craft (Heads of Workshop):* | | | | | |
| | Franz Heidelmann | 1919-20 | Alfred Arndt | 1929-31 | | |
| | Carl Schlemmer | 1921-22 | *Master of Craft (Head of Workshop):* | | | |
| | Hermann Müller (temporarily as Journeyman) | 1922 | Edwin Keiling | 1929-30 | | |
| | Heinrich Beberniss | 1922-25 | | | | |
| Photography | | | Walter Peterhans | 1929-32 | Walter Peterhans | 1932-33 |
| Theatre | Lothar Schreyer | 1921-23 | | | | |
| | Oskar Schlemmer | 1923-25 | Oskar Schlemmer | 1925-29 | | |
| Construction workshop | | | Hans Wittwer | 1927-29 | | |
| Construction Theory | | | Hannes Meyer | 1927-30 | | |
| | | | Carl Fieger | 1927-28 | | |
| | | | Hans Wittwer | 1927-29 | | |
| | | | Anton Brenner | 1929-30 | | |
| | | | Ludwig Mies van der Rohe | 1930-32 | Ludwig Mies van der Rohe | 1932-33 |
| Building and Planning, Urban Planning and Development Theory | | | Ludwig Hilberseimer | 1929-32 | Ludwig Hilberseimer | 1932-33 |
| | | | Ludwig Mies van der Rohe | 1930-32 | Ludwig Mies van der Rohe | 1932-33 |
| | | | Mart Stam | 1928-29 | | |
| Mathematics | | | Friedrich Köhn | 1926-28 | | |
| | | | *Project Supervisor:* | | | |
| | | | Erich Schrader | 1928 | | |
| | | | Alcar Felix Rudelt | 1928-29 | | |
| | | | Johannes Riedel | 1929-30 | | |
| | | | Walter Peterhans | 1930-31 | | |
| | | | Willi Saemann | 1930-32 | | |
| Physics, Chemistry, Technology and Building Material Studies | | | Wilhelm Müller | 1927-32 | | |
| Construction and Projection Drawing | Ernst Schumann | 1919-20, 1924-25 | Friedrich Engemann | 1929-32 | Friedrich Engemann | 1932-33 |
| Descriptive Geometry | | | Friedrich Köhn | 1926-28 | | |
| | | | Carl Fieger | 1927-30 | | |
| | | | Erich Schrader | 1928 | | |
| | | | Opitz (engineer) | 1928-29 | | |
| | | | Friedrich Engemann | 1929-32 | | |
| Business Operations | | | Johannes Riedel | 1929-30 | | |
| Civil Engineering Sciences (Mechanics, Statics, Strength of Materials, Iron Construction, Iron Concrete Construction, Modern Building, Construction, Estimates) | | | Friedrich Köhn | 1926-28 | | |
| | | | Carl Fieger | 1928 | | |
| | | | Alcar Rudelt | 1927-32 | Alcar Rudelt | 1932-33 |
| | | | Friedrich Engelmann | 1929-32 | Friedrich Engelmann | 1932-33 |
| Technical Drawing | Carl Fieger | 1921-25 | Carl Fieger | 1927-28 | | |
| | | | Johannes Niegemann | 1928-29 | | |
| Free Painting Classes | Otto Fröhlich | 1919-20 | Paul Klee | 1927-31 | | |
| | Lyonel Feininger | 1921-25 | Vassily Kandinsky | 1927-32 | Vassily Kandinsky | 1932-33 |
| Sport | | | Karla Grosch | 1928-32 | | |
| | | | Otto Büttner | 1932 | | |
| Other Teachers and visiting Lecturers: | Gertrud Grunow (Harmonisation Theory) | 1919-23 | Wilhelm Dehnhardt (heating and ventilation) | 1930-31 | | |
| | Ernst Schumann (Construction and Projection Drawing) | 1919-20, 1924-25 | *Visiting Lecturers:* | | | |
| | Ludwig Hirschfeld-Mack (Colour Seminar) | | Artur Krause (metal production) | 1931-32 | | |
| | Adolf Meyer (Workshop Drawing, Architecture Studies) | 1920-25 | Paul Artaria (individual house construction) | 1930 | | |
| | Paul Klopfer (Elementary Forms in Architecture) | 1919-20 | Edward Heiberg (architecture) | 1930 | | |
| | Wilhelm Köhler (Art History Course) | 1919-20 | Karlfried Graf Dürckheim (psychology) | 1930-32 | | |
| | Otto Rasch (Anatomical Drawing) | 1919-20 | Wilhelm Ostwald (colour) | 1927 | | |
| | Paul Dobe (Nature Studies) | 1919-20 | Hermann Duncker (labour movement) | 1929 | | |
| | | | J. M. Lange (labour movement) | 1930 | | |
| | | | Fritz Kuhr (figurative drawing and human figurs) | 1929-30 | | |
| | | | Hermann Schneider (physics and electrical installements) | 1930-31 | | |
| | | | Richard Vogel (welding), Max Peiffer (construction) Hans Schmidt (architecture), | | | |
| | | | Otto Neurath (image statistics) | 1929 | | |
| | | | Rudolf Carnap (philosophy) | 1929 | | |
| | | | Hans Volger (graphical representation and standards) | 1930 | | |
| | | | Dr. Lohmann (business operations) | 1929 | | |
| | | | Konrad von Meyerburg (labour fundamentals) | 1929 | | |
| | | | Karel Teige (litterature and typography) | 1929-30 | | |

# Bauhaus – Archives, Collections and Museums

Bauhaus-Archiv, Museum für Gestaltung
Klingelhöferstr. 14
D-10785 Berlin
Germany
+49-(0)30-254002-0
www.bauhaus.de

Stiftung Bauhaus Dessau
Gropiusallee 38
D-06846 Dessau
Germany
+49-(0)340-6508250
www.bauhaus-dessau.de

Stiftung Meisterhäuser Dessau
Meisterhaus Kandinsky - Klee
Ebertallee 69-71
D-06846 Dessau
Germany
+49-(0)340-6610934
www.meisterhäuser.de

Klassik Stiftung Weimar/Bauhaus-Museum
Theaterplatz
D-99423 Weimar
Germany
Tel. +49-(0)-3643-546161
www.klassik-stiftung.de

Bauhaus-Museum Weimar
Am Theaterplatz
D-99423 Weimar
Germany
+49-(0)-3643-546161
www.kunstsammlungen-weimar.de

Zentrum Paul Klee Bern
Monument im Fruchtland 3, Postfach
3000 Bern 31
Switzerland
+ 41 (0)31 359 01 01
www.paulkleezentrum.ch

Busch-Reisinger Museum
32 Quincy Street
Cambridge, MA 02138
USA
617.495.2317
www.artmuseums.harvard.edu/busch/html

The Josef and Anni Albers Foundation
88 Beacon Road
Bethany, CT 06524
(203)393-4094
www.albersfoundation.org

The Moholy-Nagy Foundation
1204 Gardner Avenue
Ann Arbor, MI. 48104
www.moholy-nagy.org

Utsunomiya Museum of Art
1077 Nagaoka-cho
320-0004 Utsunomiya
Japan
http://u-moa.jp/jp/index.html

Misawa Bauhaus Collection
1-1-19 Takaido-nishi
Suginami-ku Tokio
Japan
Tel. 03-3247-5645
www.bauhaus.ac

# Index

The numbers in bold indicate images.